Paris Tourism and Vacation Guide

Traveler's Pocket Guide

Written by
Sampson Jerry

Copyright©2022 Sampson Jerry
All right Reserved

Global Print Digital
Arlington Row, Bibury, Cirencester GL7 5ND,
Gloucester, United Kingdom

ISBN: 978-1-7392634-0-9

Table of Content

Chapter One

Introduction

Paris is a city that cannot be compared to any other. Culture, history, and natural splendor are in abundant supply here. While the Louvre, the Eiffel Tower, and Notre Dame are all popular tourist destinations in Paris, the city's cobblestone alleyways are where visitors will find the city's true charm. Young and old wait in line both in the morning and in the evening for a fresh baguette from the local boulangerie. Here, the ins and outs of daily life are played out like chic mothers on bikes pedaling their children to school, artists posting up in cafés with a notebook, and so forth. It is probably everything you imagined, and then more, since while Paris is a city with a strong cultural identity, it also houses individuals from all over the world who contribute their own culture and customs to the mix. This means that it is likely everything you thought, and then some. Because of this, going to the most famous landmarks in Paris is not nearly enough to get a feel for the city. Instcad, you should wander the city's streets, which are where the spirit and allure of Paris can be experienced to the fullest.

You'll find that as you wander the streets of Paris, you'll find yourself walking the hills of Montmartre in search of that perfect crepe spot or meandering through Belleville, a Chinese neighborhood interspersed with hip, young Parisians and elaborate murals. Both of these places can be found as you make your way through Paris. When you cross the Seine, you might find yourself sipping a glass of wine at a café in Saint-Germain-des-Prés or wandering the meandering streets of the Latin Quarter. Both of these activities are located on the other side of the river. It does not take much effort to become completely submerged in the culture of this remarkable city. Read through our Paris travel guide, in which we detail all there is to know about tourism in Paris, whether you're there for business, a vacation, a honeymoon, or any other type of visit, so that you won't miss a thing.

People who are interested in history will be amazed by the wealth of a city that has been through two major revolutions and has been home to several of the most powerful kingdoms in all of Europe. Art enthusiasts may spend a lifetime exploring the halls of the world-famous Louvre Museum, the Musee d'Orsay, or any of the city's myriad other lesser art museums. You can give in to absolutely any kind of gastronomic extasy if you have the gourmet in you. Small bistrots, charming cafés, exquisite restaurants, and delicious patisseries can all be found in Paris. The city is known for its culinary diversity. Those who have a passion for fashion will feel like they've died and gone to heaven in Paris' most upscale department stores and boutiques.

The Charles de Gaulle Airport, often known as Roissy, is located to the northeast of the city, and Orly Airport is located to the south of the city. Both of these airports serve the city of Paris. Both of the airports have access to the Metro, also known as the Regional Express Rail (RER), as well as buses, taxis, and other forms of public transportation. Administratively, the city of Paris is broken up into twenty different sections known as "Arrondissements," with the first one starting in the heart of the city and working its way outward. You can tell which neighborhood you are in by looking at the street signs, and most hotels, restaurants, and other facilities advertise this information along with the location of the closest metro stop. There are over 300 metro stops in total. The Euro currency is used in France, which is a country that is a part of the European Union. Both automated teller machines and banks can be found in abundant supply in Paris. The majority of hotels also provide guests with the option to have their money converted to the nation's currency. Both the Charles de Gaulle and the Orly airports are equipped with automated teller machines.

Paris History Overview

Over a period of more than 2,000 years, Paris has been subjected to assaults by foreign invaders, devastation by disease, and strife caused by religious conflict; however, it has also served as the location for some of the most significant cultural, political, and artistic achievements in the history of the world. All of this contributes to a lengthy and eventful history.

The city was formerly known as Lutetia; however, around the year 212 AD, it was renamed after the Parisii, who were a Celtic tribe who had established in the region in the third century BC. Invaders from the Roman Empire, the Franks (a Germanic people who lived north and east of the Lower Rhine), and the Normans (the people for whom the region of Normandy in France is named) came in the centuries that followed, and in 451, there was a near brush with the armies of the notorious plunderer Attila the Hun. Attila was able to be lured away from Paris as a result of a prayer marathon that was organized by Saint Genevieve, who is now venerated as the city's patron saint. This helped preserve Paris.

Christianization had started about the year 250 AD, but it wasn't until 1163 that construction on medieval cathedrals such as Notre Dame began. These cathedrals took nearly two centuries to finish being built. The cathedrals of Notre Dame and Saint-Chapelle, both of which are renowned for the stained glass in their interiors, are among the most identifiable symbols of the city as well as some of the greatest specimens of Gothic architecture in Europe.

Late in the 14th century and early in the 15th century brought war with England, the devastating Black Death pandemic, as well as internal revolts stemming from popular discontent with the power of the monarchy and excessive taxation. Also during this time period, the Black Death pandemic spread throughout Europe. Beginning in the early 16th century, violence between Catholics and Protestants engulfed the city. This violence reached its climax in the St. Bartholomew's Day Massacre of 1572, in which an estimated three thousand Protestants were killed by Catholic mobs who were encouraged to carry out their attacks by King Charles IX. However, the 16th and 17th centuries were also the height of the French Renaissance (which literally translates to "rebirth"), which was characterized by a number of significant developments in the fields of philosophy as well as the fine arts such as painting, music, and architecture.

The end of the French monarchy was signaled by the French Revolution in 1789, which was followed by the Reign of Terror, a period of anarchy and executions that lasted for ten years and came to an end when Napoleon Bonaparte took control in 1799. Before he was defeated in 1814, Napoleon, who viewed Paris as a "New Rome," created a number of public monuments, some of which were deliberate reproductions of great Roman buildings. These monuments included the Arc de Triomphe and the Louvre.

The beginning of an era of rapid expansion can be attributed to the Industrial Revolution. Paris became the second largest metropolis in Europe after London as a result of the migration of workers from rural areas into the city. The population of Paris increased to 900,000 during this time. In the middle of the 19th century, Baron Haussman, who had been given the task of modernizing Paris by Emperor Napoleon III, began demolishing large portions of the old city in order to create a New Paris that featured wide, straight boulevards, expansive gardens, and uniform building heights. This was the beginning of Paris' transition toward its current look and layout.

Paris reached new heights and new depths during the Belle Epoque period, which spanned the latter half of the 19th century. Impressionist painting and art nouveau architecture (French for "new art") contributed to the city's unique identity. So did brothels and cabarets like the Moulin Rouge, which contributed to Paris' hedonistic reputation as the "sin capital of Europe." Moreover, the city was home to some of the world's most famous impressionist painters and art nouveau architects. The "Lost Generation" of English-speaking writers, which included personalities like as Ernest Hemingway, James Joyce, and Gertrude Stein, as well as painters such as Pablo Picasso and Salvador Dali, made Paris their home in the years following World War One. Paris was conquered by German Nazi forces in 1940, marking the beginning of an occupation that would last for a total of four years.

The city has changed very little over the past sixty years, but during the administrations of Presidents George Pompidou (1969–1974), Francois Mitterrand (1981–1995, during which time he ordered the construction of the Louvre pyramid by Pei), and Jacques Chirac, the city has made significant strides (19952007). Today, Paris is a major worldwide city and a corporate hub, and it possesses a mystique that places it among the top three most visited cities in the world, along with London and Bangkok.

Paris Architecture

Haussmann. The main thoroughfares of Paris, their straight avenues beginning at the Place de l'Etoile, and their freestone structures with grey slate roofs are all thanks to this 19th-century architect. Napoléon III hired him in 1853 to remodel Paris in an effort to improve traffic flow, promote economic development, and make the city "revolution proof" by making it more difficult to erect barricades. The wide, tree-lined boulevards and enormous parks that Paris is known for today were created by Haussmann by razing much of the city's decaying apartment buildings and old, winding streets. The amount of criticism Haussmann received at the time led to his eventual dismissal in 1870. Le Marais, L'île de la Cite, L'île Saint-Louis, and the Latin Quarter are the only remnants of the old Paris that are still present today. Additionally, Montmartre has retained its sense of an old village. It couldn't be demolished by Haussmann's rigid architecture because it was on a hill.

It's interesting to observe that Haussmann's impact can still be felt on a basic level. As part of Haussman's innovation some might perhaps say obsession to make the old Paris a clean city, water periodically gushes from artificial artesian springs to clear the gutters of the city's streets and boulevards. He also organized the flow of the city's effluent. It's also intriguing that the USA would ask Pierre l'Enfant, a Parisian, to make similar changes to Washington, DC's urban architecture.

Despite the extensive renovation, the pre- and post-Haussmann structures and monuments in Paris are spectacular and well-preserved. You must visit the French Renaissance Louvre with its cutting-edge glass pyramid, the opulent Neo Baroque (Napoleon III) Opéra de Paris constructed by Garnier in the second half of the 19th century (a good tour for those who don't have time to visit Versailles), the iron Eiffel Tower built for the 1900 World's Fair, the Hightech Modern Centre Georges Pompidou with its exterior multicolored infrastructure that gives the impression that it was constructed "inside out," and the o

Don't miss the Grande Arche of the Défense (a nearby suburb of Paris), which stands directly in front of the Arc de Triomphe, the Champs-Elysées, the Tuileries Carousel, and the Louvre's pyramid; also, the French National Library (Bibliothèque François Mitterrand), which is situated on the left bank of the Seine, close to Bercy, and features L-shaped towers of books (symbolizing open books)

Churches, Chapels, and Cathedrals

Paris's religious structures, which are listed under "Architecture" rather than "Religion" here, captivate people of all faiths and may be one of the reasons that Paris is regarded as one of the "great" cities of the world alongside Rome, London, Florence, Madrid, Vienna, Moscow, Montreal, and Venice. They were once among the pinnacles of Western civilization and unquestionably depict vision of the greatest kind. They can now provide a cool, peaceful, and quiet refuge in the heat of a summer vacation in addition to astonishment or a rare sense of connectedness to an ancient past. The size of their enormous organs will literally move you on a Saturday or Sunday night. Additionally, in the spring, summer, and fall, organizations of classical musicians offer free or extremely inexpensive performances of everything from Bach and Vivaldi concertos to Mozart's "Requiem" by complete choirs and orchestras. Typically, the "cheap seats" cost 1015 euros, while front-row seating costs

2025 euros. These musical treasures are announced in handbills and monthly travel periodicals.

The "great dame" (who invented the term?) is the Notre Dame Cathedral in Paris. Possibly the only location in this list that defies description. It needs to be observed, circled, entered, and lived. The most well-known example of Middle Age French Gothic art, rivaling any basilica, cathedral, or church elsewhere in the world in terms of sheer size and both internal and outdoor architecture. Among numerous significant historical occurrences, Napoleon's misbehavior here in 1804 may be the most well-known. On the site of the Cathedral of Saint-Etienne (528), construction got underway in 1163 and continued for centuries.

Basilica of the Holy Cross: The architects of what is arguably THE architectural feature, whose pure white travertine can be seen from all over Paris and from which almost all of Paris can be inhaled, were motivated by location, position, location, and a vision for the majesty and grace that Montmartre deserves. They were propelled by the innumerable donations from all walks of life and all regions of France made in honor of those who lost their lives in the Franco-Prussian War and in gratitude that Paris was spared. (When they weren't enough, the government took over.) The exterior is as airy, ethereal, and lofty as a cloud. Inside the ceiling dome's (apse) dome is a massive gold Byzantine mosaic that appears to be moving. The 19ton "Savoyarde" bell is amplified by the tower of this church. Consecrated in 1919, one year after the end of World War I, but constructed in the Romano-Byzantine style between 1875 and 1914.

Stain glass dominates the walls of the French Court Gothic La Sainte-Chapelle. The light coming through these windows can be blinding on sunny days as well as some cloudy ones. If you come in at ground level, do not be disappointed. Located upstairs! You know you're there when it seems like you're inside a jeweled crown. close to Notre Dame. 124648 was constructed under King Louis IX (Saint Louis). You can attend one of the many (nearly nightly) classical music concerts there if you wish to have a special experience there.

Napoleon reimagined La Madeleine
(Sainte Marie Madeleine), a 1764 construction project inspired by the Pantheon, as the "temple to the grandeur of the Grande Armée" in 1806. (Napoleon later replaced the Arc de Triomphe in this function.) Louis XVIII decided in 1815 that the building would become a church. It was "repurposed" to become a train station after he passed away. It changed into the current church in 1842.

The biggest and most elaborate Jesuit-style church is Saint-Sulpice. churches have stood at the same location since at least the ninth century. presently more well-known for its significant role in a contentious book and film. Look for the sign that reads, "This is not a remnant of a pagan temple, despite imaginative assertions in a recent novel. Such a temple has never existed here. It was never referred to as a "roseline." It does not line up with the meridian that runs through the center of the Paris Observatory, which is used on maps to determine whether a longitude is East or West of Paris. Nothing supernatural can be inferred from this. The church was well-known for possessing the biggest organ in Europe even before the publication of the book (Notre Dame has since surpassed it). Yes, the "Astronomical Gneoman," whose meridian line was used to determine the precise dates of the solstices, equinoxes, and Easter, was given formal commission to do so. What should you believe since we already know what it is not? Built 16461745.

Sainte Eustache: This enormous Gothic building with flying buttresses and columns next to Châtelet Les Halles is less well-known and repaired than others in Paris. However, it is still stunning. The current version, which stands where its predecessor did at the start of the 13th century, was constructed between 15321637. The interior of this Gothic building is dark and void-like, although the decor is Renaissance. With 8,000 pipes, it boasts a large organ. Molière, Richelieu, and the marquise de Pompadour are buried here. Basilique Saint-Denis: A few kilometers from central Paris, it is sort of the royal necropolis of France (in the location outside is Henri de Miller's enormous modern head and hand sculpture, but that's another tale). The 12th century saw the start of the present version, which was finished in 1270. It is also the first significant Gothic and Carolingian church. The first monastery was established here during the 7th century and was given the name of the slain first bishop of Paris. The royal remains were unearthed (a polite term) and interred in a communal burial after the church was looted during the revolution. Napoleon first renovated it, followed by Louis XVIII. St. Denis' chancel is magnificent right now. From magnificent Renaissance graves to Medieval recumbent statues, it houses the tombs of the French kings. However, they're empty.

La Abbatiale Saint Germaindes Prés is a Gothic and Romanesque structure, maybe the oldest in all of Paris. It is not among the largest. The old abbey, which is said to have held St. Vincent's garment, was a popular pilgrimage site in the sixth century. Normans destroyed it in the ninth century, and it was restored as a Benedictine abbey in the eleventh and twelfth centuries. It was torched during the revolution, as were other French churches, and was looted. Both in the 1990s and the late 18th century, there were significant restorations. The choir and the biggest of the three towers are still standing today. The church still serves as the focal point of one of Paris's most romantic and intellectual neighborhoods, which many French people believe to be one of the cradles of very modern French civilization. The final resting place of various Merovingian rulers and René Descartes' heart (!). Also, the church's superb premicrophone acoustics made it a wonderful location for evening concerts.

Catholic Cathedral of the Invalids: L'Église des Soldats (16761679) and L'Église du Dôme are part of the complex (16761706). The magnificent golden-domed French Renaissance veterans' hospital church, built by Louis XIV in 1670, dominates the scene as it is approached from the Esplanade des Invalides, a broad lawn that runs from the end of the elaborate Pont Alexandre III on the Seine to the cathedral. The spire rises 101 meters. In 1989, it underwent its fifth regilding, utilizing 550,000 gold leaves, or more than 20 pounds of gold. Napoleon Bonaparte is indeed laid up in all his incomparable glory here. His conquests, including Moscow, which is not listed anywhere else on Napoleon's victory side of the ledger, are etched surrounding the monument.

Saint-Augustin: This church, which is relatively new compared to the other ancient structures mentioned here, provides a haven from the bustle of the busy boulevards Malesherbes and Haussmann, where cars zoom by at dizzying speeds, as well as from the shopping at the two most renowned department stores of Paris, which are only 200 meters away. Napoleon III ordered it, and it was the first edifice with a steel superstructure, constructed between 1860 and 1871. The principal outside feature is a gigantic dome that is nearly 100 meters high and bewildering to gaze at from inside. The conspicuous steel framing and other metalwork, a hallmark of the industrial era, is another defining interior feature. On a human level, this chapel has a lot of features that honor and are created by the young members of its congregation. a highly kind greeting in a setting that might ordinarily conjure the epithet "gaping." (However, it is incredibly light and airy throughout due to its big round windows.)

La Sainte-Trinité Church: This is the one you've seen if you arrived in town or left for CDG airport via public transportation. It is not particularly huge; rather, it is situated at the intersection of many significant thoroughfares. If you contrast how many people have seen it so many times with how few have actually entered, it might be one of Paris's best-kept secrets. It is a young building by Parisian standards, having been finished in 1867, yet it doesn't appear to be. Some claim that its outside resembles a church built upon another church (and so forth), and that neither a vertical nor a horizontal surface is empty. In contrast to what one might think based on the external coverage, the interior is serene and much lighter. The façade is light stone that has recently been cleaned, and the interior is filled with vibrant colors that are highlighted by the bright light. It was used to film a scene for Truffaut's Les Quatre Cent Coups.

Paris Cultural Awareness

Some people contend that the terms "Paris" and "culture" are interchangeable. Some people might even add the term "style" as a third. Through a variety of mediums, including architecture, cuisine, decorative arts, diplomacy, theatre, fashion, language, literature, music, painting, politics, and sculpture, Paris has made a significant contribution to Western culture for centuries. Paris serves as a global definition of what it means to be French in many ways.

Today, Paris is a tremendous melting pot of ethnic communities that enrich its own cultural life in addition to its identity on the global arena. The Northeastern region of the city is home to areas like Belleville and La Goutte d'Or that showcase many of the subcultures that make up the overall Parisian scene. You can see it all while strolling down Belleville's main thoroughfare, rue Belleville, in the 19th arrondissement: live chickens at butcher shops, colorful head scarves, crispy Peking Duck, and smokers at hookah cafes. Strasbourg In Saint Denis, which is located in the 2nd, 3rd, and 10th arrondissements, you can get dreadlocks and visit the bustling Passage Brady, a full street devoted solely to Indian cuisine. In addition to having a sizable Jewish population, the Marais is well known for being the LGBT community's center of entertainment.

Paris has always been a city for intellectuals and fresh ideas despite its enormously diverse populace. The first Surrealists gathered in the renowned Café de Flore in Saint Germaindes Prés on the left bank. It served as a hub for international collaboration between filmmakers, painters (Picasso, Giacometti), publishers, writers, and philosophers (Sartre) in the 1930s. The numerous jazz clubs in the Latin Quarter made it the place to be after the war. Here, Miles Davis, Juliette Gréco, and Boris Vian all performed.

Paris is renowned for its Cafés, even outside of the well-known hangouts. Locals spend hours relaxing on terraces drinking little cups of espresso and conversing with passersby. Paris, one of the world's artistic centers, is home to thousands of art museums, both large and small. There is something for everyone, from the classics at the Louvre to the contemporary shows at the Pompidou.

Paris is a city bursting with performing arts. You may always find street performers in the areas surrounding Beaubourg. There are numerous theaters where ballets, dramas, and operas are presented, including the renowned Opéra Garnier (home of the Phantom). You will be awed by the abundance of creativity if you have the opportunity to visit Paris during one of its major cultural events, such as "Les nuits blanches" (an all-night event dedicated to the arts around the city the first weekend of October) or "Paris plage" (a summer event with many selected performances on the banks of the Seine beginning typically mid-July and ending mid-August).

Fans of classical music have the opportunity to attend low-cost performances held in cathedrals such the Notre Dame Cathedral and Sainte Chapelle, providing a singular opportunity to hear baroque music in a baroque setting. Many Parisians think that the only sporting event worth attending is a soccer match at the Parc des Princes stadium. Be aware that when the Paris team (PSG) plays storied rivals like Marseilles, it can get fairly rowdy inside and outside the stadium (OM). And exercise considerably more caution when English teams and their boisterous fans visit! (Don't be alarmed; you'll hear them approaching!)

Etiquette has a lengthy tradition in this capital city. Parisians typically have high standards for proper conduct in public and appreciate it when visitors follow them. There are always going to be exceptions to the rules in a major metropolis, but these are some general principles: Check your volume because most people are reserved and quiet in public. They frequently dress in black and neutral hues. Both men and women use scarves for the most of the year. They are a simple way to spruce up an outfit, so it's not a terrible idea to pack one in your suitcase. When entering a store, be it a boutique or a bakery, it is considered courteous to say "bonjour" or "bonsoir" to the customer service staff. To assume that everyone speaks English is disrespectful. Many people do, but a little "Parlezvous en anglais?" can get a long way.

An appropriate gratuity for a restaurant lunch is a couple of euros. Although many people don't offer tips for drinks, tiny coins will do if you want to. At the conclusion of a dinner, you must ask for your bill ("l'addition, s'il vous plaît"). Expect efficient courtesy from waitstaff rather than friendly faces and lively conversation. Although there are some unkind servers out there you're likely to run into at least one they're not necessarily being frigid; it's just how they do things. The blatant PDA is another cliché of Paris that you will probably see. Romance in Paris pours out onto the streets, whether you find it endearing or uncomfortable.

The Economy

Paris has been an important city in Europe since the Middle Ages, but it wasn't until the second half of the 19th century that it began to take on its current form. Its population doubled to reach more than 2 million during the 40 years following 1850, when it experienced its greatest expansion. It peaked in 1921 (2,906,500), at which time residents started leaving the city. Since then, the most of the growth has taken place in the suburbs, where a sizable section of the blue-collar work force resides, as residences have been replaced by offices in the heart of Paris. A total of 2 million people commute everyday, with around half going from the suburbs to the city center and the other half going from downtown Paris to the suburbs.

Paris's economic operations are more significant and complex than those in any other region of France. The city is home to over 65 percent of the country's bank and company headquarters. The majority of the industry in central Paris is small-scale craft-based, skill-based, and frequently family-owned. Numerous of these sectors produce high-end products like perfumes, furs, gloves, jewelry, toys, apparel, wooden objects, and other luxuries.

In the heart of Paris, printing and publishing books are significant industries. The suburbs are home to heavier industries. These include the production of processed foods, electric and electrical items, chemicals, railroad rolling stock, machine tools, and automobiles. Additionally crucial are building and the manufacture of building supplies. However, the city's primary source of wealth comes from tourism, which makes it one of the top tourist destinations in Europe.

Paris Safety and Health Wise

Paris is thought to be a very safe city. Nearly all neighborhoods are safe for wandering with very little chance of being mugged. Some places are safer than others, though. Le Marais, the Latin Quarter, and the Louvre neighborhood, which is in the heart of Paris and where most tourists congregate, are all very safe areas because it is a busy region both during the day and at night.

Les Halles can be a little unsettling at night because it's a notorious hangout for drug dealers, but it's getting safer now that it's under police supervision all the time. On weekends, be on the lookout for big groups of youths; they are frequently suburban gangs traveling to Paris in search of mischief. The opulent, primarily residential western section of the city the 17th, 8th, and 16th arrondissements can get rather deserted and unsettling at night because of its luxury. Although not very dangerous, these areas could leave you feeling rather alone, especially at night.

At least during the day, the Champs-Elysées is very bustling and not too dangerous. There are many offices, therefore businesspeople are who you'll mostly run into. Even so, you should exercise caution on this wide boulevard, especially at night when it is particularly busy and a prime location for pickpockets. Additionally, because the majority of Paris' nightclubs are located in this region, you can run into inebriated individuals or groups of young people looking to cause problems. The Champs Elysées is safe to walk on, but not after midnight.

Montmarte is a safe neighborhood, and if you travel down the hill to Pigalle, the Red Light District, you won't need to worry too much because it's very busy and touristy, even in the wee hours of the morning. Avoid spending too much time on the main boulevard because there are also inebriated individuals and drug dealers there (be especially cautious if you are a female). The safest part of Paris is not in the north. You should always keep a watch on your wallet around Gare du Nord and Gare de l'Est. You should only visit La Goutte d'Or during the day if you wish to explore the area, which is rather impoverished.

African and North African communities in Belleville and Menilmontant have improved in safety over the past five years. Young "bourgeoisbohèmes" (also known as "bobos") who moved here to avoid the exorbitant rents of other hip neighborhoods like Bastille are fond of them.

East Paris is generally secure.

Due to the lively atmosphere of Bastille's many cafés and bars, you may stumble into inebriated individuals who exhibit excessive behavior at night, although nothing particularly harmful. The 13th arrondissment, which includes the Chinese quarter, Montparnasse, and the south of Paris are all secure regions to explore on the other side of the Seine.

A stroll along the stunning Seine banks is a must-do when in Paris. Even during the day, it is safer to go up the sidewalk as opposed to down the quays and directly along the bank. Although it appears to be beautiful, there are some unpleasant personalities down there, and if you do run into trouble, it will be much more difficult to escape than if you are up on the roadway. Whenever you do down the quayside: Before going down the stairs or ramp, remember to: 1 glance about, 2 always check for the next exit up, 3 don't go alone, and 4 never go into the tunnels under the bridges, even if they seem short and you can see through the other side. Unfortunately, some homeless individuals reside there and may turn hostile if you enter "their" territory.

Of course, there are some fundamental guidelines to follow in order to feel truly safe in the city:

Keep an extra eye out in the subway and close to popular tourist destinations: Watch your baggage, keep your money and passport out of your pockets, ignore those wanting you to sign their petition and keep going, or pretend to be French by saying "non merci" (don't do this or they'll rob you). Make sure no one is seeing you type your access code when you take money from a cash dispenser, then swiftly grab your card and the cash and put them away in your pocket. Never walk about with a banknote in your hand.

Don't carry your handbag too far away from your body, like in your hand, as pickpockets would be able to steal it too easily. Watch out for motorbikes on walkways and pedestrian areas. Be especially cautious if you carry a backpack because pickpockets can easily access them in crowded places like the metro and flea markets (pickpockets can operate on a moto). Beware of con artists! Do not comply if someone asks you to tie a string around their finger or wants you to do any other amusing things. These individuals are typically not a threat, but once they are done with your "free" bracelet, they will demand an exorbitant price and seize your arm until you pay the sum. Just be alert and keep an eye on your belongings. At the Place de la Concorde, a young woman played a prank on visitors by picking up a ring off the ground in front of them and offering it to them as good luck. Possibly after you put it on, she blames the visitor of stealing it.

Additionally, there are a lot of persons who congregate beneath the Eiffel Tower who will employ every scheme at their disposal to steal money from you. These individuals are not permitted to be in this area, and it is usual for them to entirely disappear when a police patrol passes by before reappearing a short time later. However, they do sell some interesting stuff, and if you buy it from them you won't get in trouble. The only piece of advice I can give is to avoid purchasing any imitation goods from one of these people (don't buy any apparel or handbags) and to haggle the price down to one that YOU are willing to pay. Regardless of what they claimed to be the original price, they will typically accept practically any sum you are ready to give them because they are aware of their competitors.

When traveling to and from the airport, avoid using the elevators at Gare du Nord. despite not being alone yourself. Pickpockets may find them to be a sanctuary. You might see young men with hoodies, hands-free phones, and white plastic carry bags no luggage occasionally accompanied by young women. So, before you exit the elevator, keep an eye on your baggage and be alert of the people entering and exiting the building if you truly don't want to battle with your luggage on the escalators.

Système d'Accueil des Victimes Estrangées (S.A.V.E.

With the twenty-language Reception System for Foreign Victims program, any police civil servant may now record complaints from foreign tourists and issue them with a receipt in their native tongue, making the visitor's subsequent procedures at the embassy or in their home nation easier.

If someone approaches you...

Some con artists may pose as police officers and solicit your identity and cash. Remember that a genuine police officer will never demand payment. Ask to view their white plastic, multicolored ID card that says "Police" in the lower quarter, has a diagonal blue, white, and red ribbon in the top left corner, and has various holographic graphics on it.

Follow these recommendations to stay safe.

The Police Department provides some valuable tips and helpful phone numbers to ensure you navigate the city as safely as possible.

Useful telephone numbers

Emergency police calls.................. 17
Paramedics (SAMU)........................ 15
Fire Department............................ 18
Poison Emergency Center.............. 01.40.05.48.48
Emergency Medical Assistance....... 01.47.07.77.77
Drug Squad Hot Line....................... 0 800 14.21.52 (tollfree)

Paris Convention & Visitors Bureau

127, avenue des ChampsElysées, 75008 Paris
RERA and Métro lines 1, 2 and 6 Charles de Gaulle Étoile station
Phone: 08.36.68.31.12 (€ 0.34/minute)

Information & Security Department

Telephone information service Mon. Fri., 09:00 a.m. 7:00 p.m.
Reception by appointment only Mon. Fri., 9:00 a.m. 12:30 p.m. and 2:00 p.m. 5:30 p.m.
Phone: 01.49.96.30.07

Lost Property Service (Le Service des Objects Trouvés)

Préfecture de Police 36, rue des Morillons, 75015 Paris
Métro station: Convention, line 12
Tram stop: Georges Brassens, line T3; Bus lines: 62, 89, 95
Mon. Wed., 8:30 a.m. 5:00 p.m.; Thurs., 8:30 a.m. 12 noon; Fri., 8:30 a.m. 4:30 p.m.; closed Sat. & Sun.
Phone: 08.21.00.25.25 (€ 0.12/minute) or 3430 (€ 0.06/minute + cost of call)

Every day, 600 to 700 objects are turned in to the police, after being found on Paris city streets, in the three surrounding departments (92, 93, 94), on RATP transports, at the three Paris airports, in taxicabs, and other public places. On average, about 150 items are restored to their owners daily. The web site (in French only) offers tips about reporting a loss. Items lost on SNCF trains and RER lines C/D/E are handled by the SNCF, not the police.

Lost or stolen credit cards

MasterCard: 08.00.90.13.87

Visa: 08.92.70.57.05

Visa Premier: 08.92.70.57.05

American Express: 01.47.77.70.00

Eurocard: 01.45.67.84.84

Diner's Club: 08.10.31.41.59

Lost or stolen mobile telephones

Contact your service provider as soon as possible in order to have your line suspended:

- Orange

  Service (including subscription) 08.25.00.57.00 (€ 0.15/minute from a fixed line)
  Mobicarte: 08.92.70.17.22 (€ 0.34/minute from a fixed line)
  Over the Internet: www.orange.fr mon abonnement SOS mobile
  Access from abroad: +33 6.07.62.64.64 (price of an international call)

- Bouygues Telecom

  Fixed price: 08.00.29.10.00 (toll free from a fixed line)
  Nomad card: 06.68.63.46.34 (price of a call towards a Nomad mobile phone):

Set price subscriptions: +33 1.46.10.86.86

Nomad Card offers: +33 6.68.63.46.34 (price of the foreign provider)

SFR

Option including subscription: 06.10.00.19.00 from a fixed phone (7 days a week, price of a call to an SFR mobile phone)

SFR Card option: 06.14.00.19.00 (6 days a week, price of a call to an SFR mobile phone)

Universal Music Mobile option: 06.12.00.12.00 from a fixed line (6 days a week, price of a call to an SFR mobile phone)

Over the Internet: www.sfr.fr

Access from abroad:

Options including subscription: +33 6.10.00.19.00

SFR Card offers: +33 6.14.00.19.00

UMM offers: +33 6.12.00.12.00

Public places & public transportation

- Do not leave your bags and luggage unattended, and do not accept any bags or packages from a stranger.
- In case you discover any suspicious item, do not touch it and immediately approach the police services.
- Do not let any individual go through a turnstile/gate directly behind you.

- Never buy tickets from scalpers who will charge you extra (up to ten times their value). Use ticket counters or ticket issuing machines in train/bus/subway stations.

Be careful in the street

- Carry a small bag or a waistbag/fannypack, rather than a backpack.
- If an assailant tries to snatch your bag, do not resist, or you may be injured.
- Do not put your phone and/or portable music player in an outside pocket of your bag or garments.
- Beware of individuals who may divert your attention in order to steal your personal belongings.
- Yell loudly for help if you feel you are in imminent danger or threatened/accosted by anyone.
- Steer clear of commotions and street demonstrations.

In restaurants and cafés

- Do not leave your methods of payment in cloakrooms or in your coat on a chair (a pickpocket could sit behind you and steal your belongings).
- Never lay your bag at your feet.
- Do not leave your mobile phone or your wallet on the table.

Your money

- Carry as little cash as you can.
- Use small denominations, credit/debit cards, or travelers' checks for any purchases.
- Carry your money in several places (bags, pockets, moneybelt...)
- Do not put your wallet in your back pockets; a front pocket (on pants) or inside jacket pocket is better.
- Keep the PIN code numbers of your credit cards confidential and note them down in a safe place, in case of loss or theft.
- Use ATMs at reputable banks, in welllit areas.

Your personal identification documents

- Remember to photocopy your passport and any other identification papers to facilitate their reissue; keep the copies in your hotel or your temporary place of residence.
- In case of loss, contact your country's consulate; in case of theft, also declare it to the police.
- Note down the address and phone number of your hotel or temporary residence, and keep them with you.

Your vehicle

- Close windows and lock doors, including the luggage compartment.
- Do not leave any valuable items in full view (mobile phone, camera, shopping bags, clothing items...)

Always know where to find the police in your neighborhood

- In every arrondissement of the capital city, the Police Prefecture offers various services to the general public.
- Central Police Stations and the SARIJ (division charged with processing and investigating complaints) are open 24 hours a day, 7 days a week.
- The local police units (UPQ) are open Monday through Friday, 9:00 a.m. 8 p.m. These services can provide you with immediate assistance such as: information, aid to victims of crime, and processing complaints.

What to do if you become the victim of an assault or theft

- During an assault, try to make the attacker go away by making as much noise as possible (shouting/screaming).
- Take refuge in the nearest shop and ask someone to call the police.

- Give a description of your attacker: sex, approximate age, hair color & cut, height & weight, distinctive features (beard, scars, tattoos, glasses, etc.).
- Indicate how and the direction in which the attacker fled. In the case of a vehicle, specify the color, brand and if possible the license plate number (even partially).
- Police officers will take you to the nearest police station so as to record your complaint. They will issue you a receipt/copy of the complaint in your own language.
- In the case of physical assault, an officer will also provide you with a written document allowing you to get examined at the medical legal emergency unit (open 24/7 at 1, place du Parvis Notre Dame, 75004 Paris; M4: Cité, RERB: St. Michel Notre Dame; phone 01.42.34.82.85). They will issue an official certificate to be added to your file.
- An investigation will then be opened to look for the assailant(s).
- In the case of a theft, go to the nearest police station to lodge a complaint. Save your receipt for insurance purposes.

Police stations in each arrondissement

SARIJ = (Service Accueil Recherche Investigation Judiciaire; UPQ = Unité de Police de Quartier)

	ADDRESS	PHONE	HOURS
1st Arrondissement			
CENTRAL POLICE STATION	45, place du Marché SaintHonoré Pyramides lines 7, 14	01 47 03 60 00	24 hrs., 7 days/wk.
SARIJ	10, rue Pierre Lescot Les Halles	01 44 82 74 00	24 hrs., 7 days/wk.
UPQ "Vendôme"	45, place du Marché StHonoré Pyramides	01 47 03 60 10	Mon. Fri., 9:00 a.m. 8:00 p.m.
Reception and Criminal Processing Unit	24, rue des Bons Enfants Louvre	01 44 55 38 00	Mon. Fri., 9:00 a.m. 8:00 p.m.
UPQ "Les Halles"	10, rue Pierre Lescot Les Halles	01 44 82 74 00	Mon. Fri., 9:00 a.m. 8:00 p.m.
2nd Arrondissement			
CENTRAL POLICE STATION	18, rue du Croissant Bourse line 3; Grands Boulevards lines 8, 9	01 44 88 18 00	24 hrs., 7 days/wk.
SARIJ	18, rue du Croissant Bourse, Grands Boulevards	01 44 88 18 00	24 hrs., 7 days/wk.
UPQ	18, rue du Croissant Bourse, Grands Boulevards	01 44 88 18 00	Mon. Fri., 9:00 a.m. 8:00 p.m.
3rd Arrondissement			
CENTRAL POLICE STATION	4bis6, rue aux Ours Etienne Marcel line 4	01 42 76 13 00	24 hrs., 7 days/wk.
SARIJ	4bis6, rue aux Ours Etienne Marcel	01 42 76 13 00	24 hrs., 7 days/wk.

UPQ	4bis6, rue aux Ours Etienne Marcel	01 42 76 13 00	Mon. Fri., 9:00 a.m. 8:00 p.m.
4th Arrondissement			
CENTRAL POLICE STATION	27, boulevard Bourdon Bastille lines 1, 5, 8	01 40 29 22 00	24 hrs., 7 days/wk.
SARIJ	27, boulevard Bourdon Bastille	01 40 29 22 00	7 days a week, 8:25 a.m. 8:00 p.m.
UPQ	27, boulevard Bourdon Bastille	01 40 29 22 00	7 days a week, 8:25 a.m. 8:00 p.m.
5th Arrondissement			
CENTRAL POLICE STATION	4, rue de la Montagne Sainte Geneviève Maubert Mutualité line 10	01 44 41 51 00	24 hrs., 7 days/wk.
SARIJ	4, rue de la Montagne Ste Geneviève Maubert Mutualité	01 44 41 51 00	24 hrs., 7 days/wk.
UPQ	4, rue de la Montagne Ste Geneviève Maubert Mutualité	01 44 41 51 00	Mon. Fri., 9:00 a.m. 8:00 p.m.
6th Arrondissement			
CENTRAL POLICE STATION	78, rue Bonaparte Saint Sulpice line 4	01 40 46 38 30	24 hrs., 7 days/wk.
SARIJ	12, rue Jean Bart Saint Placide	01 44 39 71 70	24 hrs., 7 days/wk.
UPQ"Odéon"	12, rue Jean Bart Saint Placide	01 44 39 71 70	Mon. Fri., 9:00 a.m. 8:00 p.m.

UPQ "St. Germaindes Prés"	14, rue de l'Abbaye Saint Germain des Prés	01 44 41 47 47	Mon. Fri., 9:00 a.m. 8:00 p.m.
7th Arrondissement			
CENTRAL POLICE STATION	9, rue Fabert Invalides lines 8, 13, RERC	01 44 18 69 07	24 hrs., 7 days/wk.
SARIJ	9, rue Fabert Invalides	01 44 18 69 47	24 hrs., 7 days/wk.
UPQ "Invalides"	33 ter, avenue Dusquesne St François Xavier	01 40 62 70 10	Monday/Friday 9:00 a.m. 8 p.m.
UPQ "Gros Cailloux"	6, rue Amélie (location closed on 17 Jan. 2011) La Tour Maubourg	01 44 18 66 10	Mon. Fri., 9:00 a.m. 8:00 p.m.
UPQ "St Thomas d'Aquin"	10, rue Peronnet Saint Germain des Prés	01 45 49 67 70	Mon. Fri., 9:00 a.m. 8:00 p.m.
8th Arrondissement			
CENTRAL POLICE STATION	1, avenue du Général Eisenhower ChampsElysées Clémenceau lines 1, 13	01 53 76 60 00	24 hrs., 7 days/wk.
SARIJ	210, rue du Fbg StHonoré Ternes	01 53 77 62 20	24 hrs., 7 days/wk.
UPQ "ChampsElysées"	5, rue Clément Marot Franklin Roosevelt	01 53 67 78 00	Mon. Fri., 9:00 a.m. 8:00 p.m.
UPQ "Madeleine"	31, rue d'Anjou Madeleine	01 43 12 83 83	Mon. Fri., 9:00 a.m. 8:00 p.m.
UPQ "Europe"	13, rue de Lisbonne Europe	01 44 90 82 90	Mon. Fri., 9:00 a.m. 8 p.m.

UPQ "Faubourg du Roule"	210, rue du Fbg StHonoré Ternes	01 53 77 62 20	Mon. Fri., 9:00 a.m. 8:00 p.m.
Vigie Gare StLazare	Plateform 1 cour de Rome Saint Lazare	01 53 42 05 22	7 days a week, 5:30 a.m. 1:30 a.m.
SATJ Gare StLazare	Plateform 1 cour de Rome Saint Lazare	01 45 22 17 89	Mon. Fri., 9:00 a.m. 8:00 p.m.
9th Arrondissement			
CENTRAL POLICE STATION	14 bis, rue Chauchat Richelieu Drouot lines 8, 9	01 44 83 80 80	24 hrs., 7 days/wk.
SARIJ	5, rue de Parme Place de Clichy	01 49 70 82 60	24 hrs., 7 days/wk.
UPQ "St Georges"	5, rue de Parme Place de Clichy	01 49 70 82 60	Mon. Fri., 9:00 a.m. 8:00 p.m.
UPQ "Faubourg Montmartre"	21, rue du Faubourg Montmartre Grands Boulevards	01 44 83 82 32	Monday/Friday 9:00 a.m. 8 p.m.
UPQ "Rochechouart"	50, rue de la Tour d'Auvergne Richelieu Drouot	01 49 70 87 17	Mon. Fri., 9:00 a.m. 8:00 p.m.
10th Arrondissement			
CENTRAL POLICE STATION	26, rue Louis Blanc Louis Blanc lines 7, 7bis	01 53 19 43 10	24 hrs., 7 days/wk.
SARIJ	14, rue de Nancy Jacques Bonsergent	01 48 03 89 00	24 hrs., 7 days/wk.
UPQ "Hôpital St. Louis"	40, avenue Claude Vellefaux Colonel Fabien	01 44 52 74 80	Mon. Fri., 9:00 a.m. 8:00 p.m.

UPQ "Porte Saint Denis"	45, ruc de Chabrol Gare de l'Est	01 45 23 80 00	Mon. Fri., 9:00 a.m. 8:00 p.m.
UPQ "St Vincent de Paul"	179, rue du Faubourg Saint Denis Gare du Nord	01 44 89 64 70	Mon. Fri., 9:00 a.m. 8:00 p.m.
UPQ "Porte Saint Martin"	45, rue de Chabrol Gare de l'Est	01 45 23 80 00	Mon. Fri., 9:00 a.m. 8 p.m.
Vigie Gare du Nord	18, rue de Dunkerque Gare du Nord	01 55 31 58 08	Mon. Sat., 7:30 a.m. 11:00 p.m.
Vigie Gare de l'Est	Rue du 8 mai 1945 Gare de l'Est	01 55 31 58 74	Mon. Sat. 7:30 11:00 p.m.
SATJ Gare du Nord	18, rue de Dunkerque Gare du Nord	01 40 82 74 00	Mon. Fri., 9:00 a.m. 8:00 p.m.
SATJ Gare de l'Est	Rue du 8 mai 1945 Gare de l'Est	01 46 07 06 37	7 days a week, 9:00 a.m. 8:00 p.m.
11th Arrondissement			
CENTRAL POLICE STATION	107, boulevard Voltaire Voltaire line 9	01 44 93 27 30	24 hrs., 7 days/wk.
SARIJ	19, passage Beslay Parmentier	01 49 29 59 60	24 hrs., 7 days/wk.
UPQ "Folie Méricourt"	19, passage Beslay Parmentier	01 49 29 59 60	Mon. Fri., 9:00 a.m. 8:00 p.m.
UPQ "Roquette"	10, rue Camille Desmoulins Voltaire	01 55 25 47 10	Mon. Fri., 9:00 a.m. 8:00 p.m.

UPQ "Ste Marguerite"	10, rue Léon Frot Charonne	01 58 39 38 60	Mon. Fri., 9:00 a.m. 8:00 p.m.
12th Arrondissement			
CENTRAL POLICE STATION	80, avenue Daumesnil Gare de Lyon lines 1, 14, RERA&D	01 44 87 50 12	24 hrs., 7 days/wk.
SARIJ	80, avenue Daumesnil Gare de Lyon	01 44 87 50 12	24 hrs., 7 days/wk.
UPQ "Belair"	36, rue du Rendez-Vous Picpus	01 53 33 85 15	Mon. Fri., 9:00 a.m. 8 p.m.
UPQ "Picpus"	30, rue Hénard Dugomier	01 56 95 12 81	Mon. Fri., 9:00 a.m. 8:00 p.m.
UPQ "Quinze-Vingt"	80, avenue Daumesnil Gare de Lyon	01 44 87 51 94	Mon. Fri., 9:00 a.m. 8:00 p.m.
UPQ "Bercy"	2022, rue de l'Aubrac Cour Saint Émilion	01 53 02 07 10	Mon. Fri., 9:00 a.m. 8:00 p.m.
Vigie Gare de Lyon	80, allée de Bercy Gare de Lyon	01 53 02 94 00	24 hrs., 7 days/wk.
SATJ Gare de Lyon	80, allée de Bercy Gare de Lyon	01 53 02 94 01	Mon. Fri., 9:00 a.m. 8:00 p.m.
13th Arrondissement			
CENTRAL POLICE STATION	144, boulevard de l'Hôpital Place d'Italie lines 5, 6, 7	01 40 79 05 05	24 hrs., 7 days/wk.
SARIJ	144, boulevard de l'Hôpital Place d'Italie	01 40 79 05 05	24 hrs., 7 days/wk.

UPQ	144, boulevard de l'Hôpital Place d'Italie	01 40 79 05 05	Mon. Fri., 9:00 a.m. 8:00 p.m.
Vigie BNF	160, avenue de France Bibliothèque François Mitterrand	01 44 23 23 20	7 days a week, 7:30 a.m. 10 p.m.
Vigie Olympiades	32, rue du Javelot Porte d'Ivry	01 53 79 07 17	7 days a week, 11:00 a.m. 12:30 p.m. and 6:00 7:30 p.m.
14th Arrondissement			
CENTRAL POLICE STATION	114116, avenue du Maine Gaîté line 13	01 53 74 14 06	24 hrs., 7 days/wk.
SARIJ	114116, avenue du Maine Gaité	01 53 74 11 76	24 hrs., 7 days/wk.
UPQ "Montparnasse"	114116, avenue du Maine Gaité	01 53 74 11 21	Mon. Fri., 9:00 a.m. 8 p.m.
UPQ "Montsouris"	50, rue Rémy Dumoncel Gaité	01 40 64 70 60	Mon. Fri., 9:00 a.m. 8:00 p.m.
15th Arrondissement			
CENTRAL POLICE STATION	250, rue de Vaugirard Vaugirard line 12	01 53 68 81 00	24 hrs., 7 days/wk.
SARIJ	250, rue de Vaugirard Vaugirard	01 53 68 81 00	24 hrs., 7 days/wk.
UPQ "Javel Grenelle"	3840, rue Linois Charles Michel	01 45 78 37 00	Mon. Fri., 9:00 a.m. 8:00 p.m.
UPQ "Necker"	45, boulevard Garibaldi Sèvres Lecourbe	01 53 69 44 00	Mon. Fri., 9:00 a.m. 8 p.m.

UPQ "St Lambert"	250, rue de Vaugirard Vaugirard	01 53 68 81 00	Mon. Fri., 9:00 a.m. 8:00 p.m.
Vigie Gare Montparnasse	17, boulevard de Vaugirard Gare Montparnasse	01 40 48 13 01	7 days a week, 6:30 a.m. 11:30 p.m.
SATJ Gare Montparnasse	11, boulevard de Vaugirard Gare Montparnasse	01 42 79 40 50	Mon. Fri., 9:00 a.m. 8:00 p.m.
16th Arrondissement			
CENTRAL POLICE STATION	62, avenue Mozart Ranelagh line 9	01 55 74 50 00	24 hrs., 7 days/wk.
SARIJ	75, rue de la Faisanderie Porte Dauphine	01 40 72 22 50	24 hrs., 7 days/wk.
UPQ "Auteuil"	74, rue Chardon Lagache Charandon Lagache	01 53 92 51 00	Mon. Fri., 9:00 a.m. 8:00 p.m.
UPQ "Muette"	2, rue Bois le Vent La Muette	01 44 14 64 64	Mon. Fri., 9:00 a.m. 8:00 p.m.
UPQ "Chaillot"	4, rue du Bouquet de Longchamp Boissière	01 53 70 61 80	Mon. Fri., 9:00 a.m. 8:00 p.m.
UPQ "Porte dauphine"	75, rue de la Faisanderie Porte Dauphine	01 40 72 22 79	Mon. Fri., 9:00 a.m. 8 p.m.
17th Arrondissement			
CENTRAL POLICE STATION	1921, rue Truffaut La Fourche line 13	01 44 90 37 17	24 hrs., 7 days/wk.
SARIJ	1921, rue Truffaut La Fourche	01 44 90 37 17	24 hrs., 7 days/wk.

UPQ "Batignolles"	1921, rue Truffaut La Fourche	01 44 90 37 17	Mon. Fri., 9:00 a.m. 8:00 p.m.
UPQ "Ternes Monceau"	3, avenue Gourgaud Perreire	01 44 15 83 10	Mon. Fri., 9:00 a.m. 8:00 p.m.
18th Arrondissement			
CENTRAL POLICE STATION	7981, rue de Clignancourt Marcadet Poissonniers lines 4, 12	01 53 41 50 00	24 hrs., 7 days/wk.
SARIJ	34, rue de la Goutte d'Or Barbès Rochechouart	01 49 25 48 00	24 hrs., 7 days/wk.
UPQ "Clignancourt"	122124, rue Marcadet Marcadet Poissonniers	01 53 41 85 00	Mon. Fri., 9:00 a.m. 8:00 p.m.
UPQ "Goutte d'Or"	50, rue Doudeauville Marcadet Poissonniers	01 53 09 24 70	Mon. Fri., 9:00 a.m. 8:00 p.m.
UPQ "La Chapelle"	18, rue Raymond Queneau Porte de la Chapelle	01 53 26 47 50	Mon. Fri., 9:00 a.m. 8:00 p.m.
Vigie Mont Cenis	74 bis, rue du Mont Cenis Jules Joffrin	01 53 09 97 20	Mon. Fri., 9:00 a.m. 8:00 p.m.
19th Arrondissement			
CENTRAL POLICE STATION	35, rue Erik Satie Ourcq line 5	01 55 56 58 00	24 hrs., 7 days/wk.
SARIJ	3/5, rue Erik Satie Ourcq	01 55 56 58 00	24 hrs., 7 days/wk.
UPQ "Pont de Flandre"	37, rue de Nantes Corentin Cariou	01 53 26 81 50	Mon. Fri., 9:00 a.m. 8:00 p.m.

UPQ "Amérique"	14, rue Auguste Thierry Place des Fêtes	01 56 41 30 00	Mon. Fri., 9:00 a.m. 8:00 p.m.
UPQ "Combat"	10, rue Pradier Buttes Chaunont	01 44 52 79 30	Mon. Fri., 9:00 a.m. 8:00 p.m.
20th Arrondissement			
CENTRAL POLICE STATION	48, avenue Gambetta Gambetta lines 3, 3bis	01 40 33 34 00	24 hrs., 7 days/wk.
SARIJ	66, rue des Orteaux Alexandre Dumas	01 44 93 85 20	24 hrs., 7 days/wk.
UPQ "Belleville"	46, rue Ramponneau Belleville	01 44 62 83 50	Mon. Fri., 9:00 a.m. 8:00 p.m.
UPQ "Père Lachaise"	46, avenue Gambetta Gambetta	01 40 33 34 60	Mon. Fri., 9:00 a.m. 8:00 p.m.
UPQ "Charonne"	48, rue Saint Blaise Porte de Montreuil	01 53 27 38 40	Mon. Fri., 9:00 a.m. 8:00 p.m.

Chapter Two

Traveling to Paris

Summarizing Paris Transport System

Three airports, six main train stations, and several bus stops serve Paris.

By Air

Paris has two major airports: Roissy Charles de Gaulle and Orly (ORY) (CDG).

Major airline companies are more likely to get you to Charles de Gaulle Airport from overseas flights. If you're flying with a low-cost airline or are coming from another French or European city, you might land in Orly. Northwest of Paris, Beauvais Tillé Airport (BVA) only flies to locations in Europe.

By Train

When commuting between towns or nations, trains are much more common in France than buses. A city like Marseilles (505 miles from Paris) may be reached in under three hours with the help of the TGV (high speed rail). Other cities outside of France where you can travel by rail include Brussels, Cologne, Amsterdam, Berlin, Luxembourg, and Portugal.

By choosing the "Borne Libre Service" when purchasing train tickets on the SNCF website, you can pick up your tickets at the automated ticket dispensers in your departure station. Make sure you go to the correct train station because Paris has six of them spread all over the city. Use the RATP website to make your route there. Each is reachable via RER.

By Coach

Coaches, or autocars in French, come in handy if there is an SNCF strike, which happens frequently, or if you're on a tight budget. Eurolines is the primary coach provider in France, and there are numerous boarding locations at bus stops and bus terminals (gare routières) throughout Paris. Where to board will be specified when you purchase your ticket.

Getting Downtown

From the airport, you can go to Paris via rail, bus, shuttle bus, taxi, or rented vehicle..

*Public Transit**

You can take public transportation from each airport to reach Paris.

The cheapest alternative for transportation from Charles de Gaulle Airport is the new easy Bus from easyJet bus service, which offers seats for as little as 2€ when ordered online (stops at Le Palais Royal/Louvre area and Place Andre Malraux) Alternately, spend €9.80 for a six-zone metro pass and board the RER train (a regional rail) straight. If you arrive at the platform early in the morning, it's probable that all you'll notice are a number of vending machines selling train tickets in front of you. Although some of these machines can accept credit cards, more and more of them are only designed to accept European-style chip and pin cards.

Continue along the platform to the ticket booths if you are having trouble using the machines. There, you can purchase your ticket to Paris (you may need to tell the ticket agent your card has to be swiped on the side of the credit card machine not inserted into the bottom). A return ticket (alle retour, pronounced allay raytour), while not less expensive, may spare you from standing in line on the way back. It takes about 40 minutes to get to Gare de Nord, though it may take longer in the morning when there are more stops. When you get at your station, keep in mind that since elevators are uncommon, you could have to carry your stuff up multiple flights of steps. The Air France Bus departs from all terminals and costs €15 for a single ticket; route 4 travels to Gare de Lyon and Gare Montparnasse, while route 2 makes stops at Porte Maillot and Etoile (Arc de Triomphe).

The Roissy bus from Charles de Gaulle to downtown is another option (stops at the Opera square). The cost is €10 one-way for each passenger. The bus makes stops at each airport terminal before taking passengers directly downtown without making any more stops. Two RER lines, two buses, and Orly are all connected to Paris. You will have the opportunity to board the extremely advanced autonomous shuttle called Orlyval if you ride the RER B. (your kids will love sitting in the front). To get to Paris, the Orly bus costs €6,40, while the Air France Bus costs €11,50. (or 18,50 roundtrip).

For €15, Paris Beauvais provides a shuttle service that travels in roughly an hour and a half from Paris (Porte Maillot stop) to the airport. The SNCF also operates an express regional train that travels to Beauvais's city center, from whence you may take a taxi to Paris.

More public transit details listed below.

Cabs

All three airports have taxi services available. Depending on where you're going in Paris, the typical ticket from Charles de Gaulle is around €4050, and the trip takes approximately one hour. The typical fare from Orly is roughly €35. It is not advised to take a taxi from central Beauvais due to the high cost.

Shuttle service

You might find this helpful: Typically, employing a shuttle service in Paris allows you to plan your vacation days, even weeks, in advance while still being cost-effective.

Car rental

It is not advised to rent a car in Paris because the city's traffic may be chaotic, parking can be difficult to come by, and public transportation is quite effective. However, you can locate car rental agencies (Royal Car, Avis, Hertz, Rent a Car, Budget) in every train station and at the airports if you need a vehicle. For a weekend, rates range from €85 (Hertz) to €230 (Holidays Auto). Give yourself at least two hours to drive from the suburbs into the city if you plan to return your rental car in Paris. The "extra day" fee for returns that are more than 30 minutes late (as defined by Europcar) can be pricey..

Getting Around

Despite having many Michelin-starred restaurants and upscale boutiques, Paris is only 6.2 miles long and 7.5 miles wide, making it simple to travel around on foot or by public transportation. Officially, Paris is split into 20 arrondissements, or districts, with numbers ranging from 1 to 20 in a clockwise spiral from the city's center. It's crucial to keep in mind that the city includes Zone 15 of the six Ile de France zones when purchasing specific rail tickets.

RATP is in charge of managing the metro, bus, tram, and a portion of the RERexpress train networks for public transportation. The Transilien suburban trains and the remaining RER network are operated by SNCF. The entire fare system is integrated, and you may purchase any ticket or pass at any RATP or SNCF ticket kiosk.

Walking

Undoubtedly, the best way to experience the City of Light is by walking. You can go around Paris in a few hours because it is a small city, but you'll probably spend more time at one of the many cafés and boutiques. You might have to walk in single file down the sidewalk because the majority of the city's oldest streets are incredibly narrow, with only enough room for small cars to slip past. If you become lost, ask a local hotel's concierge if he knows English to see if he can point you in the right direction.

Metro

Another quick and straightforward method for getting around Paris is the metro. There are 16 lines in it, each with a unique color and number. Every metro station will have two platforms, one for each direction, for each line. The terminus station, or the last station on the railway, designates the direction of the train. On the platform wall is a metro map. Locate your present station and your desired station, then follow the line to its terminus station. If you change lines, you'll know which line to take (and in which direction) if you keep the terminus station in mind.

It is more cost-effective to purchase 10 tickets at once (locals refer to the pack as a "carnet") rather than a single ticket. A carnet costs €14,10, compared to €1,80 for a single ticket. Every ticket is only good for one journey (including changes within the metro system). It is not permitted to change to a bus while using the same ticket. Additionally, a one-day Mobilis pass is available for €7.00; prices vary depending on how many zones you will go through (most tourists can stick to zones 1 and 2). Remember that the metro stops between 12:30 and 1 a.m. and between 1.30 and 2 a.m. on Friday and Saturday nights if you enjoy staying out late.

Buses

The only challenging part of using the bus in Paris is figuring out exactly where your bus will stop. The same tickets that are used in the metro can be purchased in a metro station. If you purchase your ticket onboard the bus, you will not be eligible for a free transfer, even if a normal "t+" ticket allows transfers between buses for up to 90 minutes after the initial ride. Additionally, there are no transfers from the bus to the metro.

Bus lines 299, 350, and 351 as well as Balabus, Noctilien, Orlybus, and Roissybus require special tickets that must be purchased at the bus stop and are priced according to the length of the trip. Typically, buses come to a stop between 9 and 10 p.m. Buses operated by Noctilien, which run all night, continue to provide reduced service.

RER Train

Although it has fewer lines and stops, the RER is still a fantastic alternative. RER trains are best used for getting to adjacent suburbs, while they can also be used to quickly cross the city. For instance, the "Champ de Mars Tour Eiffel" stop on the RER is the closest train stop to the Eiffel Tower.

The same tickets you use for the metro only work on the RER within zone 1. (within Paris). At the station, you must purchase a more expensive ticket if you are traveling outside of zone 1. Also, if your metro ticket has a "2," it does not denote zone 2 but rather refers to a time when the Parisian subway had both first and second classes.

Commuter rail (Trains de banlieue)

Use SNCF commuter trains if you need to travel to areas that are even further away from Paris or to suburbs that cannot be reached by RER. Gare Saint Lazare serves the western and southwestern suburbs of Paris, Gare de l'Est serves the eastern suburbs, Gare du Nord serves the northern suburbs, Gare de Lyon serves the southeastern suburbs of Paris, Gare Montparnasse serves the southwestern suburbs, and Gare d'Austerlitz serves the southern suburbs.

Boats

A boat tour of Paris is a lot of fun. With eight stations along the Seine, including the Eiffel Tower, the Musee d'Orsay, the Louvre, and Notre Dame, the Batobus is a distinctive route.

Bicycle

VELIB, a contraction of the French terms velo (bike) and libre, is the name of the nearly free bicycle system in Paris (free). You can check out a bike at any of the bike stations located throughout the city, ride it, and then return it to a dock when you're done. The bikes are constantly maintained, but before choosing one, take a quick glance to make sure the tires, chains, brakes, or seat are in good working order.

You must purchase a short-term membership card (either for a day or a week) with a chip-embedded credit card in order to use the VELIB system; magnetic-stripe-only cards are not accepted. Your membership number is printed after the processing of the €150 bond (refunded at the conclusion of the rental period) is complete. To check out a bike, you create a personal identification number (PIN).

It's surprisingly simple to bicycle around Paris. Many roads have bicycle lanes (identified by a painted bike emblem), including a lovely one next to the Seine. Use a designated bus or taxi lane if you can't find a bicycle lane.

Taxi

Finding a taxi in Paris is difficult because there aren't as many yellow cabs as in New York. The best chances are near taxi stands or on broad boulevards. Although there is no standard color or style for taxis, authorized cabs have a unique sign that reads Taxis parisiens. The automobile is available if the sign is illuminated.

Sharing a Ride

You can book a seat on BlaBlaCar, decide how much you want to communicate while driving, view the car and driver, learn the driver's musical tastes, agree on a pricing and meeting location, and more. The prices are really affordable. Prices are restricted in compliance with law so that drivers only cover their operating expenses (without turning a profit). It is specified how much luggage is permitted and how many persons can fit.

Paris Arrival and Departure

Paris Charles de Gaulle Airport Paris

Paris is served by two major airports: Roissy Charlesde Gaulle and Orly. Major airline companies' foreign flights are more likely to bring you to Roissy CDG. If you are flying with a low-cost airline or are coming from another French or European city, you might land in Orly. The airport at Beauvais Tillé, northwest of Paris, only flies to locations in Europe.

Paris may be reached from Roissy Charles de Gaulle International Airport (CDG) via train, bus, vehicle, taxi, or shuttle. The RATP, the Paris regional public transit authority, operates the RER regional trains, RoissyBus, and Noctilien night buses as the primary modes of public transportation. The cost of these modes of transportation between Paris and CDG airport is the lowest. The trip to Gare du Nord, the first significant train station in Paris, takes the RER trains roughly 2530 minutes from CDG Terminals 1 and 2.

Several large companies offer rental car transportation immediately from CDG Terminals 1 and 2, however be advised that traffic congestion and a lack of parking are frequent occurrences in central Paris. There are taxis accessible in Terminals 1 and 2. Depending on the location inside Paris, the average taxi charge will be around 4050€. The typical road trip lasts 60 minutes. A transportation firm called Discovery Mundo provides shared and individual service for transfers in Paris. A person with a sign bearing your name will be waiting for you at the airport after you have prearranged and paid for your transfer in USD.

Ground Transportation for CDG: By obtaining a Paris Metro Pass for 6 Zones and using the RER train straight, one can travel from Charles de Gaulle Airport to central Paris for the least amount of money. The RER travels to central Paris in around 40 minutes. Please be aware that depending on where your station is, you could have to carry your luggage up multiple flights of steps (elevators are limited to certain stations in Paris, which may be some distance from where you want to be).

Another option is the Air France Bus, which runs between 6:00 and 22:30 depending on the itinerary and serves all terminals and airlines. Gare de Lyon, Gare Montparnasse, and Etoile are the drop-off locations for Route 4, respectively (Arc de Triomphe). Another option is the Roissy Bus, which operates nonstop to Terminals 1, 2, and 3 from Opera (corner of rue Scribe and rue

Auber) from 6 a.m. to 11 p.m. Tickets are available from the driver on board and cost 10 Euros.

Two buses and two RER lines connect to Orly Airport (ORY). Your kids will love sitting in the front and pretending they are riding it if you take the RER B since you will have the opportunity to join the very high tech autonomous shuttle known as Orlyval. At Orly, you can also rent a car or a taxi. The approximate cab fare from the heart of Paris is 35€.

Tram and subway connect Orly Airport (ORY) to central Paris.

One tram and one metro ticket is the incredibly affordable method to travel to central Paris. The total price is under 4 euros. Great if you're only bringing a few things, however it takes more than an hour. If you arrive at Orly West, take the free Orlyval shuttle to the Orly Sud terminal, and then seek for the direction sign T7 (tramway 7) It's downstairs and not well marked upon entering the terminal building. The T7 tram will take you to Villejuif Louis Aragon on Metro Line 7, where there are frequent departures for the center of Paris (Chatelet Les Halles)

The Aéroports de Paris website has all the information you require for Roissy CDG and Orly; go here for RER and bus schedules. Paris Beauvais has a shuttle service between Paris (Porte

Maillot) and the airport for 17€ per person. You must board the shuttle at least three and a half hours before the scheduled departure of your flight because Beauvais is around one and a half hours from Paris. The SNCF also offers a fast regional train (TER) service to the airport from the Beauvais city center. It would be expensive to take a taxi from central Paris to Beauvais, so we don't advise it.

Buses and Trains

In France, trains are much more common than buses for commuting between cities. The TGV (High Speed Train) makes it possible to travel 815 kilometers (505 miles) from Paris to a place like Marseilles in about three hours. You will need to get to one of Paris's six train terminal stations, depending on where you are going. Each of them is easily accessible by bus, RER, or metro and is situated in a distinct part of the city.

When you book your ticket, don't forget to check your departure station. If you choose the "Borne Libre Service," which requires you to pick up your tickets from the automated ticket dispensers in your departure station, you can purchase tickets on the SNCF website with any major credit card.

However, coaches (also known as "autocars" or "cars" in French) can be beneficial in the event of an SNCF strike or if you are on a tight budget. Eurolines is the leading coach provider in

France. It provides service to numerous French cities, all of Europe, as well as additional locations including Morocco. The majority of the boarding locations in Paris are bus stops or bus stations (gare routières), not train stations. When you purchase your ticket, you will be informed of where to board. A extremely cost-effective coach company owned by SNCF is called iDBUS.

Paris Downtown Guide for Incomers

More than 2 million tourists from all around the world visit Paris annually as a romantic travel destination in Europe. The most well-known and biggest international airport in France for travel to central Paris is Charles de Gaulle. Most foreign visitors arrive in Paris via CDG airport on one of the several international aircraft services. Travelers can take the metro, a shuttle bus, or a taxi to get to central Paris from Charles de Gaulle Airport.

Metro buses. It is the most well-liked and well-known form of public transit in Paris, serving customers from 05:30 a.m. to 01:15 a.m. midnight on Monday through Thursday and from 05:30 a.m. to 02:15 p.m. on Friday and Saturday. There are sixteen lines in the metro system, each with a unique color, number, and line name. Since rush hour runs from 5:00 p.m. to 8:00 p.m., it is not advised to take the metro during those hours. Travelers may waste crucial time as a result. The metro lines 2 and 6 are excellent options for getting to the heart of Paris and visiting the Eiffel Tower and Sacre Coeur, which are both close to the Bir Haheim station. Travelers may simply purchase tickets at RER, Metro, and Tramway stations.

shuttle buses. The Charles de Gaulle airport offers a variety of bus shuttle services, including Air France, Night, and RATP or Roissy buses. From 6:00 a.m. to 8:45 p.m., most buses depart from CDG Airport and arrive there every fifteen to twenty minutes. The trip to central Paris will take about 45 minutes if you use all the buses at Charles de Gaulle airport terminals 1, 2, and 3. It costs roughly ten euros to get to Paris.

Taxi. At Charles de Gaulle Airport's arrival gate, there are numerous public and private cab services accessible. Private companies and individuals operate the cabs. Asking the driver if credit cards are accepted as a form of payment is advised. Some cabbies will not take credit card payments. Although there are numerous taxi services at CDG airport, it is advised to select a very reputable and trustworthy taxi service. A one-way cab ride to central Paris will cost you between 45 and 55 euros. Some taxi services can be negotiated depending on the traveler's budget.

Moving About within Paris

Paris is only 12 km wide and 10 km across (inside its walls, that is inside the roughly oval area covered by the Périphérique).

The RATP and SNCF French Railways are two state-owned businesses that control the majority of Paris' transportation infrastructure. The RERexpress train network and a portion of the metro, bus, and tram networks are all under the control of RATP. The Transilien suburban trains and the remaining RER network are operated by SNCF. The entire ticketing system is interconnected, so you may purchase any ticket or pass at any RATP or SNCF ticket counter.

In Paris, walking and taking advantage of the first-rate public transportation are the finest ways to get around. Driving would not be recommended because parking in the city is difficult and traffic is frequently severe. As previously mentioned, the public transit is fantastic. It makes it possible to connect quickly and easily to any location in Paris and its environs. During rush hour, the Paris metro runs every two minutes and is quite widespread. Even if it could be a little busy, you can always count on getting where you need to go fast. Try the number 14 if you wish to ride a modern, automatic metro line. It is the most recent metro line, and surprisingly enough, it smells good! But wary of the high-speed people movers at Paris' RER connector stations. It is a flat people movers that moves quite quickly. Before walking upon it, you must be ready to avoid falling or injuring yourself.

At 1:00 a.m., the Métro stops operating. There may be a gate switch on the wall or at the inside side of the gate if you are caught in a station after hours with the gates closed and need to exit. After midnight, there is now greater service than there was in 2005. Every 17 minutes throughout the week and every 12 minutes during the weekends, two circular bus lines connect Gare de l'Est, République, Bastille, Gare de Lyon, Austerlitz, Montparnasse, Invalides, Champs Elysées, Gare Saint Lazare, Pigalle, and Gare de l'Est. Numerous radial night lines pass through the city, and some of them travel as far out as the CDG Airport. Regular tickets and passes are accepted. Overall, the service is effective, albeit some visitors and tourists may feel uneasy in certain of the nighttime buses' environments. The best course of action is to confirm which night bus route you must take if you want to make sure you get back to your accommodation as soon as possible. You may do it right there on the RATP website.

Since 2007, the Velibs program has also allowed bike rentals in Paris. You can purchase a ticket for a day (1.70 euros) or a week to have access to those bikes for free. It is quite simple and affordable, and it is a great way to see Paris without getting too exhausted. In Paris, there are stations every 300 meters, so finding one won't be an issue. Simply switch bikes every 30 minutes to avoid having to pay an additional euro. Just be aware of the traffic because some Parisians don't drive very carefully !

VELIB biking in Paris

In addition to the Metro and BUS, there is a fantastic way to get around Paris.

VELIB bicycles They are all around us! Usually, distances of no more than two or three blocks. You can use them for free for 30 minutes after purchasing 8 euros for the week, after which you'll be charged for each additional 30 minutes. The ticket (which includes a code number and a password) can be purchased online or in person at each parking space.

The best feature is the Velib' app, which shows you where parking spaces are near you, how many bikes are available, and whether any spots are open for free parking (sometimes the location is full).

As a supplement to the subway and BUS, the system is actually very helpful. For instance, after getting off at TROCADERO station, you can rent a bike and ride around the Eiffel Tower for at least 30 minutes to obtain all the views you desire. Biking along Boulevard Saint Germain and the "Quartier Latin" will take you to Notre Dame. It's very affordable and great!

Excellent when used in conjunction with a PARIS VISITE ticket that provides multiple days of Metro and Bus travel. Although you can also go quickly and see more on a bike than on foot. Consider riding a bike along the Seine river. the Champs Elysées area.

Some simple precautions:

1. Try to stay away from crowded areas. The worst pedestrians are those in heavily traveled areas. High traffic areas should also be avoided, though they are usually not too bad.

2. Use the basket and lock that the bike has. Secure all of your possessions. There are many pickpockets in Paris.

3. Avoid areas where there are only one or two bikes. They might be bald tires.

4. Always inspect the bicycle before using it. You will need to wait a few minutes before renting another one if it doesn't function.

5. Before returning your bike, make sure it is located and that the GREEN LIGHT IS ON. If not, you can incur a warranty fee.

6. When renting a bike, don't try to force it out; you just have a few seconds, and occasionally the back wheel needs to be lifted

slightly to make the bike move. You will waste time and it won't come out if you force it out of desperation.

7. Try to stick to a half-hour limit; switching bikes is less expensive. Remember that the first 30 minutes are free!

8. It's not a bad idea to wear a helmet. You'll feel and be safer.

These straightforward suggestions should enable you to have a pleasant ride. Recall that this is only intended to supplement other transportation options for short distances. But it's really practical, affordable, and easy to use.

Urban Transportation

Metro

The best way to travel quickly and conveniently throughout Paris is the subway. The city is covered by 16 lines, including 2 "bis." A different color and number are on each line. Therefore, even though a metro map's multitude of lines initially seems daunting, it soon becomes simple once you grasp how it operates. Every Metro line will have two platforms at any given Metro station, one for each direction. The terminus station, the last station on the railway, designates each direction.

Find a Metro map on the wall of the platform after entering a Metro station line. Find the station you are at right now, then the one you are going to. Follow the Metro line to its terminus, which will be the direction name you're looking for for this Metro line, after finding the target station on the map. You can know which Metro lines to change to and in which directions to go by keeping the terminus stations in mind while changing Metro lines.

You may find a table with the current metro ticket costs below, although as the table shows, the price is lower if you purchase 10 at once (locals refer to this as a "carnet"). Then, you have a wide range of options for passes that are much more convenient and affordable than buying individual tickets (1 or multiple days, 1 week, or even 1 month: pass navigo). Please be aware that each ticket is only good for one trip if you don't have a pass (including changes within the Metro system).

Metro, Bus and Tram Tickets	Euros
1 ticket	1,80
Carnet of 10 tickets full fare	14.10
Carnet of 10 tickets reduced fare (children under 10)	7.05
1dayticket "Mobilis" full fare, Zone 1+2	7.00
1dayticket "Mobilis" full fare, Zone 13	9.30
1dayticket "Jeunes", Zone 13	3.85
(only valid on SAT/SUN/public holidays,	

only for agegroup under 26)	

Zones

There are 5 concentric zones that make up the Ile de France region. Zone 15 includes the Paris metro region. Orly and Versailles are in Zone 4 whereas CDG Airport is in Zone 5. Zone 1 of the Périphérique is the city of Paris. Depending on the mode of transportation you use, a single ticket has a different range of validity.

Regardless of the station's zone location, a single Métro ticket is good for one trip to any Métro station. It is not permitted to use the same ticket to transfer to a bus or tram. A single metro ticket on the RER is only good for travel inside Zone 1 (within Paris). Do not be misled if there is a "2" on your ticket; it does not indicate Zone 2 and is now obsolete (it actually means 2nd class, at a time there were 2 classes on the Paris Metro).

On buses and trams, a single ticket marked "sans correspondence" and not purchased on the bus itself is good for one hour and thirty minutes in a single direction with interchanges to other buses or trams. Certain bus lines (Balabus, Noctilien, Orlybus, Roissybus, and lines 299, 350, and 351) do not accept a single ticket and instead require round-trip tickets that may be purchased at the bus stop. One ticket is sufficient, for instance, if taking the Line 1 of the métro to La Défense (located in Zone 3). You must purchase a little more expensive ticket if you take the RER's Line A..

Paris A La Carte (International Visitors Card)

The Paris Visite Card might be one of the least expensive ways to travel if you are coming from outside. The cost of this card varies depending on how many days and zones you plan to travel in. It allows you to travel as frequently as you like. Most crucially, these are valid from the first day of use, unlike the Passe Navigo/Carte Orange (rather than from Monday to Sunday). Therefore, it can be ordered in advance to prevent standing in line at the last minute.

All metro and RER stations, sales offices, bus terminal booths, SNCF Transilien stations, Paris airports, and all Office de Tourisme de Paris locations sell Paris Visite. It is marketed by tour guides and tourist agencies abroad.

Adult fares as of January 2014 were as follows, while children's (411) fares are roughly half as much as adult fares. The card also offers a number of 2for1 deals and discounts; these extra perks may make buying the Paris Visite card well worth it.

Zones	1 day	2 days	3 days	5 days

	Adult	Adult	Adult	Adult
	Euros	Euros	Euros	Euros
13	11,15	18,15	24,80	35,70
15	23,50	35,70	50,05	61,25

Preordering the Paris A la Carte or Paris Visit Card as a Redeemable Voucher or having it simply delivered to your house. The RATP adds that if you obtain this international visitor card, you may receive a discount on entrance tickets to various Paris landmarks, like the Arc de Triomphe, Army Museum, Open Bus Tour, etc.

Orange/Passe Navigo Découverte

There is no sliding week; they are purely weekly (Mon-Sun; no sliding month) or monthly (as stated above; no sliding week). If you intend to make frequent use of the transportation system, they offer the best value for the money. In recent years, the pass has evolved from a paper card and reusable magnetic ticket to a plastic smart card (Passe Navigo Découverte) and a paper card with a foldover, self-adhesive plastic insert that has your handwritten name and a 3-cm-tall, 2.5-cm-wide photo.

Buses

Buses are another excellent choice because they let you travel while taking in the sights of the city. Since there are so many buses in Paris, you can take a bus practically anywhere. The only challenge is figuring out where they stop! Finding bus stops is more difficult than finding metro stations. The tickets are identical to those used in the metro. The bus fare structure was recently modified (in July 2007) to permit a certain number of bus transfers. If you purchase a carnet in a Metro station, you will obtain a "t+" ticket, which permits bus transfers for up to 90 minutes after the initial trip. There are no transfers, though, if you purchase a ticket while on the bus. Additionally, there are no transfers from the bus to the metro.

Remember that the Parisian buses typically cease between 9 and 10 pm, with restricted service continuing on night buses and Noctilien buses. The Parisian metro stops between 12:30 and 1 am. Before using it, always look for your night bus schedule.

RER

The RER is a reliable means to travel quickly from one location to another. However, there are fewer stops as well as lines. Although it's mostly utilized to get to adjacent suburbs, it can be useful to quickly cross the city. The nearest access to the Eiffel Tower is by an RER stop, despite the fact that BirHakeim on Line 6 has a metro station there (Champ de Mars Tour Eiffel). Tickets are identical to those for the metro, however you must be cautious if you travel outside of Zone 1 because you will need a billet Ile-de-France rather than a regular Ticket t.

Transit rail (Trains de banlieue in French)

Use SNCF commuter trains if you have to travel to a suburb that is a little outside of Paris or is otherwise inaccessible by RER. There are trains to the suburbs at each of the six Parisian train stations. Gare Saint Lazare serves the western and southwest suburbs; gare de l'Est, the eastern suburbs; gare du Nord, the northern suburbs; gare de Lyon, the southeast suburbs; gare Montparnasse, the southwest suburbs; and gare d'Austerlitz, the southern suburbs. Some TER trains that go through non-Ile de France cities cross paths with commuter trains (e.g. those to Vernon for Giverny, Fontainebleau, or Chartres).

Boats

The boat is a unique and entertaining method to go around Paris. With 8 stations along the Seine, the Batobus is a distinctive service. Batobus makes stops at all significant city landmarks (including the Eiffel Tower, Orsay Museum, Louvres, and Notre Dame). Adults pay 16 euros for a one-day pass.

Trains (Mainline Grandes Lignes in French) (Mainline Grandes Lignes in French)

Gare Saint Lazare, Gare du Nord, Gare de l'Est, Gare de Lyon, Gare d'Austerlitz, and Gare Montparnasse are the six train stations in Paris. Each one of them serves a particular region of France, and some of them also work abroad. Access to all of them is provided by RER or metro services. The 8th arrondissement's Grands Magasins neighborhood includes the Gare Saint Lazare, which is close to the Opera Garnier. The suburbs of Paris and Normandy in the west and southwest are served by its trains.

The 10th arrondissement of Paris is where you'll find Gare du Nord. It also provides service to all of France's northern cities, Brussels, Cologne, London (Eurostar), Amsterdam (Thalys), and Berlin. In the 10th arrondissement, the Gare de l'Est is located directly across from the Gare du Nord. The eastern suburbs of Paris and eastern French cities are mostly served by its trains. But there are also some cross-border connections for Central Europe, Germany, and Luxembourg (Orient Express).

The 12th arrondissement of Paris is where you'll find Gare de Lyon. It includes the Paris suburbs to the southeast, Lyon, Burgundy, Franche-Comté, the entirety of southeast France (TGV Méditerranée), as well as Switzerland and Italy. Gare d'Austerlitz is situated in the 13th arrondissement, southeast of Paris. It encompasses France's center. There are also former night trains for Spain and Portugal.

The 15th arrondissement, in the southwest of Paris, is where you'll find Gare Montparnasse. By using the TGV, it primarily serves the western and southwestern suburbs of Paris, as well as the entire west and southwest of France. On the SNCF site, you can see all the train timetables and costs. To purchase tickets and train passes from afar,.

Velib/Cycling

The VELIB (a portmanteau of Velo = bike and Libre = free) bicycle system in Paris is a great way to move around the city, especially for quick visits. On the system's official website, you may discover more details (perhaps easier for English speakers).

Non-French speakers can use Velib with ease thanks to the terminal's language selection. Basically, all you need to get a temporary membership is a credit card with a chip inserted in it (cards with a magnetic stripe do not work) (one day or 7 days). Your membership number is printed once the 150 Euro bond (reversed at the conclusion of the rental period) is processed. The following step is to enter your unique identification number (PIN).

To check out bikes from the many stations located across the city, you must enter your membership code and PIN. When you're done, you simply need to put the bike back into an open dock. You might need to push firmly in order to activate the locking tab. After around 5 seconds, the system acknowledges its return with a buzzer and a green light.

Despite being well-maintained, give the bike a brief inspection before choosing it because it can have issues with the tires, chains, brakes, or seat. The bikes have three gears and are heavy, powerful, and solid. The seat height is the only change that is possible. Simple locks are included with the bikes; all you need to do is insert the cable end of the lock into the slot and remove the key. However, the city typically has enough stations that you can just return the bike straight away and board another one as soon as you need to.

Every Velib station has a helpful map of the neighborhood that also shows the locations of the other Velib stations nearby, which is helpful because occasionally the entire station won't be working and there won't be any bikes left to take out or, in some cases, there won't be any empty spaces left to return the bikes!

When your free half-hour hire is about to expire, it will be easier for you to find the closest dropoff station if you ask the tourist office for a huge fold-up map of Paris showing the locations of all the Velib stations. This map will save you time because parked cars sometimes block your view of the stations' covert locations. Given that the bicycles are gray, the stations do not stand out in the distance.

It's surprisingly simple to bicycle around Paris. The painted bicycle markers on the road will help you choose a lane if there isn't a designated bicycle lane; otherwise, use the dedicated bus and taxi lane. There are numerous bike lanes, including a lovely one next to the Seine. The only challenge is navigating the numerous one-way streets or entering a crowded pedestrian area. A fascinating method to observe the ebb and flow of the city is to observe the Velib system. Why are there no bikes at some stations at particular times of the day? Why are some stations almost always empty?

The Louvre, the Eiffel Tower, and the Musee d'Orsay can all be seen at night while traveling through Paris on a Velib throughout the summer between 9 p.m. and midnight. The streets are quieter but not so quiet at extremely late hours; after all, this is Paris.) however, they switch off the lights at the busy places.

Metro RATP and RER Security Measure

The RER regional express trains and the RATP Metro, the city's vital public transportation system, will be used by the majority of visitors. Most tourists believe the Paris Metro to be safe, however riders should be aware of some safety precautions when utilizing the public transportation system.

Key Facts:

- Pickpockets are active on the Metro network (particularly in line 1 : the most touristic one)
- Certain stations have become known as crime 'hot spots'
- Thieves are good at what they do. Vigilance is required in order to beat them
- Security on the Paris Metro has been under closer security since recent terrorist outrages in Europe.
- Thefts of backpacks on RER from CDG to Paris. According to police common occurrence. Happened with significant loss of electronic items etc.

Most Common Problems:

- Theft of hand bags. These are usually snatched from the victim by a person outside the train as the automatic doors are closing or while entering or exiting through turnstyles. This is a common offence on many underground train systems
- Theft of wallets/personal effects from jackets
- Theft of wallets from trouser back pockets
- Theft of personal effects from hand bags
- Theft of money directly from a person's hand some people actually remove money from their wallets whilst on the Metro

- Mugging
- Thieves work in teams. One will often prevent the Metro doors from closing, while an accomplice will snatch a bag or purse just as they are trying to close. This enables them to escape quickly with the doors closing immediately behind them, leaving the victim and others locked inside of the train as it pulls away. If you see anyone keeping the doors open by force, know they are scanning your railcar for a victim.

This is just a no brainer. Do not even think about carrying your wallet in your back pocket when on a Metro train.

Stations that pose a higher risk:

It is challenging, if not impossible, to distinguish between "safe" and "unsafe" Metro stations in Paris. Generally speaking, you won't run into any issues anyplace, but some stations have a greater crime rate than others. Try the software BeSafe if you have an iPhone or iPad it might be a smart idea! which, in addition to rating the riskiness of Parisian districts, identifies the city's most hazardous subway stations using information on the city's public transit.

The following stations have been reported as having a higher risk:

- Châtelet Les Halles: This is a very large station which adjoins a shopping centre. You may see gangs wandering around the station or shopping center, but they are not usually the people responsible for theft and pickpocketing. Simply speaking, larger stations mean a higher incidence of crime by definition.
- Charles de Gaulle Étoile: The station is at one end of Champs Elysées directly below the Arc de Triomphe. It is a very busy station and thieves are 'expert' at identifying tourists. Upon reaching street level, you will often be approached by women asking, "Speak English?" Don't answer and keep walking.
- Barbès Rochechouart
- Gare du Nord This station is served by Eurostar, Thalys, SNCF, RER and the Paris Métro.
- Gare de l'Est Metro and SNCF trains, use caution when walking from Gare de l'Est to Gare de Nord.
- Pigalle This station serves the Pigalle "Red Light" district.
- Anvers This station is close to the Montmartre funicular and the Basilica of Sacré-Coeur.
- Republique

Possibly more secure stations:

Some stations have more transit security than others. If you are nervous about Metro travel, you may wish to stick to them.

- La Defense A closely guarded station in the business district outside of Paris.
- Musee d'Orsay Very popular with museum guests, this station is closely watched by the transport Police.
- George V, Franklin Roosevelt, Champs Elysées Clémenceau, alternative stations which are less busy than Charles de Gaulle Étoile for visiting Champs Elysées.

The RER:

Due to the additional security, some stations in downtown Paris have more vigilance. RER lines pass through stations including Charles de Gaulle Étoile and Châtelet Les Halles that are categorized as having a higher risk of injury.

- The most popular RER line with tourists is RER A (which terminates at Marnela Vallée Chessy, Parc Disneyland) is probably the safest line. It travels through good neighbourhoods and the largest stations are closely guarded. The final station, Marnela Vallée Chessy, is also served by TGV and Eurostar and is therefore notably more secure.
- The RER B line which serves Paris CDG and Orly Airports is considered safe but at certain times of the day is

frequented by beggars which often use children and small puppies to illicit an emotional response from people to open their purses or wallets do not give them money, just look away and ignore.

- Visitors using RER C are advised to consult train guides closely to make sure they are on the correct platform and taking the right train. Trains on RER C have many different destinations and some trains do not stop at every station between their origination and destination. Trains can be identified by names such as ELBA, MONA, ROMI. The RER C serves Versailles a popular destination for visitors wanting to visit Place de Versailles.
- RER D may not be for the faint of heart. Due to a high number of incidents and social disturbances.
- RER E does not appear to be frequented by tourists.

Secure Yourself:

You can take precautions to protect yourself when riding the Métro. Be watchful and conscious of your surroundings. If a train is making you uncomfortable, get off and wait for the next one. Paris trains run often, so there is no need to sit next to someone who makes you feel uneasy or intimidated.

- Take back packs off and carry them in front of you.

- If you are a smaller female, or petite, consider hanging your handbag between yourself and your partner, or between yourself and the building you are walking alongside.
- Invest in travel locks miniature padlocks which make theft very difficult. Lock up you bags with them, but keep the keys handy as your bag may be searched by Police who will not be very understanding when you tell them that you cannot find the keys.
- Take wallets and passports out of your back pocket.
- Keep personal documents like passports close to your person, in a pocket where you can feel them.
- If you are keeping your wallet or mobile phone in an inner jacket pocket, make sure your jacket is buttoned up.
- Do not walk around brandishing a mobile phone, iPod, PDA or any other valuable item. It has been increasingly reported that mobiles such as iPhones being used to play games or text while on the Métro have been stolen out of peoples' hands as the Métro doors are closing.
- Keep things like watches, pendants and expensive jewellery out of sight.
- If you set your bag down on the floor, do not take your hand off it even if it is just for a second. Thefts happen extremely quickly.

- Do not take money out whilst travelling on the Metro (including when faced with a beggar including children begging for money). Keep your wallet and its contents to yourself.
- If possible, leave passports, flight tickets and personal information in a safety deposit box at your hotel.
- Hold bags, purses, luggage in front of you when passing through turnstyle exits, or automatic door exits.
- Particularly if a train is packed, do not stand with your purse or valuables against the doors as they could be easily stolen as the doors are closing.

Do not Worry:

Avoid being afraid to use the metro. In compared to networks in other cities, it is fairly secure. Depending on where you are visiting from, your assessment of its relative safety will vary. It is highly trustworthy and thorough. It is the simplest and least expensive method of getting about Paris. This manual's author frequently employs it. Acting naturally is the best course of action; avoid flaunting your possessions or drawing attention to yourself. A thief will likely leave you alone if he cannot identify you as a tourist.

Transiting from Eurostar

Transfer between Paris Gare du Nord and Paris Gare de Lyon:

Take the RER line D (D2 direction of Melun or D2 direction of Malsherbes) This takes approximately 8 minutes. This is the quickest and most direct route.

A taxi takes approximately 15 to 20 minutes depending on the time of day.

Transfer between Paris Gare du Nord and Gare Montparnasse:

Take Metro line 4 in the direction of Porte d'Orleans, this will take approximately 40 minutes.

Or you can take RER line B in the direction of Robinson/ St Remy to Denfert Rochereau, then Metro line 4 in the direction of Porte de Clignacourt. This will take approximately 15 minutes.

A taxi will take between 40 and 50 minutes depending on the time of day.

Or you can take bus route 96 which will take about 50 minutes.

Transfer from Paris Gare du Nord to Paris Gare de L'Est:

Take Metro Line 4 (direction Porte D'Orleans) or Metro Line 5 (direction Place D'Italie) approximately 5 minutes Direct.

Or take Bus no. 65, 46 and 38 approximately 10 minutes.

Or walk out of the main exit and turn left. Cross over the road continuing left up to the crossroads. Turn right along Rue de Faubourg then left at MacDonalds. Approximately 510 minutes.

Transfer between Paris Gare du Nord and Paris Gare d'Austerlitz:

Take Metro line 5 in the direction of Place d'Italie.

Or you can take the RER Line B in the direction of Robinson/ St Remy to St Michel Notre Dame. Then take Line C in the direction of Massy Paliaiseau/ Dourdan/ St Martin. This will take approximately 25 minutes.

A taxi will take between 15 and 30 minutes, depending on the time of day.

You can also take bus route 65 which will take about 40 minutes.

Transfer between Paris Gare du Nord and Gare St Lazare:

Take RER line E in the direction of St Lazare. On the return journey, take the same line in the direction of Chelles Gournay or Villiers-Sur-Marne and get off at Magenta.

A taxi will take between 15 and 20 minutes depending on the time of day.

Or you can take bus route 26 which will take about 25 40 minutes.

Transfer between Paris Gare du Nord and Gare de Bercy:

Take RER line B in the direction of Robinson/ St Remy to Denfert

Rochereau, then Metro line 5 in the direction of Nation. Cross over Rue de Bercy and the station is on the left. This will take approximately 50 minutes.

A taxi will take between 15 and 25 minutes depending on the time of day.

Transfer from Paris Gare du Nord to Disneyland Paris:
The RER service from Paris Gare Du Nord to Disneyland involves one change, and the journey takes approximately 4050 minutes.

From the Gare Du Nord take RER line B (direction Chatelet Les Halles), then take RER line A4 to Marne Le Vallee.
This station adjoins the Disneyland complex.

Transfer to Gare du Nord from Charles de Gaulle Airport:
Charles De Gaulle airport is located on the RER line B (station Aeroport Charles de Gaulle 1 RER in Rue de la Haye), just a few stops away from the Gare Du Nord Terminal.

Take the RER line B direction Saint Remy les Chevreuse, which stops at Gare du Nord.
Allow at least 1hr 15 minutes to cross Paris, plus train check in time.

Chapter Three

Places to Visit in Paris

Museums in Paris Organized by Arrondissement

The art collections in Paris could keep visitors occupied for an entire vacation (or a lifetime). There are over 150 museums in the city, many of which are world-class institutions. The highlights of the Louvre Museum require several days to explore. Tourists frequently get lost in the seemingly endless galleries filled with Western Civilization masterpieces. A guided tour of the Louvre is recommended for first-time visitors.

Other museums are dedicated to specific artists or genres, such as Impressionist art at the Musée d'Orsay, medieval art at the Cluny Museum, and modern art at the Pompidou Center. There are also interesting small museums in Paris, such as the Musée Jacquemart Andre and the Musée de l'Orangerie.

Traveling Suggestions: Many museums are closed on Mondays and Tuesdays, while others (such as the Musée Marmottan Monet) stay open late on specific days and others (such as the Centre Pompidou) are open late every day. On July 14th, a national holiday, admission to the Musée du Louvre is free. On the first Sunday of each month, admission to the Musée d'Orsay, the Centre Pompidou, and the Musée de Cluny is free.

A Paris Museum Pass grants unlimited access to most museums for two or four days. Aside from taking an Art History course before the trip, what is the best way to appreciate the museum collections? When possible, sign up for guided tours. Guides who are knowledgeable enrich your experience by providing historical context and sharing unique insights.

1er Arrondissement

Musee de l'Orangerie

The art collections in Paris could occupy an entire vacation (or a lifetime) for visitors. The city has over 150 museums, many of which are world-class. It takes several days to explore the highlights of the Louvre Museum. Tourists frequently become lost in the seemingly endless galleries filled with Western Civilization masterpieces. A Louvre guided tour is recommended for first-time visitors.

Other museums focus on specific artists or genres, such as Impressionist art at the Musée d'Orsay, medieval art at the Cluny Museum, and modern art at the Pompidou Center. There are also some interesting small museums in Paris, such as the Musée Jacquemart Andre and the Musée de l'Orangerie.

Travel Advice: Many museums are closed on Mondays and Tuesdays, while others (such as the Musée Marmottan Monet) stay open late on specific days and others (such as the Centre Pompidou) stay open late every day. On July 14th, a national holiday, admission to the Musée du Louvre is free of charge. On the first Sunday of each month, admission to the Musée d'Orsay, Centre Pompidou, and Musée de Cluny is free.

A Paris Museum Pass gives you unlimited access to most museums in Paris for two or four days. Aside from taking an Art History class before the trip, what is the best way to appreciate the museum collections? Whenever possible, sign up for guided tours. Experienced tour guides enrich your experience by providing historical context and sharing unique insights.

Musee de l'Orangerie Hours and Admissions

- The museum is open every day (except Tuesdays, May 1 and December 25) from 9:00 a.m. to 6pm

- Admissions are 7.50 euros for adults; 5.50 euros for students under 26 years of age and free on the first Sunday of the month.

Musée des Arts Décoratifs

This museum in the Louvre's western wing is a must-see for those who appreciate fashion and the finer things in life. The Musée des Arts Décoratifs (Museum of Decorative Arts) houses a large collection (around 150,000 items) of decorative arts objects dating from the Middle Ages to the Art Nouveau movement.

Visitors marvel at the variety of objects on display, which includes medieval altarpieces and Renaissance wedding chests, as well as 18th-century tapestries and First Empire tableware. With its Mediterranean menu (inspired by the cuisine of the French Riviera, Italy, and Sicily), stylish dining room, and pleasant garden terrace seating, the museum's chic restaurant, Loulou, embodies the essence of Parisian art devivre.

The Musée Nissim de Camondo, located at 63 Rue de Monceau in the 8th arrondissement, is affiliated with the Musée des Arts Décoratifs. This magnificent Belle Epoque private mansion houses a remarkable collection of 18th-century French decorative art objects and paintings, including sparkling chandeliers, gilded clocks, Sèvres porcelain, and Marie Antoinette's vases. The

Ateliers du Carrousel, which offers art workshops for children and adults taught by professional artists, is also supported by the Museum of Decorative Arts.

Address: 107 111 Rue de Rivoli, 75001 Paris (Métro: Palais Royal Musée du Louvre, Tuileries or Pyramides station)

Musée du Louvre

- The Louvre is open everyday except Tuesday, January 1st, May 1st, November 11 and December 25. The hours are from 9 a.m.6 p.m., and until 9:45 p.m. on Wednesday and Friday.

o The main entrance to the museum is through the Pyramid in the main courtyard, the Cour Napoleon. There is also an entrance through the Carrousel du Louvre, the elaborate, underground shopping mall, which has three accesses:

1) by Metro tunnels at station Palais Royal/Musee du Louvre.

2) from rue de Rivoli.
3) by stairs leading down on either side of the Arc de Triomphe du Carrousel.

Another entrance during regular hours, though closed on Friday, is through the Porte des Lions, located in the southern wing.

The Passage Richelieu has an entrance during regular hours for those who already have tickets for the museum.

- Admission price is 12 euros. The museum is free for those under 18 years of age; free for those under 26 years of age if a citizen of an EU country; and free for everybody on the first Sunday of the month from October to March.
- Admission for the temporary exhibits is 13 euros. Combination of museum and temporary exhibit admission is 16 euros.
- Tickets are valid the entire day which allows you to leave the museum and return.
- The full price ticket also allows a sameday entrance to the National Museum Eugene Delacroix. The Delacroix museum is open everyday, except Tuesday, from 9:30 a.m.5:00 p.m.
- Free facilities include a coatcheck, firstaid, a small luggage room, wheelchairs and a lost and found.
- The museum is handicapped accessible and there are floor plans indicating elevators and easy wheelchair access.

There are several museum personnel working at the Louvre who are responsible for enforcing the rules. These rules are primarily intended to conserve the vast and priceless collection..

- Do Not Touch The Art. That includes the sculptures and artifacts, which are generally not protected by glass casings. Accumulation of oils from the skin have a damaging affect on marble, bronze and, of course, paint. There is a "Tactile Room" where you are invited to touch sculptures. It is located in the Lower Ground Floor of the Denon Wing.
- Cumbersome objects and animals are not allowed in the museum.
- Eating and drinking are prohibited in the museum, except in the cafés, the restaurants and the food court. Smoking is permitted only on the outdoor terraces of the cafés.

The Louvre is the ideal location to just let your feet carry you wherever they want to go if your preferred method of exploring museums is to simply meander and follow your curiosity.

However, if there are specific artworks or works of art that you must visit, it is in your best interest to use the helpful maps and plans on hand at the information desk in the main foyer, located beneath the spectacular Pyramid entrance. The plans, which are available in a variety of languages, clearly depict the arrangement of the museum's three main wings. The highly helpful CyberLouvre, with computer terminals and online information on the museum, is located along the passageway of the underground Carrousel du Louvre.

The Palace

The Louvre was once a fort that King Philippe Auguste constructed in the late 1100s and early 1200s along with the city's first stone enclosure wall to protect the Seine river banks from invaders coming from the north. The Donjon, also known as the Keep, was a cylindrical tower that stood in the middle of the square fort's high, thick walls. In the Sully wing of the museum, the Medieval Louvre display includes archeological finds from the old fort.

Charles V expanded and embellished this fort in the fourteenth century, turning it into the most renowned castle in all of Europe. However, François I partially destroyed this in the 16th century to create place for a massive new building designed in the Renaissance style.

The Palais des Tuileries is a castle to the west that Catherine de Medici constructed in 1567. The Grand Gallery, now known as the Denon wing and housing the collection of Renaissance works by Italian and Spanish artists, was built between the Palais du Louvre and the Palais des Tuileries during the reign of Henri IV.

The medieval Louvre fort's north wing was destroyed by Louis XIII in the early 17th century, and the Lescot wing was built in its stead. His architect, Jacques Lemercier, built the clock-shaped Pavillion de l'Horloge.

The Cour Carée, or Square Court, was enclosed by Louis the XIV. However, when he left the Louvre in favor of Versailles in 1678, work was put on hold. The Cour Carée's north, south, and east buildings were left without roofs until Louis XV started up where Louis XIV had left off in 1756. On August 10, 1793, the Louvre, then known as the Central Museum of the Arts, made the Academy of Painting's exhibits and the collections of French nobles who had left France permanent. The Salon Carée and the Grande Galerie served as the exhibition spaces.

Following the Revolution, Napoleon I and succeeding French emperors resided in the Tuileries Palace, while the Louvre served as both a museum and an office complex for the French Ministry.

The Tuileries Palace, the center of aristocratic power at the period, was set ablaze and completely destroyed during the Paris Commune revolt in 1871. This actually created the magnificent perspective of the Grand Axis that is enjoyed today, spanning from the Place de la Concorde to the Arc de Triomphe du Carrousel, the Tuileries Gardens, and, on a clear day, the Grande Arche de La Défense.

The Louvre underwent a significant refurbishment and extension in the 1980s. I.M. Pei, an architect, entirely repositioned the main entryway and topped it with a glass pyramid. Like all exceptional things, it sparked some debate, but it has subsequently turned out to be a big success. Another iconic and well-liked building in the Parisian environment is the pyramid. The Richelieu wing of the museum, which opened in 1993 and has an exhibition space of almost 60,000 square meters, 15 acres, or 645,800 square feet, makes the Louvre the largest museum in the world.

The Collection

It's hard to imagine the size of the Louvre Museum's extensive collection. Over 30,000 works of art are on display, and the collection has more than three times as many cataloged items. The collection features outstanding artwork from many ages. The museum's oldest object dates back 9,000 years. It is referred to as the "Statue from Ain Ghawn" and was found in Jordan in 1985. The Louvre's permanent collection is divided into eight parts, each of which thoroughly examines a certain time or subject in the development of the arts. A permanent collection database and online catalog have just been finished by the Official Louvre Website. This website comes highly recommended for an experience that is truly thorough..

Collection History

The Louvre was never meant to be a public museum. The royal residence's collections of antiques, drawings, and paintings, established by Louis XIV in 1671, were reserved for a select few. When Louis XIV moved the Louvre to his chateau in Versailles, it was transformed into a "Palace of the Arts" and used by resident artists. The Palace of the Muses, also known as the "Musée," was founded in 1747 to house the royal collections. The concept of a "museum" was relatively new at the time, but with the influence of the Enlightenment, its time had come. The arts were becoming a people's right and patrimony, and a new egalitarian spirit opened up a world previously reserved for royalty.

The French Revolution was supposed to carry out the already advanced plan of making existing collections available to the public. The task of organizing the "Musée Central des Arts," which opened in 1793, was delegated to a commission. Apart from the king's and the Academy's collections, it also included property seized from the Church. Many works of art arrived at the Louvre as war spoils after 1794. In July 1798, masterworks from Italy arrived in Paris. The museum had to be reorganized due to the large number of these. In 1803 it was renamed the "Musée Napoleon." Under Vivant Denon's leadership, it expanded through commissions, purchases, and war booty. Following Napoleon's defeat, however, the collection shrank dramatically as many works were returned to their countries of origin and former owners.

During the Restoration, the museum, which had lost its most important works, launched a vigorous campaign to restore the collection, beginning with the "Venus de Milo." Renaissance and modern sculptures from the Musée des Monuments Français (1824), Egyptian works collected by Jean François Champollion (1826), the Musée Naval (1827), Louis Philippe's Spanish collection, and Assyrian antiquities from Paul Emile Botta's excavations (1847) were added. The collection was expanded even further during the Second Republic and Napoleon III's Second Empire. The museum's collections continued to grow as more of it became accessible to the public. The Etruscans, Ancient Greece, and the Ancient Orient were added as new departments.

Architect Visconti completed the Palace during Napoleon III's reign. The Nouveau Louvre, which opened in 1857, completed the "Grand Dessin," or Grand Design. That is, until the Tuileries Palace was destroyed by fire in 1871. The Tuileries Palace ruins were demolished in 1882, effectively ending the Louvre's function as a palatial residence. As a national museum, the Louvre has continued to enrich and display its collections throughout the twentieth century.

By the 1970s, the museum's popularity had outgrown its available space. The majority of French artists' post-1848 works were relocated to the new Musée d'Orsay on the opposite bank of the Seine in 1986. The Louvre was then renovated. The new design in 1989 was intended to allow as many people as possible access to the museum. The grand reception area beneath the Glass Pyramid is an impressive and welcoming first impression of the museum. The Louvre Palace has rediscovered a rich and animated life in the heart of the city by revitalizing its function as a museum.

3eme Arrondissement

Musée Carnavalet / The Carnavalet Museum

The Carnavalet Museum is housed in a magnificent old palace in the heart of the Marais district. The palace, which was built in 1548, was once home to Madame de Sevigné, a 17th century marquise and letter writer whose correspondence has left us with a unique and lively glimpse of court life in the 1600s. The Museum is divided into two buildings that are linked by a gallery on the second floor. The Hôtel Carnavalet is the larger of the two structures, while the Hôtel le Peletier de Saint Fargeau is smaller but no less beautiful. When you enter the courtyard from the rue des Francs Bourgeois, you are greeted by a small, beautifully designed garden with gravel paths..

This is the Court of Flags.

The buildings have some interesting architectural elements, such as a large medallion and statues on the eastern facade. A covered walkway separates the Court of Flags from the Court of

Victory, so named for the dramatic statue of Victory holding out her laurels. If, however, you enter by the main entrance on rue de Sevigne you are greeted by one of the few statues of royalty to have made it through the Revolution, that of King Louis XIV, created in 1689 by Antoine Coysevoux.

Basrelief sculptures by Jean Goujon that symbolize the four seasons and are inscribed with the astrological signs associated with each season adorn the wall behind the statue. The four elements are depicted in bas-relief on the wall to the left, while the four winds are depicted in sculpture on the wall to the right. The author of these was Gerard Van Obstal. The ultimate museum dedicated to Parisian history is the Carnavalet Museum. This collection serves as an example of how the city has changed over time, from prehistoric to modern times. The Carnavalet Museum portrays daily life in Paris in a way that is both endlessly fascinating and endearingly personal. Walking around the Carnavalet Museum's chambers conveys the idea that the history of Paris is a tale of the lives of millions of famous and anonymous people over the years.

The prehistoric origins of Paris were first discovered during Baron Haussmann's time as a city planner and the improvements that Napoleon III ordered. Even though the fields of archeology and paleontology were still young, the committed researchers who worked for Baron Haussmann were thorough in their work. Crews discovered remnants of the past while dismantling large portions of Paris in order to complete the process of city planning, pushing the knowledge of human occupancy on the banks of the Seine back thousands of years.

Human artifacts from the Old Stone Age, or 500,000 BCE, when humans coexisted with woolly mammoths and saber tooth tigers, can be found at the Carnavalet Museum's Orangerie collection. A canoe from the Middle Neolithic period, roughly 4,000 BCE, has been found in the collection. The earliest burials along the Seine have been dated to around 200,000 BCE, and the earliest settlers to 5,000 BCE. Stone axes, spear points, and arrowheads make up the majority of the artifacts from this time period, but from 1800 BCE onward, bronze and iron objects proliferate, attesting to the region's popularity.

Coins from 100 BCE have been found, and grave sites and stone carvings that show Celtic ancestry have also been found. Additionally, there is a collection of coins and engravings from the Roman era. The rest of the home is like a time machine as you meander back through it. You may experience those eras of Parisian living in the rooms thanks to the furnishings and design.

The frequent reminders of the regular people constitute this collection's unique attractiveness. The rooms themselves, despite being furnished in a way that would have been out of the reach of the majority of the population, still reflect a working class practicality that is frequently lost when touring the mansions and homes of French royalty. This refrain can be heard in the paintings of everyday life, in the collections of street signs and shop signs, and in the paintings of everyday life.

The Carnavalet Museum Admissions and Hours

- The Carnavalet Museum is open everyday, except Monday, from 10:00 a.m.6:00 p.m.
- Admission to the permanent collection is free.
- Admission to the temporary exhibitions is 7 euros for adults; 5 euros for those over 60 years of age; 3.50 for those between the ages of 1826; and free for those under 13 years old.

Musée CognacqJay/ CognacqJay Museum

Le musee Cognacq Jay, often known as the Cognacq Jay Museum, is named after Ernest Cognacq and Marie Louise Jay, who founded the prestigious department store La Samaritaine. Ernest Cognacq donated their collection to the City of Paris after he passed away in 1928. Its original home was at 25 Boulevard Capucines in the Cognacq residence. The Cognac Jay Museum was relocated to the Hotel de Donon in 1990. Mederic Donon, Henri III's Controller of Buildings, erected the hotel in 1575. French art from the 18th century makes up the majority of the Museum Cognacq Jay collection, which was assembled between 1900 and 1925. It has artwork, furniture, sculptures, porcelain, ceramics, and paintings, many of which are portraits.

Additionally, there is a collection of inlaid cigar cutters and diamond snuff boxes. Some of the rooms are exact replicas of the salons from the Cognacq home, down to the furniture, rugs, 1750s-era chandeliers, and 1740s-era wood paneling. A visit to the attic is particularly remarkable to see the original and exposed roofing beams of the house, and the building's back garden is also accessible. It is a tiny museum dedicated to works from a certain time. Even though one is in a 16th century mansion, one feels as though they have traveled to the 18th century. Although there is no admission charge for seeing the permanent collection, there are occasionally temporary exhibits that do charge a price, typically around 4 euros.

Cognacq Jay Museum Hours and Admissions

- The museum is open from Tuesday Sunday 10:00 a.m.6:00 p.m. with the last admission at 5:30 p.m.
- It is closed on Monday and holidays.
- Admission is free to the permanent collection. A fee of 4 euros is required for the temporary exhibit.

- A coatcheck is available as well as a small bookstore.
- Photography is allowed without the use of a flash.

Musée d'Art et d'Histoire du Judaïsme/ Museum of Art and History of Judaism

Le Musée de l'Art et Histoire du Judasme, the Museum of Art and History of Judaism, is set in a gorgeous ancient edifice in the center of the Marais neighborhood. The structure itself was constructed in 1650 by Pierre Le Muet for the Count d'Avaux, who succeeded Cardinal Richelieu as Cardinal Mazarin and served as Louis XIV's French Prime Minister. A portion of the medieval city wall, built by Philippe Auguste between 1190 and 1220, is incorporated into the edifice. The Duke of Saint Aignan bought the hotel in 1688 and restored it, extending the front, creating a grand staircase, and adding dwelling apartments on the first level.

The architect Le Notre, who also created the Grounds of Versailles and the Gardens of the Tuileries, also expanded and rebuilt the gardens. It was shut down in 1795 during the Revolution, but it was reopened and used as a hub for small business and trade before gradually becoming into a hub for Jewish artists from Romania, Poland, and the Ukraine. The Jewish Art and History Museum opened in the Hotel Saint-Aignan in 1986. To accommodate the collection, it underwent partial renovation in 1991.

The Collection

The majority of the collection's origins are the Jewish Art Museum, which was founded in 1948 and was located in the 18th arrondissement, and the Rothchild collection of burial objects, which was a part of the Middle Ages Museum's collection. A portion of this collection is also kept in the Pompidou Center's Museum of Modern Art. Marc Chagall and Amedeo Modigliani's works can be found in the department of modern art.

The collection consists of over 6,000 items, of which 1,500 are displayed here. The Jewish community was historically located in the West and North Africa, according to the Museum of Art and History of Judaism, which spans the Middle Ages to the present. A lovely visit and opportunity to learn about culture are provided by the museum's well-decorated and captioned rooms, which each relate to a theme or time period in the history of the Jewish community.

- Metro: Hotel de Ville Arrondissement: 3eme, 71 rue du Temple
  Hours: Monday- Friday 11 a.m.6 p.m., Sundays 10 a.m.6 p.m.

Musée de l'Histoire de France Archive Nationales

At 60 rue des France Bourgeois, respectively, the Hotel de Soubise and the Hotel Rohan house the National Archives and the Musee de l'Histoire de France. Except for Tuesdays and holidays, the Museum of the History of France is open from 1:45 a.m. until 5:45 p.m. every day. One of the most stunning homes in the Marais neighborhood is still the Hotel de Soubise. It was constructed for the Princess de Soubise between 1705 and 1708. The towers are the only physical reminders of a much earlier medieval structure that stood where the mansion now stands.

Some of the most well-known artisans and artists of the time, including Boucher, van Loo, and Lemoyne, decorated the interior of the structure. The Princess's private apartments are quite fascinating and offer a genuine look into early 18th-century aristocracy. For the Archbishop of Strasbourg, construction on the Hotel de Rohan began. Documents from the Merovingian period's fifth and sixth centuries all the way up to the twentieth century can be found in the National Archives. They are beautifully presented and provide any history enthusiast with something to occupy hours of research.

Among the highlights are:

- The Edict of Nantes of 1598, which established freedom of religion in France ending the Wars of Religion

- The Treaty of Westphalia of 1648 which ended the Thirty Years War
- The Declaration of Human Rights of 1789 at the overthrow of the French Monarchy
- The Last Wills of Louis the XIV and Napoleon Bonaparte

The diary of Louis XVI is another item of lasting relevance. There is only one item for July 14, 1789, the day of the Bastille's storming and the start of the French Revolution: "Rien," which means "Nothing." a good museum in one of Paris's most gorgeous neighborhoods. Definitely worth the $4 admission price.

Musée des Arts et Métiers

The interesting history of the devices created by engineers and scientists from the 1500s to the present is on display at the Musee des Arts et Metiers. The Conservatoire des Arts et Metiers was established in 1794 by Abbot Henri Gregoire and was intended to house a collection of devices, instruments, and models developed in the disciplines of technology and science. A school and the precursor to the Musee des Arts et Metiers, the Conservatory was founded in 1802 and housed in the former priory of Saint Martin des Champs. The first Gothic building in Paris was the Benedictine priory and church of Saint Martin des Champs, which was constructed in the middle of the eleventh century. The current church, which was constructed in the 13th century, took its place when this was demolished.

Through the years, improvements were made; Henri III built the substantial entranceway on Rue St. Martin; Mansart constructed the high altar in the apse in 1626; and a cloister was finished in 1720. The priory was looted and the monks were killed during the French Revolution, leaving it vacant until the Conservatory moved in there in 1802.

Archaeological findings made in 1993 during renovations proved that a Merovingian necropolis, dating from the 6th and 7th centuries, existed beneath the nave of the medieval church. There were found to be around 100 plaster coffins. The Scientific Instruments, Materials, Construction, Communication, Energy, Mechanics, and Transportation departments make up the Musee des Arts et Metiers' organizational structure. The order of each department is chronological. The museum's first section, Scientific Instruments, features astronomical instruments for locating the sun in the zodiac, weights and measures, including Charlemagne's Pile, the imperial scale used at the end of the 15th century, and Pascal's calculators, which were created by the 19-year-old Blaise Pascal.

The tools from Antoine Lavoisier's lab from the middle of the eighteenth century are on display. The father of modern chemistry is acknowledged as being Lavoisier. The tools that

Foucault used to measure the speed of light in 1862 while working at the Observatory of Paris are on exhibit. Numerous further displays trace the advancement of robotics and science up until the 1990s. The development of glass, masonry, and fabrics, as well as the looms and factories that manufacture the great majority of the materials used today, are all covered in the Materials department.

The model used in 1690 to build Jules Mansart's Eglise du Dome at the Hôtel les Invalides is on display at the museum's Construction area. The dome construction model for the Bourse, the structure housing the Paris stock exchange and situated next to the Garden of Les Halles, which was the Wheat Market in 1809, is also on display. One of the first metal buildings in France was this dome, which was erected in 1763.

A model of the Telstar, which allowed the first live trans-Atlantic television transmission from New York to England in 1962, is on display in the Communication department along with printing presses, typewriters, telephone equipment from the early 1900s, telegraph systems from 1860, radio development from 1924 onward, and the history of cameras, phonographs, recording instruments for producing sound for cinema. The history of the equipment used to harness every type of energy, including steam, wind, electrical, atomic, and solar energy, is on display in the energy area. With its collection illustrating the evolution of mechanical technology, the Mechanics department of the Musee des Arts et Metiers is outstanding. Here are a few "hands-on" exhibits where people can use gears, pumps, and pulleys.

Everything from bicycles to rocket ships is on display in the transportation category. This is the last piece of the museum that was seen, and it is remarkable. It is housed in the chapel of the former church. Here, in stark contrast to the ceiling of this medieval church, are the earliest "horseless carriages," steam-powered trains, racing automobiles with propellers, modern cars sliced in half, and whole airplanes that are strung overhead.

A moving Foucault Pendulum can also be found in this section of the museum. This 156-year-old demonstration still astonishes and serves as tangible evidence of the Earth's rotation. This display features and protects the exact orb that Foucault used on February 3, 1851 at the Paris Observatory, during his first-ever public demonstration of his pendulum. Audio consoles with recordings depicting the lives, investigations, experiments, speeches, or snippets from written works of the scientists and innovators may be found everywhere across the Musee des Arts et Metiers. The majority of the exhibits have a visual monitor that demonstrates how the device on display works. A interesting and instructive trip through time is the Musee des Arts et Metiers. There are available guided and audio tours.

- The Musee des Arts et Metiers Hours and Admissions

- The museum is open Tuesday Sunday from 10 a.m.6 p.m. and until 9:30 p.m. on Thursday.
- It is closed on Monday and on French holidays.
- Admission is 6.50 euros for adults and 4.50 euros for students under the age of 26.

Musée Picasso

The Hotel Sale, a 17th-century structure designed by architect Jean de Bouiller for General Aubert de Fontenay, now houses the Musee Picasso, or Picasso Museum. The Gaspard brothers, Balthazar Marsy, and Martin Desjardins carved the ornaments for the main staircase. The Hôtel Salé, often known as the Salted Hotel, got its name from the occupation of Pierre Aubert, the first lord of Fontenay and a salt tax collector. Beginning around the end of the 17th century, the hotel served a variety of functions. The National Library, the Embassy of the Republic of Venice, a youth center, the Ecole Centrale des Arts et Manufactures, and Balzac's school were all once located there. The structure was purchased by the City of Paris in 1964, and in 1968 it was designated as a Historical Landmark.

One of the masters of 20th-century art is Pablo Picasso, properly Pablo Ruiz Picasso (October 25, 1881–April 8, 1973). The hotel was leased to the government in 1975, two years after

Picasso's passing, with renovations being completed between 1975 and 1984. Following a competition, the Musee Picasso in the Hotel Sale was designed by architect Roland Simounet in 1976. Diego Giacometti specifically designed the furniture, including the tables, benches, and seats, for the Picasso museum.

Public access to the museum began in 1985. Over 200 paintings, 190 sculptures, 80 ceramic pieces, and more than 3000 drawings, engravings, and manuscripts are included in the Musee Picasso's collection. His personal art collection, which includes pieces by Cézanne, Matisse, Corot, Chardin, and Renoir, is also on display. There are New Guinean Nimba masks, Iberian bronzes, and drawings by Degas and Giorgio de Chirico. In place of inheritance taxes that the Picasso family owes to France, these works and collections of Picasso are given to the nation-state of France. When Picasso's widow, Jacqueline Picasso, passed away in 1990, more than 40 paintings from her legacy were added to the collection.

From the basement to the top level and outside into the garden, the hotel is completely covered in this enormous collection of artwork from a highly prolific artist. There is a tiny outdoor café in the yard. A few times a year, the Picasso Museum also hosts transient exhibitions. A unique cinema shows movies, and a library is accessible. The Picasso Museum's bookshop and boutique are open during the same hours as the museum and are open to the public; admission to the museum is not necessary.

4eme Arrondissement

Centre Pompidou Musée National d'Art Moderne

This Center Between 1971 and 1977, the Renzo Piano, Richard Rogers, and Gianfranco Franchini-designed Georges Pompidou, often known as the Pompidou Center, was built. The Bibliothèque Publique d'Information, a sizable public library, and the Musée National d'Art Moderne are both located there (National Museum of Modern Art).

Here, art movements including Fauvism, Cubism, Surrealism, and Abstract Expressionism are among many that are represented. 1,500 to 2,000 of the museum's 50,000 art pieces, including paintings, sculptures, drawings, and photographs, are on display. The structure is quite recognizable. The phrase "an oil refinery in the middle of the city" has been used to describe it. A unique aspect of the structure is the colored outside pipe. Electricity lines are yellow, water pipes are green, and air conditioning ducts are blue. The white ducts are ventilation shafts for the underground spaces, while the escalators are red. Even the steel beams that support the framework of the Pompidou Center are external.

The architects wanted to flip the building inside out by situating the numerous service components (electricity, water, etc.) outside of the structural framework. The indoor area for the presentation of art pieces is made extra spacious and clutter-free by this design. Georges Pompidou, who served as president of France from 1969 to 1974, is honored by the center's name. On January 31, 1977, it debuted.

Organizationally, it is linked to IRCAM.

In the 1970s, Pierre Boulez established the Institut de Recherche et Coordination Acoustique/Musique (IRCAM). One of the most significant institutions in Europe for research on music and sound as well as contemporary electroacoustic art music is this Paris-based institution.

IRCAM located next to the Centre Pompidou.

Street performers including jugglers, acrobats, and mimes are frequently seen on the Place Georges Pomidou, which located in front of the Center. It's a pretty fun place to be. Musée d'Art Moderne de la Ville de Paris is the name of Paris's other modern art museum.

Centre Pompidou Hours and Admissions

- The Centre Pompidou is open from 11 a.m.10 p.m. every day except Tuesday and May 1.
- Museum tickets cost 12 euros. For those between ages 1825 the price is 9 euros.
- Under 18 years of age are admitted free.
- Everyone is admitted free on the first Sunday of the month.

Crypt Archeologique Notre Dame de Paris

One of the biggest archeological crypts in all of Europe is located beneath the square in front of Notre Dame de Paris. The area in front of the Cathedral of Notre Dame was crowded with structures before the 1860s, some of which were from the medieval ages. Remains of foundations and artifacts from pre-Roman periods were recovered when the buildings were demolished. Humans have lived in this region along the banks of the Seine since the early Paleolithic Period, or about 500,000 years ago.

First discovered during Napoleon III's reconstruction of Paris were artifacts from the Gallo-Roman era that had been forgotten. During this refurbishment, excavations near Parc de Bercy and along the Seine's banks turned up items that stretched the dates of human settlement way back into the mists of prehistory.

A highly fascinating exhibit on the prehistory of the area may be seen at the Musée Carnavalet. There is no charge to enter this museum. The City was well aware of the archaeological wealth that might be there when excavating started in the area in front of Notre Dame. Parts of Roman defences, chambers heated by a system of underground furnaces and pipes, medieval cellars, and the remains of an orphanage hospital were all revealed during excavations beneath the square.

Along with other intriguing historical photographs of the area taken before the 1880s, these are on exhibit. Directly in front of the Notre Dame church across the square is where you'll find the Crypt of Notre Dame.

Hours and Admissions to the Crypt of Notre Dame

- The Crypt of Notre Dame is open everyday, except Monday, from 10 a.m.6:00 p.m. The ticket booth closes at 5:30 p.m.

Admission prices are:

- 3.30 euros for adults; 1.60 euros for teens; under 13 years of age are admitted free.

Maison de Victor Hugo

In the southeast corner of Place des Vosges, beneath the arcades, sits the Maison de Victor Hugo, also known as the Home of Victor Hugo. Every day from 10 a.m. until 5:40 p.m., excluding

Mondays and holidays, it is open. The permanent exhibitions of this City of Paris museum are free to view. From 1832 through 1848, Hugo resided here. It was the first residence of a writer in Paris to be opened as a museum in 1902.

Hugo's original manuscripts, first edition books, numerous sketches, paintings, sculptures, posters for theatrical performances, and several rooms' worth of his furniture, including a writing desk, are all on display.

The most significant Romantic writer in the French language was Victor Hugo, who was a French author who was born on February 26, 1802, and died on May 22, 1885. The novels "Notre Dame de Paris" (also known as "The Hunchback of Notre Dame"), "Les Misérables," and a substantial body of poetry are among his best-known creations.

He was born in the Franche Comté area in Besançon. During Napoleon III's reign, he lived in forced and later self-imposed exile in Jersey from 1852 to 1855 and in Guernsey from 1855 until his return to France in 1870. Hugo first gained popularity in France as a poet, even though he is more known in the English-speaking world as a novelist.

The success of his book "Notre Dame de Paris" contributed significantly to the revival of interest in the Cathedral of Notre Dame and the eventual restoration of the structure in the mid-

1800s. Hugo passed away on May 22, 1885, in Paris. The French government decided to designate the Panthéon in Paris as a place of honor for the great men (and Madam Marie Curie) of France as a result of his passing and the subsequent period of national sorrow. In its necropolis, he is interred.

Memorial de la Shoah

The Tomb of the Unknown Jewish Martyr was the prior name for the Shoah Memorial. On January 25, 2005, President Jacques Chirac opened the Mémorial de la Shoah. The architects Alexandre Perzitz, Georges Goldberg, and Léon Arretche created the Tomb of the Unknown Jewish Martyr, which was constructed between 1953 and 1956. Inauguration day was October 30, 1956. In 1992, architect Jean Pierre Jouve refurbished it.

The Shoah Memorial honors the six million European Jews who perished in the Holocaust during World War II. The Memorial also pays tribute to the 76,000 persons who were assisted by the Vichy government in being transported to detention camps while the Germans were occupying Paris.

It is also known as the Museum Center of Contemporary Jewish Documentation (Musée Centre de Documentation Juive Contemporaine). One must pass through two locking doors into an enclosed courtyard in order to access the Memorial. This gives off a certain sense of confinement and imposed security, as if the builders intended for the visitor to feel temporarily confined.

The Memorial has a sizable bronze cylinder in its courtyard. The names of the Warsaw Ghetto and the principal concentration camps are written on it. The cylinder stands in for the extermination camp chimneys. Seven depictions of the Holocaust have been sculpted in basrelief along one side of the courtyard on bronze plaques set into the stone wall by artist Arbit Blatas. In 1982, they were positioned here.

A Wall of Names, part of the Memorial, lists the names of the 76,000 Jewish men and women, including 11,000 children, as well as their birth and capture years. There is a model of the Warsaw Ghetto and a reconstruction of the façade of a concentration camp barracks when you descend the stairs to the crypt.

The largest, black marble Star of David in the crypt is holding an Eternal Flame, and it is the most stirring piece. This is a powerful metaphor for the unburied victims' tombs. On February 24, 1957, Chief Rabbi Jacob Kaplan buried the ashes of victims from the Warsaw Ghetto and the death camps on soil that he had brought from Israel.

The history of Jews in France, the years of Jewish persecution during World War II, the history of anti-Semitism in

Europe, narratives of Jewish resistance, and more are all covered in exhibits past the crypt. These exhibitions include newspapers, documents, diaries, picture exhibits, texts, and videos.

A Memorial of the Children Killed in the Shoah is also on display.

The Center of Contemporary Jewish Documentation is situated inside the Memorial to the Shoah. A bookstore, a café, a multimedia learning center, meeting spaces, temporary and permanent exhibits, and reading rooms are all located here.

In another room, from 1941 to 1944, the Vichy Government police files on Jews are kept. Experiences at the Memorial to the Shoah are potent and deeply moving. It is a location to remember and learn. Once more passing through a set of double locking security doors is required to exit the Memorial. It offers the feeling of being set free, which is something that the majority of people who were detained in concentration camps never felt.

- The Memorial is open Monday Sunday from 10 a.m.6 p.m. and until 10 p.m. on Thursday. It is closed on Saturday and national and Jewish holidays.
- There is no admission fee. Appropriate attire is requested.

5eme Arrondissement

Institut du Monde Arabe (Arab World Institute)

In striking contrast to the historic structures of the medieval Latin Quarter is the Institut du Monde Arabe. This distinctive Parisian monument is a modern adaptation of Islamic design. The south facade is embellished with mashrabiyas, which resemble mosaics or filigree work and are influenced by geometric designs from the Arab world and allow light to enter the inside.

The institute was founded to foster dialogue between Eastern and Western cultures through lectures, music performances, film screenings, dance and theater productions, poetry readings, and transient exhibitions that are accessible to a wide audience. The institute's Centre de Langue et de Civilization collaborates to offer Arabic language classes.

The institute's museum is divided into three sections: Islamic Art, which exhibits ceramics, calligraphy, ancient manuscripts, traditional carpets, textiles, and jewelry; Ethnography, which offers exhibits on society, culture, and daily life in various Arab countries; and Modern and Contemporary Art, which showcases works by Muslim artists dating back to the 1920s.

The institute's museum offers a thorough overview of the various Arab civilizations. The collection starts with antiquity and emphasizes the third century, when the Arabic language and the genuine identity of Arab culture develop. It also shows how the Islamic faith had an impact as early as the seventh century.

Eating in the institute's fine-dining restaurant, Le Zyriab, on the ninth floor, is among the most delightful things to do in Paris. The elegant dining area of the restaurant provides breathtaking views of Notre Dame Cathedral and the Île de la Cité. There is a self-service café for quick meals on the ninth floor as well. On the ground floor, Le Café Littéraire offers light fare and snacks. The views from the rooftop terrace span the entirety of the Parisian skyline to the Arc de Triomphe. On clear days, La Défense is visible in the distance.

- Address: 1 Rue des Fossés Saint Bernard, 75005 Paris (Métro: Jussieu or Cardinal Lemoine station)

Musée de Sculpture en Plein Air

The 5th arrondissement's Quai Saint Bernard is home to the Musée de la Sculpture en Plein Air, also known as the Museum of Sculpture in Open Air. This park-like outdoor museum stretches along the river for around 600 meters. It reaches slightly east of Pont de Sully in the west from Place Valhubert and Gare d'Austerlitz. It is situated just across the Jardin des Plantes from the Quai Saint Bernard.

Over fifty sculptures from the second half of the 20th century are housed in the museum, which was founded in 1980. Brancusi, Gilioli, and Cesar are a few of the represented artists. The sculptures are dispersed over the park, some in the fountains and others on the strips of grass. A handful people gathered on an open square that's in the middle of the park.

There are sculptures next to the playground for kids and a few right on the quay's stone and concrete edge. The sculptures are dispersed over the park, some in the fountains and others on the strips of grass. A handful people gathered on an open square that's in the middle of the park. There are sculptures close to the playground for kids and some right on the quay's stone and concrete edge. A handful of lovely houseboats are moored along the waterfront as well. This museum offers wonderful vistas and picnic areas, making it a fantastic place to unwind. It is accessible to those with disabilities and open 24 hours a day.

Musée National du Moyen Age, Thermes de Cluny

The Musée National du Moyen Age, the building that houses the Museum of the Middle Ages, was constructed in the late 1400s and early 1500s and mixes Gothic and Renaissance design. This structure has served several purposes over the years. As a repository for medieval relics, it has existed since 1833, when collector Alexandre du Sommerard purchased the land and set up his collection there.

He passed away in 1842, and the State bought the structure and the collection. On May 17, 1844, it opened as the Museum of the Middle Ages. The Chateau d'Ecouen donated its collection of Renaissance antiques to the museum in 1945, and the Parvis de Notre Dame also made donations.

The structure was built on the ruins of the "Thermes de Cluny," or Gallo-Roman baths, which date to the third century. The Frigidarium, or "cooling room," which is a Roman bath's ruins, and the Hôtel de Cluny, which holds the museum's collection, make up the Museum of the Middle Ages.

Numerous significant medieval objects can be found in the museum. It is well known for its tapestry collection, which includes the six-piece series La Dame à la Licorne (The Lady and the Unicorn). Gothic sculptures from the seventh and eighth centuries, as well as pieces made of gold, ivory, ancient furniture, and illuminated manuscripts, are among the other noteworthy items in the Museum of the Middle Ages' collection. The "Forest of the Unicorn" (Forêt de la Licorne) garden, which is situated on the grounds of the Museum of the Middle Ages and was influenced by the tapestries, features exclusively plants from the Middle Ages..

"The Lady and the Unicorn"

The sequence of French tapestries known as The Lady and the Unicorn (La Dame à la Licorne) is regarded as one of the greatest pieces of European Middle Ages art. They are believed to have been woven in Flanders during the beginning of the 16th century, around 1511.

They show the six senses taste, hearing, sight, smell, and touch as well as "A Mon Seul Désir," which is frequently seen as a representation of love. In each of the six tapestries, a noblewoman is seen with a unicorn. A lion or a monkey are also shown in some of the tapestries.

The pennants, together with the unicorn and lion's armor in the tapestry, bear the sponsor's arms: Jean Le Viste, a prominent nobleman in King Charles VII's court. The tapestries are created in the millefleurs style (thousand flowers). Prosper Mérimée rediscovered the tapestries in the Boussac Castle in 1841. George Sand, a novelist, made the tapestries in her writings more widely known.

6eme Arrondissement

Musée National Eugene Delacroix

In Delacroix's final apartment and studio, where he lived from 1857 to 1863, is where the Musee National Eugene Delacroix, or National Museum of Eugene Delacroix, is situated. It is situated on a little Square that once served as the court of honor for the abbey residence, which the Cardinal de Bourbon, the abbot of Saint Germain des Prés, erected in 1586. The palace is a beautiful structure that underwent restoration a few years ago.

In order to make it simpler for him to work on the nearby church of Saint Sulpice's frescoes, Delacroix relocated here in 1857. His final significant works, these frescoes, which are still on display in the church, were finished right before his passing in 1863.

In 1952, the studio and flat were converted into the Musee National Eugene Delacroix. Except for Tuesdays and holidays, the Musee National Eugene Delacroix is open daily from 9:45 a.m. to 5 p.m. The National Eugene Delacroix Museum houses the artist's personal items in addition to his paintings, drawings, furniture, and engravings. From the French romantic era, Ferdinand Victor Eugène Delacroix (April 26, 1798 – August 13, 1863) was a significant painter.

He was born in the Ardèche town of Saint-Maurice-en-Chalencon in France's Rhône-Alpes region. Although he received Jacques Louis David's neoclassical training from Pierre Narcisse Guérin, he was also greatly influenced by the more vibrant and richly detailed styles of Flemish painter Peter Paul Rubens (15771644) and fellow French artist Théodore Géricault (17911224), whose works introduced romanticism in art.

The emerging style of Delacroix would have a significant impact on others. The art of the Impressionist movement was deeply influenced by his use of expressive color. His first significant work, The Barque of Dante, was recognized by the Paris Salon in 1822. Two years later, with Massacre at Chios, he found widespread popularity.

The picture "Liberty Leading the People," by Delacroix, became his most famous piece in 1830. This artwork demonstrates the differences between Jean Auguste Dominique Ingres' romantic and neoclassical painting styles.

The French government purchased the artwork, but officials decided that it was too controversial because it glorified the concept of liberty and took it out of sight. Napoleon III, the newly elected president, finally displayed "Liberty Leading the People" after the Revolution of 1848 that brought an end to King Louis Philippe's reign. Now, it is displayed in the Louvre Museum.

Despite the uproar surrounding "Liberty Leading the People," Delacroix continued to be hired by the government to paint murals and ceilings. Several books by William Shakespeare, Sir Walter Scott, and Johann Wolfgang von Goethe were also illustrated by Eugene Delacroix. He is also well known for his journals, in which he shared his thoughts on a range of subjects, including art.

He visited Spain and North Africa in 1832, a voyage that had a significant impact on the themes of many of his subsequent paintings. Delacroix continued to be the foremost French romantic painter in the mold of Michelangelo and Rubens throughout his whole life.

He created the well-known portrait of Frederic Chopin, the composer.

His large-scale murals can be found in numerous Parisian churches as well as the Palais du Luxembourg. In the third arrondissement of Paris, Saint Denis du Saint Sacrement, his "Deposition" was completed in 1848. His painting "The Agony," which showcases the artist's talent in capturing light on canvas, is located in the Church of Saint Paul, Saint Louis. In Paris, Eugene Delacroix perished. In the Père Lachaise Cemetery, he rests.

Musée Zadkine

From 1928 until his death in 1967, Ossip Zadkine, a Russian-born artist who immigrated to Paris in 1908, resided and worked in this area. Valentine Prax, his wife and a painter, remained here until her passing in 1981. The home and the artwork were donated to the City of Paris at that time.

A year later, in 1982, the Musee Zadkine, the Zadkine Museum, debuted. The majority of Zadkine's abstract and cubist pieces are on display here. One of the key figures in the Ecole de Paris, also known as the School of Paris, which is the collective designation for artists who emigrated to Paris in the early 20th century, was Ossid Zadkine.

His various periods and the various materials he used are depicted in the artwork in this museum, demonstrating the steady progression of his art from his earliest stone and wood sculptures to his bronzes. Early on, it is clear that primitive painting had an influence on him.

In reality, Zadkine had phases where he worked with a variety of materials, including marble, stone, terra cotta, and bronze. He used woods including elm, walnut, cedar, acacia, pear, and ebony in his creations. He was particularly interested in wood carving. Promethée, one of his creations, is carved into a nine-foot-tall tree trunk.

The bronze sculpture "Femme a l'Eventail" (Woman with Fan), produced in 1923, is arguably his most well-known Cubist piece. Or "La Belle Servante," a stone sculpture from 1926. Many of his larger pieces are on view in the house's serene garden. Among the garden's flowers and plants are smaller pieces as well.

The artist's studio, which hosts contemporary art exhibits three to four times annually, opened its doors in 1995. It is currently being renovated (July, 2008). The collection has more than 400 pieces of art, including paintings, drawings, and sculptures. There are never more than a few on show at once. A couple of his pieces are on display in the museum's permanent collection in Paris. The Garden's largest outdoor sculptures are always on view.

The house is situated at the end of a very brief and short roadway that leads straight to the house. It is an extremely private, sequestered home. Only the trees and ivy can be seen over the garden walls that enclose the property.

"Come visit my 'folie' (madness) in rue d'Assas and you will realize how a man may be altered because of a pigeon coop or because of a tree," Ossip Zadkine wrote in a letter to a friend. The invitation still stands today, albeit without the pigeon cage. One of Zadkine's earliest known pieces, "Tete Héroque" (Heroic Head), a granite sculpture, is included in the collection.

Zadkine Museum Hours and Admissions

- The Zadkine Museum is open Tuesday Sunday from 10:00 a.m. 6:00 p.m.
- It is closed on Monday and holidays.
- Admission is free to the permanent exhibit.
- A small book store is located at the entrance to the Zadkine Museum.

7eme Arrondissement

Musée de l'Armée

The Hotel Les Invalides is home to the Musée de l'Armée, or the Army Museum. Le Musée de l'Ordre de la Libération, the Museum of the Liberation Order, and the Museum of Relief Maps are included. The Artillery Museum and the Museum of the Historic Army were combined to form the Museum in 1905.

Following the Revolution, the Artillery Museum was established. Collections from the National Library, the Louvre, the Artillery of Vincennes, the Hôtle des Monnaies, and other private collections were added to the collection after its move to Les Invalides in 1852. By 1871, the Artillery Museum had been formally established at Les Invalides.

The Sabretache Society founded the Museum of the Historic Army in 1896. At the time, its collection of antique weapons and armor was ranked third in the entire globe. Additionally, it housed a remarkable collection of items from Napoleon's army as well as the world's unique collection of tiny artillery models.

One of the largest museums of its sort in the world today is the Museum of the Army. The Museum of the Army houses collections of historical artifacts, including emblems and flags, paintings, sculptures, stamps, sketches, and pictures, as well as collections of antique weapons and armor, Louis XIV's classic collection of weapons, 19th-century weapons, and artillery.

From 1650 to 1851, the Museum of the Army covers France's military history from Louis XIV through Napoleon III. It provides a summary of the French mounted forces from 1803 to 1939 and examines the weaponry and weapons the French army has employed from 1680.

The museum exhibits the weaponry and equipment used by the army, notably those used by the guards of the royalty, and explores how the military changed between the Thirty Years War and Louis XVI's reign. Additionally demonstrated is the evolution of consistent standards beginning in the 17th century.

Twenty rooms are devoted to the First Empire's years of rule between 1789 and 1815. The campaigns in Egypt and Italy, which had a significant impact on Napoleon's destiny, are highlighted. There are displays of Napoleon's personal belongings, including his hat and coat. A recreation of one of his campaign tents is also present.

The July Monarchy's history of the Metropolitan and the African Army is described. The Second Empire period, the Crimean War, the Italian campaign, the expeditions to China and Mexico, and the Franco-Prussian War between 1870 and 1871 are also covered.

Rooms relating to World War II were inaugurated in June 2000. The displays in these 2,000 square meter rooms detail the events that occurred in France between 1940 and 1944.

The Resistance, the French army's resurgence during the Italian battles and the landings in Normandy and Provence are also examined, along with the Vichy regime. De Gaulle is given special attention. Examined are the Wars in Asia, Africa, and Russia. Additionally covered are the horrors of the concentration camps, the fall of Germany, and Japan's capitulation.

Le Musée de l'Ordre de la Libération, often known as the Museum of the Liberation Order, was established on November 16, 1940, by an order signed by General Charles de Gaulle. It was developed to recognize the soldiers who gave remarkable service in the liberation of France. Additionally, it serves as a memorial for the Deportation, the Resistance, and the Companions of the Liberation.

The Legion of Honor is France's first national Order, while the Order of the Liberation is its second. The museum occupies an area of more than 1,000 square meters, with three galleries, six halls, more than 150 exhibits, and 3,700 items and documents on display. Personal mementos, flags recovered from European and African battlefields, varied uniforms, artwork created by prisoners in concentration camps, and underground posters, pamphlets, and newspapers are among the exhibit objects.

General Charles de Gaulle is honored in a Hall of Honor within the museum. Here are 78 of his honors, his final military outfit, and the original text of his June 18, 1940, radio broadcast Appeal to the French People, which he delivered while in exile.

Le Musée des Plans Reliefs, the Museum of Relief Maps, displays 28 examples of fortified city models made between 1668 and 1875. These two museums can be entered through the Museum of the Army. The Museum of the Army also features a café, library, bookstore, and boutique.

Every day but Monday is open at the Army Museum. Additionally, it is closed on December 25, January 1, May 1, and November 1. It is open from 10:00 am until 5:00 pm. October 1 until March 31. It is open from 10 a.m. to 6 p.m. between April 1 and September 30.

Adult admission costs are 9 euros, or 7 euros on Tuesday after 5 o'clock. For those who are under 18 or under 26 if they are citizens of the EU, there is no fee. The Museum of the Army, Napoleon's Tomb, temporary displays, the Museum of the Relief Maps, and the Museum of the Liberation Order are all accessible with a single admission. 30 minutes prior to closure, no tickets are sold, and coat check is free.

The Museum of the Army hosts numerous performances in addition to banquets, galas, and symposiums. There are four locations available for these events. The Grand Salon, the Esplanade des Invalides, and the Alexandre III bridge are all visible from here, and it provides a lovely view of Paris. The Salons of Quesnoy are made up of three little salons where there are arm, uniform, and equipment displays.

The museum's east wing is home to the Auditorium, which was constructed in 1997. This space has 150 seats and a video and film projector for symposiums and lectures. Up to 550 people can attend concerts in the Soldier's Church of the Church of St. Louis, which occurs many times every week.

Museum Guided Tours

Thirteen distinct, one hour and thirty minute guided tours are available at the Museum of the Army. Reservations must be made by phone and confirmed by mail two months in advance. The form is also available on their website. Each participant must pay 3 euros. It can be reached at 33 (0)1 44 42 37 72.

The many tours include:

The Discovery Trip: This tour provides an understanding of the Museum of the Army's collection, a synopsis of the Hôtel des Invalides' history, a visit to the Napoleon section, the Ancient Arms and Armor collection, the Eglise du Dôme, and Napoleon's Tomb.

The Secrets of Les Invalides Tour explores the Hôtel des Invalides promenade, the Eglise du Dôme, and the Eglise des Soldats, also known as the Church of St. Louis, with a focus on the building's design and the life of the Hôtel's boarders in the 18th century. The Honor Room, the Rooms of Ornano, the Caves of the Governors, and the Crypt Fieschi are among the locations that are typically off-limits to the general public.

The Musée des Plans Reliefs, or the Museum of Scale Models, is the sole focus of the Vauban Tour. The Napoleon Bonaparte Tour: Napoleon I is the focus of this tour. It stops by the Eglise du Dôme and the museum's Empire Rooms. Viewing his personal mementos, investigating his role as a man of war, going to his grave, and studying his legal and administrative writings are all included.

The final days of Imperial splendor are the focus of the Napoleon III Tour. The Second Empire's rooms, period uniforms, and technological advancements that will alter battle in the 20th century are all visited. The Second World War and General de Gaulle Tour includes stops at rooms related to the conflict. The Grand Battles of Napoleon I Tour: Highlighting his military battles, military techniques, and the Wars of the Republic (1796) and Waterloo (1815), this tour concentrates on Napoleon as the Man of War. It stops by Napoleon's mausoleum and the First Empire collection. The France in Torment Tour follows France's history from 1940 to 1945. Particular attention is paid to the conflict, French factions, and the Resistance.

The Posters of World War II Tour: This tour explores the use of posters, notices, texts, and leaflets in military and civilian life between 1939 and 1945, as well as the use of radio, newspapers, and journals. The Mysteries and Traditions of Les Invalides Tour: This tour explores the mysteries and legends of Les Invalides, including the mystery of the invalid with a wooden head and the histories of Napoleon's statue and the Dome's construction. The History Trip: This tour examines French history as it has emerged from the Hôtel des Invalides' tales, including those about border life, Napoleon I's image under various regimes, and the Occupation and Resistance.

The tour, "The Women of Les Invalides," explores the impact of the women who lived at the Hôtel, including the Grey Sisters, who were interested in the 18th-century frontiers, the women of the Resistance, and previous queens and empresses. Tour of the Les Invalides through Paintings: This tour explores the military history of France through artwork from the museum and the Eglise du Dôme.

Musée d'Orsay

One of Paris's most enjoyable museums is the Musee d'Orsay, or the Orsay Museum. The Gare d'Orsay, which once served as a train station, has a structure that beckons visitors to enter and take a voyage through a most spectacular period in art history.

One is immediately struck by the museum's spaciousness, the play of light, and the magnificent sculpture show when entering into the main hall. Excellent views of the museum's main hall are made possible by the spacious aisles, the mezzanine, and the lack of any architectural obstacles.

There is a calm, leisurely mood. Although there is a lot to see here, the Louvre is not nearby. This museum may be explored in its entirety in a single visit. There are two cafés and a lovely restaurant at the Musee d'Orsay, one of which has a terrace with views of the Seine and the Tuileries Garden.

Practicalities

- Access to the museum is at Square 1, rue de la Légion d'Honneur.
- The Musee d'Orsay, is open daily from 9:30 a.m6 p.m. and until 9:45 p.m. Thursday.
  The galleries begin closing at 5:30 p.m. and at 9:15 p.m. on Thursday.
  It is closed on Monday, January 1, May 1 and December 25.
- Admission prices are:

  8 euros for adults, 5.50 euros for those 1825 years old, for everybody on Thursday after 6 p.m. and everyday after 4:45 p.m. Admission is free for those under 19 years old and free for EU citizens under 26 years old, though a ticket must be acquired at the ticket desk with proof of age.
- Your entrance is an all-day ticket allowing you to leave the museum and return.
- During the week following, your ticket gives a reduced admission to the Gustave Moreau National Museum and a reduced fee for an unguided visit to the Palais Garnier National Opera House.

- A combination same day use ticket for the Orsay Museum and the Rodin Museum is available at 12 euros, a reduction of 2 euros if bought separately.
- There is a free coat-check service available.
- Wheelchairs are available at the coat-check, free of charge.
- Photography and filming: Any shooting using a flash, an incandescent lamp, a tripod or a stand is forbidden except when special permission has been obtained.
- The museum offers maps and brochures at the reception desk inside the main entrance.
- There is a bookshop with over 6,000 titles on painting, sculpture, architecture, decorative arts, French and foreign museum collections, photography and children's books. There is also a postcard shop and a boutique.
- The Musee d'Orsay restaurant has 19th century decor and is in the very location of the hotel restaurant of the Gare d'Orsay.
- On the 5th floor, the Café des Hauteurs offers quiches, salads, hot and cold drinks.
- Above the Café des Hauteurs, the Mezzanine provides self-service snacks, sandwiches and drinks.

History of the Area and the Building

The center alley of Marguerite de Valois, Henri IV's estranged queen, was previously located in the garden behind the Musee d'Orsay, which is now known as Rue de Lille. The land was divided up and separate residences were built after her death in 1615.

Back then, log boats and other cargo were loaded onto the banks of the Seine. Near the Pont Royal, work on the Quai d'Orsay began in 1708, and it was finished during Napoleon I's Empire a century later.

The area continued to draw the wealthy, and numerous luxurious residences were constructed there. The Hôtel de Salm, which is now the Museum of the Legion of Honor and is situated directly across from the Orsay Museum's main entrance, was constructed between 1782 and 1788.

The cavalry barracks and the Palais d'Orsay were the two structures that stood where the Musee d'Orsay is today. The entire area was destroyed during the Paris Commune of 1871. The ruins of the Palais were not touched for the following thirty years.

The Station

The Orléans railroad company purchased the land from the French government in 1895 because it wanted a more central stop for trains coming from the south. Victor Laloux, an architect, was awarded the contract to construct the station after winning a competition.

Within two years, the station and its hotel were constructed, and they were finished on July 14, 1900, in time for the World Fair. Laloux covered the station's metal frame with the hotel's exterior. Cut stone was used to construct the facade, combining it with the neighborhood's architectural design.

The station itself was cutting-edge for the time, featuring ramps and elevators, sixteen underground railroad lines, and a welcoming great hall. This room had a height of 32 meters, a width of 40 meters, and a length of 138 meters. It was a huge success, and both the beauty and the usefulness of the structure were praised.

The Gare d'Orsay served as the hub of the southwest French train network from 1900 to 1939. Travelers and convention goers both utilized the hotel. After 1939, however, the station primarily provided service to the suburbs. For the newer, longer trains that were being deployed, its platforms had became too small.

From Station to Museum

The station saw a variety of uses following 1939. It served as a mailing facility during World War II that sent packages to prisoners of war. It was the station that the soldiers traveled through on their way home after the war.

It has served as a backdrop for movies, most famously "The Trial" by Orson Welles, which is an adaptation of a Franz Kafka short tale. In addition, a theater group and auctioneers both used it.

The Hotel was still in operation in 1973. As early as 1975, using the station as a museum was being discussed. It was designated as a historical landmark in 1977, mostly to prevent it from being demolished and changed into a hotel complex. It was planned to renovate it, and work got under way in 1978. On December 1st, 1986, the Musee d'Orsay was officially opened to the public.

The Collection

The artwork from 1848 to 1914 is the emphasis of the Orsay Museum. This historical period produced a wide variety of artistic forms that reflect the changes occurring in the contemporary art world. The Louvre and the Musée Jeu de Paume's vaults provide the bulk of the collection. The museum maintains established collections of furniture, architecture, and photography in addition to painting, sculpture, graphic arts, and decorative arts.

Musée du Quai Branly

One of the newest structures in Paris is the Musée du Quai Branly, which is also one of the newest museums. Native American art from the cultures and civilizations of Africa, Asia, Oceania, and the Americas is on display at the Quai Branly Museum.

President Jacques Chirac has supported the museum's concept and development since it first emerged in 1995. The Musee du Quai Branly was constructed for 232.5 million euros and debuted on June 23, 2006. Architect Jean Nouvel, who in 1986 founded the Institute du Monde Arabe, was responsible for its design.

The majority of the collection's nearly 300,000 pieces, 3,500 of which are on permanent display, come from the now-closed Musée National des Arts d'Afrique et d'Océanie (25,000 objects) and the ethnology section of the Musée de l'Homme (250,000 objects). Each year, ten unique displays are scheduled. Temporary displays will occupy at least half of the exhibition space.

This is one of the largest collections of African art in the entire world and includes pieces from sub-Saharan Africa, Madagascar, and the Maghreb. Thousands of musical instruments are also kept in the museum. The collection and the museum's development have benefited considerably from contributions from private contributors.

A research facility is also part of the Quai Branly Museum. The multimedia collection has thousands of images as well as monographs, periodicals, and magazine titles. The Claude Lévi Strauss Theatre, which has 390 seats and a movie room with 100 seats, hosts lectures in addition to music concerts and dance acts.

In its 4 rooms, the multimedia library contains hundreds of reading spaces. There are 20 interactive terminals, 150 multimedia screens, and 25,000 works available, with ten times that many works in storage. The Quai Branly Museum has a lot of unique and intriguing characteristics. A glass column called "The Tower of Music," which rises from the ground to the building's top and is located in the middle of the exhibition space, is filled with 8,700 musical instruments.

In the Quai Branly Museum's administrative area and bookstore, there are five ceiling paintings by Australian Aboriginal painters. The "Green Wall" ("Le Mur Vegetal"), a Patrick Blanc creation, is a portion of the museum's outside wall that is covered with 150 plants.

Flowers, insects, and shells wrapped in clear plastic can be discovered in the pathways that wind through the gardens around the museum. In the garden area, there is a café and an underground amphitheater.

4,750 square meters of the building's 40,600 square meters are used for exhibition space. The 210-meter-long structure is supported by beams that raise it 10 meters from the ground. The

18,000 square meter landscape contains the Musée du Quai Branly. A 200 meter long and 9 meter high glass wall divides the museum's grounds from the actual quai Branly.

The Gilles Clement-designed garden features over 100 trees, including oak, maple, magnolia, and cherry trees, as well as pathways that wind over small hills and close to ponds. It's a lovely place that is also distinctive in that the garden continues beneath the elevated museum building. There is no entrance fee to browse the bookstore or the garden.

- The Quai Branly Museum is handicapped accessible and has texts presented in braille.

Quai Branly Museum Hours and Admissions:

- The Musée du Quai Branly is open every day, except Monday, from 10:00 a.m.6:30 p.m. and until 9:30 p.m. on Thursday.
- Admission fees for the permanent or the temporary exhibits are 8.50 euros, full fare and 6 euros for students. Those under 18 years of age are admitted free.
- Admission fees for both the permanent and temporary exhibits are 13 euros full fare and 9.50 for students.
- Admission is free the first Sunday of the month.

Musée Rodin

In the Hôtel Biron, the Musee Rodin debuted in 1919. It has sculptures by French artist Auguste Rodin. He was born François Auguste René Rodin in Paris, and his works represent the pinnacle of the figurative tradition in sculpture, while sculptors after him tended to focus more on abstraction. When "The Age of Bronze," one of his earliest pieces, was finished during his time in Belgium, the sculptor was accused of surmoulage because it was so lifelike (taking plaster molds from a live model).

After battling to defend his name, Rodin was given the assignment to design the entryway for the future Museum of Decorative Arts in 1880. Despite the fact that the museum was never completed, Rodin spent almost his entire life working on his most famous piece, "The Gates of Hell," which features scenes from Dante's "Inferno" in high relief.

Many of his most well-known works, including "The Thinker" ("Le Penseur," originally named "The Poet," representing the poet Dante), and "The Kiss," ("Le Baiser"), were first created as figures for this massive landscape of eternal passion and punishment before being later displayed as independent pieces.

Rodin preferred to work with amateur models, street performers, acrobats, strong men, and dancers rather than replicating conventional academic poses. These models would move around freely in the sculptor's studio as he drew fast clay sketches that would later be fleshed out, cast in plaster, and translated into bronze or marble.

Rodin was always drawn to dance and impromptu movement; in his sculpture "John the Baptist," a preacher is seen strolling while simultaneously demonstrating two phases of the same stride. Rodin and Camille Claudel first met in 1883 when Rodin promised to oversee Boucher's sculpture class while he was away. Infatuated with his gifted student, Rodin.

Camille saw her opportunity to learn from the most talented sculptor of her time, who was just beginning to gain notoriety. Rodin used Camille as a model for many of his sad love stories and she also helped him with "The Burghers of Calais," another significant assignment ("Les Bourgeois de Calais").

Rodin refused to sever his bonds with Rose Beuret, his faithful companion during his years of hardship in Belgium and the mother of their son Auguste Eugène Beuret, born January 18, 1866, even though they shared a studio in a tiny ancient castle at 68 Boulevard d'Italie in Paris.

Rodin never followed through on a deal he made to stop talking to any other women and get married to Camille. The pair split up after nearly 15 years together. Camille followed her own artistic path but ended up alone.

When Rodin was asked to design a monument for Victor Hugo in the 1890s, he extensively covered the topic of Artist and Muse, illustrating the various facets of his turbulent and complicated relationship with Camille in "The Poet and Love," "The Genius and Pity," and "The Sculptor and His Muse."

The Victor Hugo monument, like many of Rodin's public works, encountered opposition since it did not conform to popular expectations; the 1897 plaster model was only cast in bronze in 1964. Additionally rejected was Rodin's "Monument to Balzac," which was displayed at the Champ de Mars Salon in 1898 and depicted the author wearing a morning suit. It is now situated in the Rodin Museum's Garden.

Rodin never completed another public commission as a result of this painful experience. Instead, he had his most popular pieces scaled up to gigantic proportions after 1903. As one of France's most well-known artists, he could afford to employ a sizable number of apprentices and craftspeople.

Additionally, he produced a significant number of society portrait busts, particularly for affluent American collectors, and he started exhibiting fragmentary sculptures that, in his opinion, captured the essence of his artistic statement, such as "Meditation Without Arms," "Iris, Messenger of the Gods," or "The Walking Man."

In his later years, Rodin focused on little dance studies (about 1915) and produced a huge number of loosely drawn sensual drawings without ever pulling his pencil away from the paper (nor his eyes from the model). The so-called Kessler affair, which resulted from an exhibition of these drawings in Weimar in 1906, saw Harry Count Kessler fired as the curator of the Weimar Museum.

Rodin wed Rose Beuret on January 29, 1917, but she passed away two weeks later. On November 17, 1917, Auguste Rodin passed away. In Meudon, Îlede-France, France, a cast from "The Thinker" was positioned close to their grave. The Musee Rodin was established to manage and display the enormous body of work (more than 5,000 plaster objects, more than 1,000 bronze sculptures, over 8,000 sketches, and as many pictures) that Rodin donated to the French Government through a number of actions shortly before his passing.

Most of this collection is on display in the wonderful outdoor Garden of the Rodin Museum, while a small portion is on display in the Hôtel Biron. The Villa des Brillants, where Rodin spent his final years of life and worked, is where the majority of the plaster collection is stored. Meudon is a suburb of Paris.

Rodin gave the Musee Rodin the permission to reproduce his works together with them. Only 12 copies of any work may be published as a "original edition" in accordance with French law. The Rodin Museum continues to exercise "le droit moral," or the moral right, to prevent harm to the artist's reputation from copies of poor quality even though the copyright to the artist's work ended in 1987.

From 1908 until his death, Rodin lived at the Hôtel Biron. After his death, he gave the French State the entire collection of sculptures he owned, along with paintings by Vincent van Gogh and Pierre Auguste Renoir that he had acquired, in exchange for converting the residence into a museum devoted to his work.

The majority of Rodin's notable works, including "The Thinker" and "The Kiss," are housed in the Musee Rodin. There is a section at the Musee Rodin devoted to Camille Claudel's artwork.

8eme Arrondissement

Musée Cernuschi

In June 2005, the Cernuschi Museum reopened its doors following a more than 3-year makeover that cost 7 million euros.

Collection of the Cernuschi Museum:

After the Guimet Museum, the Musée Cernuschi has Paris' second-most significant collection of Far Eastern art. The fifth-largest collection of Chinese art in Europe is kept there. The renovation kept the historic wood parquet flooring, the original staircase, and the beautiful ceiling moldings while expanding the exhibition space and enhancing lighting.

The smoking area at Cernuschi's office was created as a tribute to him. 900 of the 12,400 items in the Museum's collection are always on exhibit. Chinese bronzes from the fifteenth to the third centuries A.D. make up the majority of this collection.

The Chinese art collection at the Musée Cernuschi, which spans from the Neolithic to the 13th century, is its most notable feature. Mingqi, or tomb figures, from the Han dynasty from 206209 B.C., the Northern Wei dynasty from 386354 B.C., and the Sui dynasty from 821618 B.C. are all included.

Pottery from the Tang and Song dynasties and a unique collection of gilded copper artifacts from the Liao dynasty, 9071125 B.C. The largest bronze Jian basin outside of China as well as the bronze wine vessel from the 11th century B.C., known as "The Tigress," are noteworthy pieces in the museum's collection. Female musicians riding horses are depicted in multicolored clay sculptures that date to the Tang dynasty of the eighth century. There is also a display of restored Chinese calligraphy.

More than 3,500 paintings, porcelain, and bronze artefacts can be found in the Japanese collection. The "mingqi" collection in the Cernuschi Museum is particularly impressive. Mangqi were buried alongside the deceased with the intention of offering comfort from the earth. They are portrayed as dancers and musicians, protectors and cooks, birds and horses. These, along with the bas-relief carvings on tomb walls, provide a window into 2,000-year-old Chinese culture.

Milanese banker and philanthropist Enrico Cernuschi (1821–1896). He participated in the 1848 battle to free Milan from Austrian domination before serving a one-year term in the Roman National Assembly. He fled to France after the new government fell in 1850, where he worked in banking and business to become wealthy. He changed his name to Henri, participated in the establishment of the Banque de Paris, and attained French citizenship in 1870. He was detained and then freed in 1871 after being discovered to be a major Communard sympathizer. In September 1871, after seeing the deadly rebellion, he went to the Orient.

He started acquiring Asian art in large quantities. Eighteen months after his return to Paris, he constructed a palace close to Parc Monceau for himself and to store his collection of approximately 5,000 works of art, which included the largest bronze Japanese Buddha sculpture in Western Europe. It's the Amida Buddha from the 18th century. The sculpture, which stands

4.4 meters tall, had to be divided into numerous sections in order to be transported from Tokyo to Paris.

Cernuschi left the property and his extensive art collection which he continued to add to throughout his life to the city of Paris as part of his will. On October 26, 1898, a public museum was opened there..

Cernuschi Museum Hours and Admission

- The Museum is open Tuesday Sunday from 10:00 a.m.5:45 p.m. It is closed on Monday and public holidays.
- Admission to the museum is free

Palais de la Découverte

The Palais de la Decouverte, also known as the Palace of Discovery, was created thanks to the efforts of Jean Perrin, a physicist who won the Nobel Prize in 1926 for his research on the atom. Vice-president of the Confederation of Intellectual Workers André Léveillé was the one who first proposed the idea for such a museum.

Perrin wanted to show how science has contributed to the development of our civilization and that "only research and discovery might change destiny," which is why he founded this educational museum. In 1937, the Palais de la Découverte received

25,000 square meters, or half of the Grand Palais exposition space, for the International Exposition of Arts and Techniques in Modern Life. Between May and November 1937, 2,225,000 people visited the Palais.

The Palace of Discovery was placed under the Ministry of National Education, Research, and Technology in 1990. It is therefore overseen by scientists with the intention of educating people. This is accomplished through the use of both ongoing and passing exhibits, lectures, interactive demonstrations, experiments, and workshops for both adults and children.

The Permanent Exhibits

Ariane V's Space Odyssey is a digitally projected, three-dimensional simulation of two space missions. A 3D movie called Voyage Into the Cell immerses viewers in the complexity and beauty of a cell by transporting them there. Animal Communication uses live animals in action, including frogs, crickets, ants, spiders, Siamese fish, electric fish, and spiders, to explore this incredibly diverse and complicated world.

The evolution of Earth's topography and climate since its creation is shown in Earth and Life. Investigative research teaches us that the origin of life and the appearance of various animal and plant species are related to the various stages of Earth's evolution.

Questions of Atmosphere: Covers issues related to ozone depletion, climate change, and meteorology. A 15-meter-diameter dome that serves as the Palais' planetarium displays the night sky and all astronomical phenomena, including Earth as seen from other planets.

Each of the Planetarium's several programs lasts for roughly 45 minutes. 3.50 euros are added on as an extra charge. The Planetarium has the following hours from Tuesday through Friday: 11:30, 2:00, 3:15, and 4:30. A 5:45 p.m. session is added on Sundays, holidays, and throughout the summer.

The second-most powerful force in the cosmos, after nuclear power, is brought to life in an electrostatic presentation at the Palais de la Découverte. Only on Sundays are these demos provided at 10:00, 10:30, 1:00, 3:00, and 5:00. Workshops in chemistry, astronomy, astrophysics, mathematics, geosciences, life sciences, and physics are also offered.

Admissions and Hours of the Palais de la Decouverte

- The Palais de la Decouverte is open Tuesday - Sunday from 9:30 a.m.6:00 p.m.
- On Sunday and holidays, it is open from 9:00 a.m.6:30 p.m.
- It is closed on Monday, January 1, May 1, July 14, August 15 and December 25.

- Admission prices are:
- 7 euros for adults, 4.50 euros for students, for those over 60 years of age and for those under 18 years of age.
- Planetarium admission is an additional 3.50 euros.

Petit Palais: Musée des Beaux Arts de la Ville de Paris

Charles Giralut, an architect, built the Petit Palais for the 1900 Universal Exposition (18511932). Giralut oversaw the construction of the Grand Palais, which was built nearby for the 1900 Exposition Universelle.

Together with the Alexander III bridge, these two structures constitute a majestic whole. The Palace of Fine Arts of the City of Paris was formally opened on December 11, 1902 under the name Palais des Beaux Arts de la Ville de Paris. It recently finished a four-year, $84 million restoration. In 2005, December, it reopened.

The Petit Palais is a four-part structure enclosing an interior garden. The Gardens of the Champs-Elysées can be seen through large windows. While yet protecting the artwork, the structure is well-lit. This, along with the roomy, clean hallways and the tall, rounded ceilings, provide a feeling of space and lightness.

A short flight of stairs leading to big glass doors with gilded wrought iron frames and Ionic column frames serve as the primary entrance. Directly beneath the building's dome is where one enters. This beautiful institution is introduced in an elegant and spectacular manner. The building's interior is decorated in a neobaroque style with carved wall decorations, marble walls and columns, a lovely mosaic floor, and murals on the ceiling.

The collection of Auguste Dutuit (18121892) and his brother Eugene (18071886), who amassed over 20,000 pieces of art including antiquated ceramics, prints, drawings, rare books, and medieval artifacts, was the first significant contribution to the Palais des Beaux Arts de la Ville de Paris, as it is officially known. A fund was also left by Auguste Dutuit for the purchase of other artwork.

Ancient Greek art to works from the First World War are all included in the permanent collection. It is presented chronologically and stylistically, enabling comparisons and the identification of the influences on the many artists.

Paris 1900, the 19th century, the 18th century, the 17th century, the Renaissance, the Christian world in the west, the Christian world in the east, and Roman and Greek antiquities are some of the several eras represented in the Petit Palais' permanent collection.

Poussin, Rembrandt, Géricault, Delacroix, Courbet, Carpeaux, Guimard, as well as Pissarro, Cassatt, Renoir, Sisley, and Cezanne, are a few of the artists who are featured in this exhibit. It serves as a linking point between the Musée du Louvre and the Musée d'Orsay, one would say.

The permanent collection is located in the northern side of the structure. The temporary collections are housed in the southern part. Access to the magnificent indoor garden with its ponds and palm trees, fresh air, and peace is available from both halves of the building.

Petit Palais Hours and Admission

- The Petit Palais is open Tuesday - Sunday from 10 a.m.6 p.m. It is closed on Monday and holidays.
- The Temporary Exhibit is open on Tuesday until 8 p.m.
- Admission to the Permanent Collection is free.
- Admissions for the Temporary Exhibits:
- 9 euros for adults; 6 euros for those over 60 years of age; 4.50 euros for those between the ages of 1426 and free for those under 14 years of age.
- The building is wheelchair accessible.

9eme Arrondissement

Musée de la Vie Romantique/Museum of Romantic Life

The former residence of painter Ary Scheffer is now the Musee de la Vie Romantique, or Museum of Romantic Life (17951858). It is located where old St. Lazare-related religious structures originally existed. This region passed into the hands of the State in 1792, and a sizable park was created there. This park was separated into several lots around 1820, and one of those lots was where Scheffer's house was built.

He included two studios and a fountain to the Scheffer mansion, which was erected in 1830. The intellectuals and artists of Paris paid Scheffer visits over the course of his nearly 30-year residence here, particularly when they were in the city: George Sand, Frederic Chopin, Franz Liszt, and Charles Dickens.

Residents of the area included Delacroix and Gericault. In reality, the homes of Georges Sand and Fredrick Chopin were only a short distance apart. Additionally, Scheffer sponsored exhibitions here for painters like Rousseau, Huet, and Dupré who had been denied a display by the Salon.

Although Scheffer rented the home while he was living there, his daughter Corneila eventually purchased it. She left several of her father's creations to his hometown of Dordrecht, Holland, when she passed away in 1899. After passing to the

Scheffer family, the home was sold to the State in 1956, who set up a cultural center there. In 1983, the home was transformed into a museum devoted to works of art and literature from 18201860.

The Museum of Romantic Life is divided into two sections: the first level is devoted to Georges Sand, while the second story houses works by Ary Scheffer and other artists of his age. It features a broad collection of paintings, drawings, sculptures, furniture, ceramics, and art items. The replica of a room from her Nohant home, replete with her furnishings, rugs, tapestries, and wood paneling, is a component of the George Sand exhibition.

Plaster casts of Chopin's left hand and her right forearm are also on display. Displayed with photos of her are her rings, necklaces, earrings, pins, brooches, handkerchiefs, a necklace she crafted for her daughter, a sample of her hair, and a handwritten draft of her most recent, unfinished novel.

Additionally, there are four pieces by Eugene Delacroix, including two drawings of Sands' garden in Nohant. In these spaces, Chopin recordings are frequently heard. His paintings, sketches, pictures, artifacts, sculptures, furniture, and books are all included in the Scheffer collection. A portrait of the Princess of Joinville, painted in 1844, is one of his works displayed here.

A lengthy alley leading to the home serves as the Musee de la Vie Romantique's entrance. The studio where Scheffer worked is now utilized for transient art exhibitions. A tea room with a terrace is located in the front courtyard and is open in the spring and summer. There is also a bookstore there.

Museum of Romantic Life Hours and Admissions

- The Museum of Romantic Life is open Tuesday Sunday from 10:00 a.m. 6:00 p.m. It is closed on Monday and holidays.
- Admission to the permanent exhibit is free. A fee is charged for visiting the frequent temporary exhibits, though free for those under 14 years of age.

15eme Arrondissement

Mémorial de la Libération de Paris

The Jardin Atlantique and the Memorial of the Liberation of Paris are situated side by side on the roof of the Gare Montparnasse train station in Montparnasse, France. Le Mémorial du Maréchal Leclerc de Hauteclocque et de la Libération de Paris Musée Jean Moulin is another name for the Memorial.

On August 24, 1994, on the occasion of the 50th anniversary of Paris' liberation from German occupation during World War II, the Mayor of Paris, Jacques Chirac, officially opened the Mémorial du Maréchal Leclerc de Hauteclocque et de la Libération de Paris Musée Jean Moulin.

French commander General Maréchal Leclerc (1902–1947) fought in North Africa. Upon his return to France, he commanded the 2nd Armored Division in the liberation of Paris from German occupation in August 1944, with the assistance of the 4th Division of the American Infantry.

The Memorial of the Liberation of Paris serves as a hub for information sharing, documentation, reflection, and study. The general public, as well as organizations, associations, researchers, teachers, and schools, may access it. A council of historians and Second World War experts oversaw the design of the Memorial to the Liberation of Paris.

Some of General Leclerc's personal belongings are on exhibit in the Memorial of the Liberation of Paris, including jackets he wore in Africa and Indochina, a tropical helmet, and walking sticks. Drafts of coded messages, documents, photographs, records of Leclerc and the 2nd Armored Division under his command, and propaganda posters from Vichy and the Allies are all there. Additionally, there are reproductions of historical leaflets and underground newspapers.

Testimonies and visuals of combat are presented in audiovisual exhibitions. The visitor can watch the development of the war using a variety of charts. The Memorial relocated within a structure with an elliptical interior wall. This wall has been transformed into fourteen moving picture screens. These screens transport the viewer to the powerful cinematic presentation Occupied Paris, the Resistance of Paris, and the Liberation of Paris.

The Musée Jean Moulin is also housed in this structure. The Jean Moulin Museum keeps a record of Jean Moulin's life and career as the acknowledged head of the Resistance Movement.

In 1939, Jean Moulin (1899–1943) was chosen to serve as the region's prefect. When the German Army invaded France in June 1940, he refused to assist them, especially by refusing to sign a German paper that falsely accused the French Senegalese Army of killing civilians. The German Army detained him for it, and while he was imprisoned, he was tortured. He used a piece of glass to try to slit his throat in this effort. Soon later, he was freed from jail.

The Vichy Government ordered all prefects to oust communist mayors in November 1940. When Moulin refused, the Vichy Government had him removed from his position. Soon after, Moulin began gathering with other individuals who were opposing the Vichy regime and seeking to drive the Germans out of France. One of them was Henry Frenay, who had put together "Combat," the most significant of the early Resistance units.

Under the guise of Joseph Jean Mercier, Jean Moulin traveled to London in September 1941 to meet with Charles de Gaulle, the commander of the Free French forces in exile. Moulin was given the job of leading the Resistance by De Gaulle.

Moulin returned to France via parachute on January 1st, 1942.

The Resistance was unified by Jean Moulin. He was successful in concentrating the Movement's anti-German efforts. Because of Jean Moulin's efforts, France was spared the civil wars that Greece, Poland, and Yugoslavia went through during the war.

While having a meeting with many of the leaders of the Resistance on June 21, 1943, Moulin was taken into custody by the Germans at Caluireet Cuire, in the Rhône region, at the home of Dr. Frédéric Dugoujon. He was brought to Lyon and questioned there. The Gestapo chief Klaus Barbie then transported him to Paris for questioning. Nothing was ever divulged by Jean Moulin. On July 8, 1943, Jean Moulin passed away from torture-related wounds while he was riding the train to the concentration camp.

In Paris' Père Lachaise Cemetery, Jean Moulin was laid to rest. The Panthéon received his ashes on December 19, 1964. Temporary exhibitions are also held at the Memorial of the Liberation of Paris. The Memorial to the Liberation of Paris' permanent exhibition is free to visit.

Admission to the temporary exhibits costs 4 euros for adults and 2 euros for visitors under the age of 26. For individuals under the age of 13, it is free. The Paris Liberation Memorial is open Tuesday through Sunday from 10 a.m. to 6 p.m. During Mondays and on holidays, it is closed.

By appointment only, a document center is open from 10 a.m. to 5 p.m.

Overlooking the Montparnasse railway station's tracks lies the Memorial to the Liberation of Paris. The Memorial can be reached in a number of ways. The Gare Montparnasse serves as one entry. A staircase leading to the Atlantic Garden on the roof, which the Memorial borders on the north end, is located in the far left, eastern corner of the station's second level.

Two elevators with glass sides are also available for accessing the rooftop Garden. One is situated on the northeastern side of Gare Montparnasse, in front of 4 Rue du Cdt. René Mouchette. The other is on the northwest side of the train station, in front of 25 Boulevard de Vaugirard.

These elevators do not, however, always run. A staircase leading to the Memorial of the Liberation of Paris is located in the building across from the elevator on Boulevard de Vaugriard. There isn't a stairway that can be used instead of the elevator on Rue René Mouchette.

Musée Bourdelle

The Montparnasse Tower and the Gare du Montparnasse, the Montparnasse train station, are both nearby the Musee Bourdelle, often known as the Bourdelle Museum. One of the finest sculptors of the late 19th and early 20th centuries, Antoine Bourdelle, lived and worked at the museum.

On October 30, 1861, Emile Antoine Bourdelle was born in Montauban, Tarn-et-Garonne, France. At the age of 13, he dropped out of school to work as a wood carver at his father's cabinet shop. He studied sketching at Montauban with the Ingres Museum's creator before moving on to Toulouse's art school to study sculpture. He got a scholarship to the École des Beaux-Arts in Paris when he was 24 years old.

He rose to prominence as a pioneer of monumental sculpture in the 20th century. After becoming a huge admirer of his work, Auguste Rodin hired Antoine Bourdelle as an assistant in 1893. However, Bourdelle soon realized that "very little grows in the shadow of a great tree" and left Rodin's employ to start his own workshop and studio, where he quickly gained popularity as a teacher. His classes attracted a lot of future notable artists, which greatly influenced sculpture. On October 1, 1929, Antoine Bourdelle passed away in Le Vesinet, close to Paris. He was interred in the Cimetière du Montparnasse, a short distance from his home, where he had lived and worked since 1884.

Prior to his passing, Antoine Bourdelle envisioned a museum where his creations might be shown alongside a studio where young artists could work and receive instruction. In light of this, he decided to give many of his works and possessions to the Musee Bourdelle in addition to transferring the title of his residence to the City of Paris. His generosity has considerably improved the city of Paris.

The Musee Bourdelle has gone to great measures to retain the homey and intimate ambiance of the workshop, giving it a certain charm that makes it a top-notch museum and a befitting memorial to this brilliant artist.

In 1949, Musee Bourdelle first opened.

The Great Hall was erected in 1961 to commemorate Bourdelle's 100th birthday and was created to house and exhibit the enormous figures of which he had become a master. Though mythical figures flank you on each side as you enter the Great Hall, your attention is pulled to the far end where Bourdelle's "Dying Centaur" is located beneath the rotunda. This majestic, melancholy piece is straightforward in form with a geometrical clarity.

A replica of General Alvear's enormous creation, who was a key figure in the movement for Argentina's independence, dominates the space. The General, his horse, and the four allegorical representations of Eloquence, Force, Freedom, and Victory make up the monument's major six components. The project was first commissioned in 1913, and in 1926 it was officially opened in Buenos Aires.

The full-scale replica of "Heracles Archer," or "The Archer," as it is sometimes called, is also housed in the great hall. One of Hercules' Twelve Labors, which are depicted in this statue, was to shoot the birds of Stymphalos. The full-scale replica of the "Virgin with Child" may be found in the Great Hall.

The new reception hall was added as part of an additional restoration in 1991, and the complex's central, spectacular, four-story building was constructed. This brand-new structure, which spans around 1,700 square meters, has workshops for aspiring artists, document archives, and galleries.

Models of Antoine Bourdelle's monument to Adam Mickiewicz, the leader of Polish independence, may be found on the gallery's lower floor. Bourdelle was enthralled by the work of this poet and leader, and she was moved by it.

Today, "The Monument to Mickiewicz" is located in the park of the Cours Albert 1er in the 8th arrondissement, just east of the Place de l'Alma. In the courtyard of the Palais de Tokyo and the Musée d'Art Moderne, Bourdelle's 1925 sculpture "La France," which is tall and graceful, is displayed. Over 800 sculptures, tens of thousands of drawings, papers, and manuscripts, along with the artists' own private art collection, can be found in Musee Bourdelle. One of the few remaining examples of the numerous artist residences and studios that dotted the Montparnasse neighborhood of Paris at the turn of the 20th century is the Musee Bourdelle. The Bourdelle Museum is open Tuesday through Sunday from 10 a.m. to 6 p.m. During Mondays and on holidays, it is closed.

Free admission is offered to the ongoing collection.

It is a fascinating and magical spot because of its intimacy and feel of an ordinary person's garden. Don't miss the chance to see this little-known Parisian gem.

16eme Arrondissement

Cité de l'Architecture et du Patrimoine

The Cite de l'Architecture et du Patrimoine, also known as the City of Architecture and Heritage, examines French architectural history from the 1100s to the present. It is the French Architecture Museum. Examples from the Middle Ages, Renaissance, Baroque, and Rococo periods are all included, as are buildings from the 20th century. After more than ten years of construction, it finally opened in September 2007 and is situated in the Palais de Chaillot on the Place du Trocadero.

One of the biggest architectural museums in the world is The City of Architecture and Heritage, a collaboration between the French Institute of Architecture and the Museum of French Monuments. With a few exceptions, everything in this collection is a reproduction. The depictions of French architecture on display at this museum include plaster replicas, copies of paintings and frescoes, reconstructions, and models.

The permanent collection is presented in three major galleries:

- The Gallery of Moldings
- The Gallery of Wall Paintings and Window Panels
- The Gallery of Modern and Contemporary Architecture

The Gallery of Moldings

Viollet le Duc, who renovated the Cathedral of Notre Dame and Sainte Chapelle in the 1850s, is credited with creating the Museum of Comparative Sculpture, which served as the foundation for this collection. Castings of civic and religious buildings' facades, gargoyles, pillars, and arches from the 1100s to the 1700s are displayed chronologically in the Gallery of Moldings.

The Wall Paintings and Window Panels Gallery

The Paul Deschamps-organized Museum of French Monuments included this collection. French murals from the 12th and 16th centuries were copied between 1937 and 1962. The order and themes of this collection are displayed.

The Modern and Contemporary Architecture Gallery

This collection, which spans 150 years of architecture and is organized chronologically, starts in 1851. Here, the emphasis is on architecture's role in society as well as its design and construction. Included is a scaled-down replica of an apartment from Le Corbusier's 1952 Cité Radieuse, the Radiant City, in Marseille.

The City of Architecture and Heritage also hosts transient displays. There are classes and workshops available. Conferences, symposiums, and lectures are held in a room with more than 270 seats. The renowned Cinematheque theater, a relic from the film museums that were formerly located here, screens movies. One of the largest architecture-related book collections in Europe, with 45,000 titles, is available. This museum serves as a dynamic center for education and training.

City of Architecture and Heritage Museum Hours and Admissions

- The City of Architecture and Heritage is open everyday from 11 a.m.7 p.m. and until 9 p.m. on Thursday.

- It is closed on Tuesday and on May 1, August 15 and December 25.
- Admissions to the permanent exhibits are: 8 euros for adults, 5 euros for those between 1825 years old and free for those under 18 years old.
- Admission is free for everybody on the first Sunday of the month.
- Combination tickets for the permanent and temporary exhibits are 10 euros and 7 euros, depending on the age of the person.
- Admissions to one temporary exhibit is 5 euros and 3 euros.
- Admissions to two temporary exhibits is 8 euros and 5 euros.
- Admission is free to the temporary exhibits for those under 12 years of age.
- A café is available which offers a great view of the Eiffel Tower.

Maison de Balzac

Author Honoré de Balzac resided in The Maison de Balzac, also known as The House of Balzac, between 1840 and 1847. The father of realism in French literature is regarded as Honoré de Balzac. In this home, Balzac revised and edited "La Comédie

Humaine," one of his most well-known works ("The Human Comedy").

While residing in this location, he also completed other complete works, including "Splendeurs et Miseres des Courtisanes," "La Cousine Bette," and "Le Cousin Pons" ("A Harlot High and Low"). Many of the pages that he manually edited are on display in a space specifically designated for them. The home is situated in Passy Village, which was once some distance from central Paris. Homes were spaced apart by fields and meadows in a sparsely populated area.

Balzac came here to work in the peace and quiet but primarily to avoid paying back debts to people. He even used the alias "Monsieur de Breugnol" and had a password that only enabled his friends not his creditors to visit him.

But when the creditors tried to enter, Balzac was able to leave through the two lower floors below his flat, which he had rented to others, and make it to the street, Rue Berton, which was at the base of the building. There are rumors that Balzac had a trapdoor that led to a secret stairway. There is a trapdoor, but it doesn't lead to a secret stairway, and it's not clear if it was there while Balzac was a resident.

The only structure that Balzac utilized as one of his houses in Paris that is still standing is this one. Over the years, when he left, the house was rented out to a number of other people. Since there were still people living in the lower levels of the home when it was designated a historical monument in 1913 and turned into a museum in 1949, it wasn't made public until 1960.

The residence is situated on the side of a small hill. The home descends from the entry level to the garden level. Balzac resided on the third floor, or the garden level, of the three-story mansion. It had a kitchen, which currently serves as the entryway to the museum, a living room, his bedroom, a space for writing, and a guestroom.

His family and acquaintances, many of whom appeared as characters in his novels, are shown in portrait paintings in the museum. His library is displayed in its entirety, many of the books being first editions. The area that is probably the most spectacular is his writing room, which features his desk and chair and has been redecorated to match how Balzac had described it in his writings. It also has some of his personal items. Only five months had passed since his marriage to Ewelina Haska when Honoré de Balzac passed away on August 18, 1850. He was interred in the Paris cemetery Pere Lachasie.

Balzac's House Hours and Admissions

- The Maison de Balzac is open Tuesday - Friday from 12:30 p.m. 5:30 p.m.

- It is open on Saturday from 10:30 a.m.5:30 p.m. It is closed on Sunday, Monday and holidays.
- There is no entrance admission charged to this museum.

Musée d'Art Moderne de la Ville de Paris

The National Museum of Modern Art Centre Pompidou should not be confused with the Museum of Modern Art of the City of Paris, or Musee d'Art Moderne de la Ville de Paris. The Palais de Tokyo, which was constructed for the 1937 International Exposition, houses this city museum. Here, a museum debuted in 1961. Donor gifts are primarily responsible for its accumulation. From 1901 and later, art is on display. The pieces are a combination of Surrealism, New Realism, Cubism, and Post Cubism.

The building's interior is big and empty. The displays are set out in several rooms. The temporary exhibits are held in three different rooms. The museum's permanent displays are located elsewhere. Two of the three "La Dance" paintings "La Dance Inachevée" (1931) and "La Dance de Paris" can be found in the Salle Matisse.

The Henry Thomas Collection, which includes pieces by Auguste Herbin, Goerges Valmier, and Charles Pierrehumbert, as well as works by Robert Delaunay, Gerhard Richter, Lucio Fontana, Jean Degotter, Martin Barre, Simon Hantas, Pierre Bonnard, and Marc Chagall, are also included.

The enormous murals titled "La Fée Electricité" are displayed in the Salle Duffy ("The Electricity Fairy"). These measure 10 x 60 meters in size. Duffy finished these pieces in ten months flat. In 1964, they were put in place here.

The "Collection" is located at the museum's basement level. It houses works by Andre Derain, Maurice de Vlamnik, Georges Braque, Raoul Duffy, Pablo Picasso, Amadeo Modigliani, Leopold Survage, Ferdnand Leger, Jean Helion, Frantisek Kupka, and Francis Picaba. This is the museum's largest section.

The Jonathan Monk Room, where he is featured, is located in the lower level as well.

This museum features a store, a coat check, a cafe with outdoor seating, and other amenities.

Museum of Modern Art Hours and Admissions

- The City of Paris Museum of Modern Art is open from 10 a.m.5:30 p.m. Tuesday - Friday.
- It is open from 10:00 a.m.7:00 p.m. on Saturday and Sunday.
- It is closed on Monday and holidays.
- Admission to the permanent collection is free.

- Admission prices vary to the temporary exhibits depending on what is being presented.

Musée de la Marine

Everything maritime is the focus of the Musee de la Marine, also known as the Maritime Museum. The museum is the world's oldest institution of its sort. It serves as a museum of history, technology, and society. It focuses on French maritime history and uses both ongoing and sporadic displays to show how it developed over time. The Paris Maritime Museum examines advancements in naval construction, the growth of offshore racing and recreational boating, as well as defense and maritime research technology.

Some History

The royal collection of model ships served as the inspiration for the development of this type of museum in 1747, but it wasn't until the creation of the "Central Museum of Arts" following the Revolution that the notion became a reality. On October 31, 1678, a decree mandated the creation of ship instructional models. At the period, models served as the building blueprints rather than any written plans for ships. Due to the fact that they were true architectural masterpieces, these models quickly attracted the attention of aristocrats. The most significant collections of these models in the 18th century belonged to Duhamel du Monceau, Bonnier de la Mosson, and the duc of Orleans.

In 1739, Henri Louis Duhamel was appointed as the Navy's inspector general. The Naval School of Engineering and Construction was founded by him in 1741. Duhamel offered his 20-year collection of model ships and other marine items to King Louis XV in 1748 with the request that they be shown in the Louvre. This 132-item collection was transferred to the Ministry of the Navy's newly opened Naval Gallery on the Place de la Concorde on August 3, 1801. Charles X made the decision to build the Musée Dauphin, a maritime museum, on December 27, 1827.

The Director of Ports, Pierre Zédé, visited Brest, Toulon, Cherbourg, Lorient, and Rochefort in 1828 to choose models of various kinds, as well as tools and equipment, that would be suitable for a museum. The name of the museum was changed to the Musée de Marine, the Naval or Maritime Museum, during the brief Revolution of July 1830. The Palace du Trocadéro was constructed for the Exposition Universelle, or World's Fair, in 1878, and the Musee de la Marine was created there. The Palais de Chaillot was constructed in 1937 in conjunction with the Exposition Universelle of that year, and the Musee de la Marine was moved here. In the same west wing of the Palais, the Musée de l'Homme opened at the same time.

The Collection

The most significant collection of model ships, gunboats, and antiquities dating back to the 17th century is kept at the Musee de la Marine. Models of the final great sailing ships from the 19th century, like the "Valmy," and the inventions of the great steam ships added to the collection. Exhibited are models of commerce ships, fishing boats, and leisure watercraft from more than three centuries.

Two galleries, each 190 meters long, house the Musee de la Marine's permanent collection. The Museum French maritime history is chronicled in Under the Glass Roof from the 17th century to the demise of the great sailing ships. The Lower Gallery is devoted to the history of seafaring's technical features, including the development of navigational aids and charts, ships built in the 17th and 18th centuries, steam ship development, and modern nuclear-powered battleships.

The Musee de la Marine also includes a workshop where model ships are built. Its primary objective is to restore the museum's collection of models. Only original materials are used in the models in order to preserve their historical value. The masts are often built of Oregon pine, and the wood is either ebony or fruitwood. The rigging uses cotton instead of the original hemp, which is the sole material that was not intended for that purpose.

Visitors can watch modelmakers and restorers at work.

Musee de la Marine Hours and Admissions

- The museum is open everyday, except Tuesday and holidays, from 10 a.m.6 p.m.
- Admission for adults is 7 euros; 5 euros for students under 26 years old; it is free for those under 18 years of age and for EU citizens under 26 years of age.

Musée de l'Homme

The expansive Musée National d'Histoire Naturelle, also known as the National Museum of Natural History, includes the Musee de l'Homme, or the Museum of Mankind, which is housed in the west wing of the Palais de Chaillot on the Place du Trocadéro. When the Palais de Chaillot was constructed for the 1937 Exposition Universelle, it was established here. It takes the place of the Museum of Ethnography, which has called the Palais de Chaillot's Trocadéro Palace home since 1918.

One of the most significant museums in the world for anthropology, ethnology, paleontology, and prehistory is the Musee de l'Homme. With more than a million pieces in its collection, it houses some of the most significant French collections on these topics. One-third of the 10,000 square meters (or 108,000 square feet) of exhibition space is given over to the prehistoric and anthropological exhibits. A library with more than 180,000 books and temporary displays are housed in the remaining space..

The Musee de L'Homme has four permanent collections:

- "The Night Times", describing the evolution from the first hominoids to modern humans including exhibits of human fossils;
- "Six Billion Humans", tracing the growth of world populations and the challenges facing the future;
- "All Relatives, All Different", concerning the unity and diversity of humans through biology, genetics and linguistics;
- "Galleries of Ethnology" covering Africa, Asia the Americas, the Arctics and the Pacific Islands.

A prehistoric lithophone from Vietnam made of 10 stones that were carved into various lengths is among the outstanding array of musical instruments in the "Room of Music," which is also present. The "Cabinet of Curiosities," which belonged to French rulers since the sixteenth century, provided the museum with its initial collection. The Museum of Ethnography once housed this collection. Every official French exploration trip is actively supported by the museum, which also receives the finds.

The "Menton Man," a cast of the "Hottentot Venus," and the "Venus of Lespugue," a carving created from a mammoth's tusk, as well as rock carvings from the Algerian Sahara and medieval frescoes from Abyssinia, are also included in the museum's collection. About 35,000 skulls and hundreds of entire skeletons are kept in the museum.

The Maritime Museum, or Musée de la Marine, is also located in this west wing of the Palais de Chaillot. The City of Architecture and Heritage, or Cite de l'Architecture et du Patrimoine, is located in the east wing. The Musee de l'Homme, or Café de l'Homme, is right next door to the Museum of Mankind. Dinner is served from 7:30–11:30 p.m., while lunch is served from 12:00–2:30 p.m. From 2:30 to 6:00 p.m., it is open and serves tea, coffee, pastries, and other snacks. The view of the Eiffel Tower is spectacular.

Musée National des Arts Asiatiques Guimet

The largest collection of Asian art located outside of Asia may be seen at the Guimet Museum, also known as the Musée National des Arts Asiatiques Guimet. Emile Guimet, a businessman from Lyon, France, who founded this museum, lived from 1836 until 1918. He made his first trips to Egypt and Greece in 1865. The old structures and the beliefs of the people who gave them their inspiration deeply moved him. His participation in international anthropological and archaeology conferences quickly increased, and he joined the Asiatic Society.

He visited the Museum of Ethnography in Copenhagen in 1874 and pondered whether France may also be able to build such a museum. He was sent to Japan, China, and India in 1876 to research Eastern religions on behalf of the French Ministry of Public Instruction. Soon after, he gathered an amazing collection of 600 sculptures and 300 paintings.

A portion of this collection was displayed in Paris during the Exposition Universelle in 1878. It was such a success that a museum in Lyon dedicated to several world faiths was created as a result in 1879. In 1882, this museum's collections were moved to Paris, where Guimet constructed a new museum that opened its doors in 1889. This museum's emphasis shifted more and more toward Asian cultures.

With the return of many expeditions from various Asian nations, the collection of the Guimet Museum gradually expanded throughout the years. This museum came under the management of the French Museums Directorate in 1927. Paul Pelliot and Edouard Chavannes added artifacts to the Guimet museum after returning from journeys to China and Central Asia. The Trocadéro Musée Indochine was merged into the Musée Guimet the same year, 1927.

Artifacts were given by the French Archaeological Delegation to Afghanistan throughout the 1930s. In order to display the Khmer collection, the center courtyard was covered in 1938. In 1945, the Guimet Museum received Egyptian art from the Louvre in exchange for the Louvre's Department of Asian Arts. The Musée Guimet continues its specialized item acquisitions and structural upgrades during the ensuing years.

The Guimet Museum required restructuring by the middle of the 1990s. It had been described as a jam-packed labyrinth. The task of renovating it was handed to architects Henri and Bruno Gaudin. Skylights and stairs were added after the structure was completely demolished. The Musée Guimet reopened in January 2000 to great acclaim after three years of construction and a $50 million price tag. It is an exquisite example of a contemporary exhibition hall, with lots of windows and natural light. The rooms and the various civilizations portrayed seem to merge together while being regionally structured. It would gratify Emile Guimet.

The Collections of the Guimet Museum

The Afghanistan Pakistan Collection contains artifacts from the first century, including Gandhara art from the Great Kouchans dynasty in the first through third centuries. The Kidara Kushan and Hephtalite stucco work from the fourth and fifth centuries, discovered in Hadda, is also on display.

The Chinese Collection is made up of 20,000 pieces that span 7,000 years of art history. These pieces include paintings from the Tang and Qing dynasties as well as bronze sculptures from the Shang and Zhou dynasties, Han and Tang tomb figures, and ceramics and jades from the Neolithic period.

The Himalayan Collection contains 1,600 works of art, including bronzes and paintings from Tibet and Nepal from the 18th and 19th centuries, book covers from the 12th and 14th centuries, metal sculptures from the 11th and 19th centuries, and wooden images from the 16th and 18th centuries.

The Trocadéro Musée Indochine collection, Emile Guimet's personal collection, as well as Khmer art and Cambodian artifacts, are all included in the South East Asia Collection. The Khmer sculptures are regarded as some of the greatest works of art in history. A large Shiva from the 11th and 12th centuries is among the rare Champa sculptures that are also displayed.

The Central Asia Collection is a representation of the great Buddhist artistic centers that emerged along the Silk Road at rest stops for traveling caravans. Along with books and manuscripts, this collection also includes 250 artworks. The Korean Collection: consists of 1,000 works of art from all stages of Korean history, including the Silla Crown, bronzes from the Koryo period, and tomb sculptures from the Choson period. Silla gold and silverware dates from 57 B.C. to 668 A.D., as well as the Silla Crown.

Terracotta, stone, bronze, and wood sculptures from 3000 B.C. to the 1800s and 1900s A.D. are included in the Indian Collection. There are paintings from the 15th to the 19th centuries on display, along with Roman-related archaeological finds.

There are 11,000 works in the Japanese Collection, which spans from 3000 B.C. to the Mejira era in 1868. The Jomon, Yayoi, and Kofun cultures' terracotta vases and figurines are on display. The iconic development of the 8th–15th centuries as represented in sculpture and silk paintings is given special consideration. Kakemono, makimonon, and screen paintings from the 16th through the 19th centuries are also on show. This amazing collection also includes ceramics, porcelain, stoneware for the Tea Ceremony, and ivory objects.

Admissions and Hours of the Guimet Museum:

- The Guimet Museum is open every day, except Tuesday, from 10:00 a.m.6:00 p.m. The ticket desk closes at 5:15 p.m. The Rooms are cleared at 5:45 p.m.
- Admission prices for the permanent exhibition are:7.50 euros full fare; 5.50 euros for students under 26 years old.

- Admission for the temporary exhibitions are: 6.50 euros full fare; 4.50 euros for students under 26 years old.
- Admission prices for both permanent and temporary exhibitions are:8 euros full fare; 5.50 euros for students under 26 years old.
- Admission is free for those under 18 and for EU citizens under 26 years old.
- The museum is free to everybody on the first Sunday of the month.
- An Asian restaurant is available and has the same hours as the museum. No admission fee is required for the restaurant.
- A bookstore and gift shop is also available without admission fees and is open during museum hours.
- The library is open Monday, Wednesday, Thursday and Friday from 10:00 a.m. 5:00 p.m.

Musée Marmottan Monet

Jules Marmottan purchased the mansion where the Musee Marmottan Monet is located in 1882. After his passing, his son, Paul Marmottan, moved there. Between Parc du Ranelagh and the Bois de Boulogne, it is located. Artworks in this museum span 700 years, from the 13th century to the 20th century, and are particularly special and unique collections. The Marmottan home serves as the museum's home, and the furnishings can be readily mistaken for everyday comforts in the midst of the artwork on display. Additionally, it is a museum that provides a close-up look at the work and life of the legendary painter Claude Monet.

Paul Marmottan (1856–1922) was a poet, art historian, and art collector. Jules Marmottan (1829–1883), his father, served as the general treasurer and administrator of industry for the Gironde department of France. Paul Marmottan left his home and art collection to the Académie des Beaux Arts after his away in 1932. The Musée Marmottan, which focused on First Empire treasures, was established on June 21, 1934. For its collection of Claude Monet paintings, it is more well known today. When Claude Monet's son Michel passed away in 1966, the Musee Marmottan Monet received the majority of this collection as a memorial. It is now acknowledged to be the biggest collection of Monet artwork in existence.

The collection of Jules and Paul Marmottan, which includes paintings, furniture, bronzes, pottery, and artifacts from the Napoleonic era, is largely displayed on the ground floor of the mansion. Along with 15th-century wooden sculptures, it also contains Bourgogne Renaissance tapestries from the 16th century. Over 300 writings and paintings from the Italian, English, German, and Flemish Schools from the 13th to the 16th centuries were donated by Daniel Wildenstein in 1981 to the Musee Marmottan

Monet, which now houses this priceless collection. A room downstairs is somewhat reminiscent of the Orangerie Museum in the Tuileries Garden, which houses Monet's Grand Water Lilies, "Les Nymphéas."

Oscar-Claude Monet is located in this space, in this room. From the cartoonish sketches he created in 1857, when he was just 17 years old, to "Impression: Soleil Levant," a piece from 1873 that unintentionally gave the Impressionism movement its name, to his final paintings of his Giverny garden, which amply display his cataract-induced failing vision and his own personal frustrations with old age. There is also one of his paint-covered palettes on display.

There are two Auguste Renoir paintings in this space. One of the portraits is of Claude Monet, and the other is of Camille Monet, who was his first wife. A sizable collection of Berthe Morisot's artwork may be found upstairs on the top floor of the Musee Marmottan Monet. Berthe was the first Impressionist woman. Boudin, Edouard Manet, Camille Pissarro, Paul Gauguin, Edgar Degas, Johan Jong kind, Gustave Caillebotte, Alfred Sisley, Paul Signac, and sculptures by Auguste Rodin are among the other artists whose works may be found in this location. There are audio guides created specifically for younger visitors, making this museum "kid friendly." The museum also holds kids' monthly drawing competitions. Their website offers online games.

Musee Marmottan Monet Hours and Admissions

- The museum is open from 10 a.m.6 p.m. Wednesday through Sunday and open until 9 p.m. on Tuesday. It is closed on Monday, January 1st, May 1st and December 25th.
- Admission is 10 euros for adults, 5 euros for those over 60 years of age and for students under 25 years old and free for those under 7 years old.

No photos are allowed and cell phones are asked to be turned off.

18eme Arrondissement

Espace Dali Montmartre

On top of the Montmartre hill stands the Salvador Dali Museum, also known as Espace Montmartre. Walk uphill along the street de Steinkerque to Square Willette from Metro Station Anvers. To get to the Basilica Sacre Coeur, either take the funicular or climb the stairs. It's wonderful to stroll through Square Willette's gardens and lanes. The area is typically bustling with a variety of people taking in the sights, mingling with one another, and watching the various street performers who frequent the area.

You do have to run the gauntlet of "independent businessmen" hawking their fine selection of post cards, miniature Eiffel Towers and squishy toys. Turn left when you reach the top and make your way to the Place du Tertre. This colorful spot is alive with quick character sketch artists, landscape artists and restaurants. Keep left through the Place du Terte and you'll find yourself on rue Poulbot and soon in front of the Dali Museum. Within is a superb collection of Dali's works.

Musée de Montmartre

A cultural hub that hosts concerts and lectures, the Montmartre Museum is situated in the midst of the village of Montmartre. Here, individuals from the art and literary worlds congregate. The building's construction in the 17th century started a tradition that is continued in this fashion. Being owned by Rose de Rosimond, a well-known actor who was a member of Molière's troupe, gave it the name "Maison Rosimond." In Montmartre, it is the oldest residence. The home's magnificent grounds and rural, scenic charm have been preserved.

Numerous famous figures from the worlds of literature and art have called it their home and studio, including the painters Auguste Renoir, Maurice Utrillo, Susan Valadon, Raoul Dufy, Francisque Poulbot, the composer Erik Satie, and the novelist Leon Bloy. Scale models of the neighborhood are among the local history exhibits of the museum, which also features archeology exhibits on the nearby area. Along with these, there are old photographs, letters, and artwork. Of interest are the furnishings as well. There is a bookshop that sells both English and Spanish travel information as well as a variety of local history books and artwork. Due to its central location in Montmartre, there are cafés close by where visitors can unwind and rehydrate afterward. Go to our Montmartre Tour page to schedule a private guided tour.

Museum of Montmartre Hours and Admissions

- The Museum of Montmartre is open Tuesday - Sunday from 10 a.m.6 p.m.
- The admission is 8 euros for adults, 6 euros for those between 18 and 25 years old, 4 euros for those between 10 and 17 years and free for younger children.

Monuments in Paris Organized by Arrondissement

There are monuments all across the city of Paris. There are many options for forming these memories of the past because of the numerous significant events and people in Paris' history. These remembrances may be seen everywhere, from the massive Arc de Triomphe and the more compact Arc de Triomphe du Carrousel to the plain inscriptions in the Tuileries Garden wall honoring the valor of resistance fighters during the German occupation of Paris. There are monuments to be found practically everywhere. Plaques that are attached to structures mention a variety of people, many of whom you've probably never even heard of before, including Oscar Wilde, Pablo Picasso, Jean-Paul Sartre, and many others.

You can find yourself seeing past events as you gaze upon landmarks in Paris like the Conciergerie on the Ile de la Cité or the Colonne de Julliet in the Place de la Bastille. You can create a theme for your walks around Paris using these numerous historical places and monuments. For instance, the National Museum of the Middle Ages offers tours of Roman archaeological sites, including the Arena of Lutece and the Roman Baths.

1er Arrondissement

Arc de Triomphe du Carrousel

The practice of organizing military displays or drills primarily for the enjoyment of the royals gave rise to the term "carrousel," which means "little war." Louis the XIV, whose reign was noted for the splendor of extravaganzas like this, directed the holding of one extremely renowned carrousel in June 1662. Knights in full regalia displayed equestrian skills while being accompanied by music and song on the field between the Louvre Palace and the Tuileries Garden.

The location has retained its name, The Carrousel.

One of Napoleon I's two large arches, the Arc de Triomphe du Carrousel, was built here. This Arch was fashioned after Rome's Arch of Septimius Severus. Between 1806 and 1808, architects Charles Percier and Francois Fontaine conceived and constructed it. Three arches make up its structure. The arched structure is 24 feet deep, 73 feet wide, and 63 feet high. Beautiful rose marble that offers dramatic accents of color at various times of the day or when it becomes wet from rain makes up the columns and front paneling. Looking west through the Arc, you are treated to a stunning perspective of Napoleon's bigger arch, the Arc de Triomphe, as well as the Obelisk of Ramses in the Place de la Concorde and the great sweep of the Avenue des Champs-Elysées. In the distance, if the sky is clear, you may see the Grande Arche de la Défense. One of the best views of Paris is simply this.

An equestrian chariot pulls a team of horses at the top of the arc. The horses were originally a little memento that Napoleon had taken from the St. Mark's Cathedral in Venice. In 1815, they received a courteous return. Baron François Joseph Bosio constructed the statues that presently stand atop the Arc de Triomphe du Carrousel in 1828. They depict horses, a chariot, and a human. One can easily spend some time here exploring the arch and the adjoining hedge mazes while also taking in the magnificent view of the pyramid designed by architect I.M. Pei in the Louvre courtyard. Stairways leading down to the Carrousel du Louvre are just a few steps away, on either side of the Arc de Triomphe du Carrousel. This elaborate, marble-floored shopping center is where one can find access to Metro stations Palais Royal Musée du Louvre on lines 1 and 7, as well as the inverted glass pyramid and the lower entrance to the Louvre Museum.

Conciergerie

The Conciergerie was formerly a part of Philip IV's palace (12841314). It was an area of the palace that was looked after by a government employee, the royal palace keeper, the concierge. The Guardroom and the Hall of Menat Arms, two outstanding instances of medieval secular architecture, are the dominant features of the ground floor levels constructed during Philip's reign. The latter is particularly impressive; it is 209 feet long, 90 feet wide, and 28 feet high and used as a dining area for the 2,000 palace employees. It was lighted by several windows that are now closed up and heated by four substantial fireplaces. Additionally, it was utilized for court procedures and royal banquets.

The Great Hall, where the king held his parliamentary sessions, located immediately above the Guardroom and served as its antechamber. In 1358, the royal family left the palace and relocated to the Palais du Louvre on the other side of the river. The structure had a conversion to become a prison in 1391. Its inmates included both political prisoners and regular criminals. The treatment of convicts at the time was frequently based on their income, prestige, and connections (unlike today, of course). The wealthy or powerful convicts would be given their own cells with a bed, desk, and reading and writing tools. Less wealthy inmates could afford to pay for sparsely furnished "pistole" cells, which came with a rudimentary bed and sometimes a table.

The poorest convicts, known as "pailleux" because of the hay (paille) they slept on, would be kept in "oubliettes," which are gloomy, damp, and vermin-infested chambers (literally "forgotten places"). They were allowed to pass away in settings that were favorable for the plague and other contagious diseases, true to the name. The Caesar Tower, named after the Roman emperors, the Silver Tower, which served as the royal treasury, and the Bonbec ("good beak") Tower, where prisoners were tortured and made to "sing," are the three towers that still stand from the medieval Conciergerie. In the square tower, the first public clock in France was set up in 1370. There is now a clock from 1535.

The Conciergerie housed the Revolutionary Tribunal and held up to 1,200 male and female convicts simultaneously during the Revolution. Between 1793 and 1795, the Tribunal met in the

Great Hall and executed roughly 2,600 people. Queen Marie Antoinette was the inmate with the highest notoriety. Later, her cell was turned into a chapel. The Conciergerie and Palais de Justice underwent renovations in the mid-1800s. In 1914, the Conciergerie became a publicly accessible national historical landmark.

Conciergerie Admissions and Hours

In the months of March through October, the Conciergerie is open daily from 9:30 a.m. to 6:00 p.m. It is open from 9:00 a.m. to 5:00 p.m. the remainder of the year. The 25th of December is a holiday. Admission to the Conciergerie costs 7 euros for adults, 4.50 euros for visitors between the ages of 18 and 25, and is free for visitors who are under 18 or under 26 if they are citizens of the EU, as well as for visitors who are disabled and a companion. Conciergerie and Ste. Chapelle combined tickets cost 11 euros for adults and 7.50 euros for people between the ages of 18 and 25.

Palais Royal

Originally known as the Palais Cardinal, the Palais Royal served as Cardinal de Richelieu's residence. Its construction was started by architect Jacques Lemercier in 1629. The Comédie Française, the official theater group, has its home in the bigger theater, which has existed at both ends of the galleries since Napoleon's rule. Lemercier constructed the first theater in 1641 for

Cardinal de Richelieu. From 1660 until Molière's death in 1673, plays by Molière were performed there under Louis XIV. Following it, opera was performed there under Jean-Baptiste Lully's leadership. The palace was left to the French Crown by Richelieu. Later, the youthful Louis XIV and Queen Mother Anne of Austria made it their home. Philip II, Duke of Orleans, reigned from here as France's regent during Louis XV's minority. Louis Philip II, Duc d'Orléans, sometimes known as Philippe Egalité, his great-grandson, hired architect Victor Louis to rebuild the buildings surrounding the palace gardens and enclose the park with arcades starting in 1781–1784. He constructed boutiques among the arcades and rented them out to defray the cost of the renovation.

The public was then allowed access to the Palais Royal Garden. The Duc, however, forbade the police from approaching these lands. Nowhere else in the city could one find such freedom. Intellectuals, bankers, workers, and artists would get together and talk about the current political happenings. To learn the most recent news, people come here. The most well-known cafés could be found there, and it served as the social hub of Paris. The "Le Grand Vefour" restaurant is still present in the northwest corner. A young attorney named Camille Desmoulins informed the gathering on July 12, 1789, that Necker, the well-liked Director General of Finances and Minister of State, had been fired. He then shouted, "Citizens, To arms!" while pointing up two pistols. The Bastille was taken two days later, marking the start of the Revolution. The Palais Royal was vandalized and robbed during the Revolution of 1848. The Conseil d'État, the State Council, the Constitutional Council, and the Ministry of Culture are currently housed there.

Place Vendôme

The octagonal Place Vendome was constructed between 1686 and 1699 and was designed by Jules Hardouin Mansart, who also built the Château Versailles. The Hotel de Vendôme, where César de Bourbon, the Duc of Vendome, the son of Henri IV, lived, gave the Place its name. Mansart demolished this hotel to make room for the Place. Its original name was Place des Conquêtes. Place was renamed Place Louis le Grand in 1720 when a huge equestrian statue of Louis XIV by sculptor Girardon was erected in its center. However, on August 12, 1792, rebels who saw this statue as a representation of royal power smashed it. Following that, the location was known as Place des Piques for seven years. It acquired the name Place Vendome in 1799. Investors and financiers established themselves in the Place's buildings. The Place was already a showpiece of opulence and prestige by the 19th century, and it still is today.

Currently, banks, investment firms, the Hôtel Ritz, Cartier, and other upscale hotels, as well as jewelers, are situated near Place Vendome. Temporary art displays are frequently available in the

Place's large pedestrian area. Napoleon had the 44-meter column designed by Denon, Gondouin, and Lepére built between 1806 and 1810 as a tribute to himself and the soldiers who had fought at the Battle of Austerlitz. Both it and the July Column, or Colonne de Juillet, which is located in the center of Place de la Bastille, are replicas of Trajan's Column in Rome.

The bronze that covers the stone core was created by melting between 133 and 1250 Russian and Austrian guns that were looted from the Battle of Austerlitz, depending on who you read (1805). Bergeret's basrelief spiral sculptures of Napoleonic victories between 1805 and 1807 feature a variety of heroes and combat scenes. Antoine Denis Chaudet's statue of Napoleon wearing a Roman toga was first positioned on top. It was taken down and replaced with a portrait of Henri IV nine years later. But in 1815, this was moved and placed on Pont Neuf, where it is still today.

The fleurdelys Louis XVIII placed atop the column was later removed by Louis Philippe to make room for a statue of Napoleon dressed in uniform. This statue was transferred and now stands in the Hotel des Invalides, overlooking the Cour d'Honneur. The column was toppled but not destroyed in the 1871 Commune. The column was repositioned in the center of Place Vendôme in 1874. The statue that is currently there is a replica of the original, which depicts Napoleon as Caesar. Inside the column is a staircase that ascends to the summit, however it is not accessible to the general public.

Ste. Chapelle

Sainte Chapelle is situated on the Ile de la Cité in the center of Paris, next to Notre Dame, and is largely encircled by the Palais de Justice. A Gothic chapel called La Sainte Chapelle (The Holy Chapel) was constructed in the rayonnet style. It is thought to be the world's most authentic example of high Gothic architecture. This can be explained by the rapidity with which it was constructed. It was most likely designed by a single individual, started in 1246, finished, and dedicated on April 26, 1248.

The name of Pierre de Montreuil has historically been associated with the chapel, however the designer-builder is not specifically listed in the archives. The façade of the Notre Dame Cathedral in Paris was finished by Pierre de Montreuil, who also renovated the apse of the Abbey of Saint Denis. Louis IX served as the chapel for the royal residence and oversaw construction. The Palais de Justice now encircles the Sainte Chapelle in place of the palace itself. Important aristocracy presented their arguments to the king at the Palais de Justice. It was constructed to contain Christ's crown of thorns, which Louis IX paid 135,000 livres to purchase from Baldwin II, the Byzantine emperor.

However, Sainte Chapelle's construction cost 40,000 livres.

Later, relics and a fragment of the True Cross were added. In a sense, the structure itself served as a priceless reliquary. The construction of Ste. Chapelle was heavily influenced by politics. Louis IX believed the Emperor in Constantinople to be nothing more than a Count from Flanders. Louis IX saw an opportunity to establish his city as the primary hub of Christendom due to this and the fact that the Holy Roman Empire was at the time in a state of considerable chaos. A smaller chapel that served as the parish church for the palace's residents located directly on top of the Royal Chapel. The Palace served as the venue for the executive branch. The chapel's stained glass, whose fine brickwork serves as a frame, is its most striking visual feature. They are regarded as the best examples of their kind in existence. The upper chapel received the rose windows in the fifteenth century.

The chapel was turned into an office during the French Revolution, and massive filing cabinets were placed over the windows. Whether on purpose or by happy coincidence, these filing cabinets shielded the chapel's windows from the vandalism that had ruined the choir stalls and rood screen. Additionally, the spire was destroyed, and the artifacts were scattered. Viollet le Duc gave Sainte Chapelle its current appearance in the 19th century. He designed the new spire. Since 1862, Sainte Chapelle has been recognized as a national historic landmark.

Sainte Chapelle's opening times and prices

Sainte Chapelle is open daily from 9:30 a.m. to 6 p.m. from March through October. It is open Monday through Friday, 9:00 a.m. to 5:00 p.m. It closes on Monday through Friday between 1:00 and 2:15 p.m. The 25th of December is a holiday. Admission is 8 euros for adults, 5 euros for those between the ages of 18 and 25, free for those under 18 and under 26 if they are EU citizens, and it is also free for those with disabilities and a partner. For adults, the combined admission to Sainte Chapelle and the Conciergerie is 11 euros; for children under the age of 18, it costs 7.50 euros.

St. Eustache

The history of both the Church of Saint Eustache and the vicinity in which it is located is extensive and fascinating. A substantial sum of money was lent to King Philippe Auguste in 1213 by a trader named Jean Alais. The King granted permission for a levy on each basket of fish sold in the market to be paid to Jean Alais in order to pay back the loan. As a token of gratitude for his good fortune and to honor St. Agnes, a virgin martyr from the fourth century, Jean Alais built a chapel there with the money from this tax.

The original location of Les Halles' marketplaces was where the boats disembarked in front of the Hotel de Ville. Louis VI relocated the markets to the location of the current Fountain of the Innocents in 1108. Philippe Auguste constructed two sizable halls for the clothier trades there in 1183, and his grandson Louis IX, St. Louis, constructed two further sizable halls for the sale of fish in 1265. This enormous market of the Middle Ages developed into a thriving and active hub of social life. The chapel was elevated to the rank of a church in 1223. It became a parish church in 1303. It was given a new name in honor of St. Eustache, a Roman martyr who died in the second century and whose relics the Basilica of St. Denis presented to the parish. St. Eustache is a patron saint who is prayed to when there are problems in the family. He is also known as the patron saint of hunters because while out hunting, he had a vision of Jesus between a stag's antlers. Eustache was a Roman general at the period, going under the name Placidus. Following this vision, he converted to Christianity and adopted the name Eustatius, which means "good fortune."

His fortune was soon taken, his servants succumbed to the plague, his wife was abducted, and his two sons were taken by wolves and lions. Due to his Christianity, Eustache refused to offer a pagan sacrifice in gratitude when his fortune was returned and his family was miraculously reunited. As a result, the Emperor Hadrian had Eustache and his family burn to death. Due in large part to the local businessmen, the church was expanded in 1435 and again in 1495, making the parish of St. Eustache one of the biggest and wealthiest in all of Paris. The foundation stone for the current edifice was placed on August 9, 1532. The structure was the final Gothic-style church to be constructed in Paris when it was finished in 1637.

The church is the same size as the Cathedral of Notre Dame at 348 feet (106 meters) long, 145 feet (44 meters) wide, and 115 feet (35 meters) tall. Notre Dame, on the other hand, is 13 feet (4 meters) wide and 79 feet (24 meters) long. The St. Eustache church was converted into an agricultural temple during the Revolution. The crypt of the Virgin was completed and rebuilt in time for Pope Pius VII's visit in 1804 after the church was restored in 1795.

The bell tower sustained substantial damage during the Commune in 1871, and the current renovation determined that the roof and buttresses needed to be strengthened. Le Ventre de Paris ("The Belly of Paris") by Emile Zola illustrates the politics and day-to-day life of Les Halles markets in the middle of the 19th century. The Forum des Halles, a huge shopping mall that would soon be rebuilt itself, took the place of the old marketplaces in 1969. The old market area also includes the Jardin des Halles, popularly known as the Garden of Les Halles. The Paris Stock Exchange, or Bourse, is close. St. Eustache is still the neighborhood's parish church. The church occasionally hosts free performances. It is well known for its superb organ.

4eme Arrondissement

Colonne de Julliet

The Colonne de Juillet, also known as the July Column, is a 52-meter-tall, 170-ton steel and bronze column that stands in the middle of Place de la Bastille. Like the Colonne Vendôme, it was designed by architects Alavoine and Viollet-Duc to resemble the Trajan Tower in Rome. Inauguration day was in 1840. A wood and plaster elephant model measuring 14.6 meters tall and 16.2 meters wide had once stood here. Napoleon intended to turn this elephant into a fountain with water spurting from its trunk by turning it into bronze using the melting of Spanish artillery and cannons. Before this could be achieved, though, the Empire fell.

When the elephant was standing, it provided a haven for homeless kids like Gavroche from Victor Hugo's "Les Miserables." In addition, when the elephant was pulled down, it was the residence of swarms of rats that plagued the neighborhood. A statue known as the "Genie of Liberty" is gilded and perches atop the Colonne de Juillet. Durmont is the author. It has a star on its forehead and is holding a torch in one hand and a broken chain from a set of chains in the other. The Colonne de Juillet honors the July Revolution of 1830, a three-day fight known as "Les Trois Glorieuses" that saw Charles X overthrown and Louis Phillipe put in power. The foundation was designed with burial vaults, and the 504 revolutionaries who perished there were laid to rest (as well as a couple of Egyptian mummies which were decomposing in the Louvre). These remains were later transferred and buried in the National Library Garden.

The column bears the inscriptions of the 504 martyrs. The 196 martyrs of the 1848 February Revolution were interred at the National Library garden in 1848 with those who perished in the 1830 rebellion. The dates of the July Revolution "27 28 29 Juillet 1830" are etched on the base's northern and southern sides. " la gloire des citoyens français who s'armèrent et combattirent for the defense of public freedoms in the unforgettable days of July 27, 28, and 29," is written on the other side ("To the glory of the French citizens who armed themselves and fought for the defense of public liberties in the memorable days of 27, 28, 29 July 1830").

"The Law of December 3, 1830" and "The Law of March 9, 1833" are written on the base's opposite side. According to these two regulations, a monument honoring the July events will be built in the Place de la Bastille. There are 238 stairs inside the Colonne de Juillet that provide access to the column's top. Sadly, this spiral staircase is no longer accessible to the general public.

Hôtel de Sens

The Hotel de Sens was constructed between 1474 and 1519 as Tristan de Salazar's house, the archbishop of Sens. It is one of the very few remaining medieval homes in Paris. Another is the Hôtel de Cluny, presently housing the Museum of the Middle Ages, located at 6 Place Paul Painlevé in the 5th arrondissement. Defense-related design aspects can be seen in Hotel de Sens' architecture. A square tower acted as a dungeon, and the arched entryway has chutes built into it so that defenders can pour boiling water on attackers. Turrets were also constructed for monitoring. Queen Margot was sent here by her husband, Henri IV, in 1605. As of 1689–1743, it served as the "Seat of Parcel Delivery Service Coaches and Carriages of Lyon, Bourgogne, and the Franch Comté," or "Siege of Messageries, Coches, and Carroisses of Lyon, Bourgogne, and the Franch Comté." So to speak, it served as a stage coach office.

Up to the French Revolution, it later again served as the archbishops of Paris' palace. It was afterwards inhabited by art students and utilized as a jam factory. The Council of Paris made the decision to establish an art and design library in 1883. A location where individuals could draw, use models, and borrow books was something the Council desired to establish. During this time, businessman Samuel Fornay gave the City 200,000 francs to be utilized for funding young painters' education. The name of the Bibliothèque Fornay is given in homage to this man. The Bibliothèque Fornay was founded in 1886 and is located in the 11th arrondissement at 12 Rue Titon. Architects, bronze artisans, and artists began to frequent the library very fast.

The Paris City Council didn't choose to relocate the Bibliotheque to the Hotel de Sens until 1929. The Hotel de Sens underwent restored from 1939 until 1961. The Bibliothèque Fornay was founded in the Hôtel de Sens in 1961. Currently, the library has 200,000 volumes, 2,580 magazines, 23,000 posters, 1,110,000 postcards, 325,000 copies, 28,000 commercial catalogues, and 50,000 slides in its collection.

The Hôtel often holds temporary exhibits.

Hotel de Sens Hours and Admissions

The standard entrance charge to these displays is 4 euros for adults, 2 euros for those over 60, students under 26, teachers, librarians, and groups of ten or more, as well as free admission for those under the age of 26. Anyone under the age of 14 is admitted free of charge to the exhibitions. Open to the public Tuesday through Friday from 1:30 p.m. to 8:30 p.m. and on Saturday from 10 a.m. to 8:30 p.m. On Sunday and Monday, it is closed. Moreover, it is closed from June 29 to July 19..

Hôtel de Sully

Between 1624 and 1630, Mesme Galle constructed the Hotel de Sully. It was created in the Renaissance style with Baroque characteristics by architects Jean 1er Androuet du Cerceau and Yves Boiret. The Hotel received its current name thanks to a purchase made in 1634 by Maximilien de Béthune, the first duc de Sully, who served as Henri IV's minister of finance and superintendent of construction. His grandson Maximilien, the second duc of Sully, also constructed a new wing in 1660. The family kept ownership of the Hotel de Sully up until the middle of the 18th century. The Hotel de Sully then changed owners on a number of occasions. It was altered to make room for tradespeople and businesses throughout the 19th century when it was utilized as an investment property.

It was designated a historic monument in 1862, and the State finally acquired it in 1944. Restoration work started then and didn't end until 1973. The Office of National Monuments and Historical Sites' main office later moved there, becoming the Caisse Nationale des Monuments Historiques et des Sites. This changed into the Centre des Monuments Nationaux, or Center for National Monuments, in 2000. This organization oversees more than 100 national monuments and produces literature on national heritage. Two courtyards exist at the Hôtel. The first one divides the mansion from the street and opens onto rue Saint Antoine in the past. The

Center of National Monuments Information Center is on the right side when you enter from Rue Saint-Antoine. Here you may find out more about museums and monuments and pick up free maps and brochures.

The Center of National Monuments' Information Center is open Monday–Friday from 9 a.m.–12:45 p.m. and from 2–6 p.m., as well as on Friday until 7 p.m. A bookstore selling books on all things French may be found beneath the second arch. Its major patio, the second courtyard. There are various benches here for relaxing and taking in beautiful courtyard from the 17th century. The four lawns are ornately bordered. This is where Jeu de Paume Site Sully's exhibition space is. The Jeu de Paume museum, whose main location is in the northwest part of the Tuileries Garden, hosts its transient photographic exhibitions here.

Depending on the exhibit, prices and schedules change.

The four seasons and the elements are represented by the basrelief sculptures that line the courtyard's walls. These exact season-themed basrelief sculptures may also be seen on the exterior of the Hôtel Carnavalet. There is a structure that served as the hotel's original orangerie, or greenhouse, along the back of the courtyard. Now it serves as office space. The door leading to Place des Vosges is located in the corner of the Orangerie's right side, near to the courtyard wall.

Hotel de Sully Hours and Admissions

- Hotel de Sully is open Monday Thursday from 9 a.m.12:45 p.m. and from 2 p.m.6 p.m. On Friday it is open from 9 a.m.12:45 p.m. and 2 p.m.5 p.m.
- Admission is free.

Memorial of the Shoah

The Tomb of the Unknown Jewish Martyr was the prior name for the Shoah Memorial. On January 25, 2005, President Jacques Chirac opened the Mémorial de la Shoah. The architects Alexandre Perzitz, Georges Goldberg, and Léon Arretche created the Tomb of the Unknown Jewish Martyr, which was constructed between 1953 and 1956. Inauguration day was October 30, 1956. In 1992, architect Jean Pierre Jouve refurbished it.

The Shoah Memorial honors the six million European Jews who perished in the Holocaust during World War II. The Memorial also pays tribute to the 76,000 persons who were assisted by the Vichy government in being transported to detention camps while the Germans were occupying Paris. It is also known as the Museum Center of Contemporary Jewish Documentation (Musée Centre de Documentation Juive Contemporaine).

One must enter an enclosed courtyard through two sets of locking doors before reaching the Memorial. This gives off a certain sense of confinement and imposed security, as if the builders intended for the visitor to feel temporarily confined. The Memorial has a sizable bronze cylinder in its courtyard. The names of the Warsaw Ghetto and the principal concentration camps are written on it. The cylinder stands in for the extermination camp chimneys.

Seven depictions of the Holocaust have been sculpted in basrelief along one side of the courtyard on bronze plaques set into the stone wall by artist Arbit Blatas. In 1982, they were positioned here. A Wall of Names, part of the Memorial, lists the names of the 76,000 Jewish men and women, including 11,000 children, as well as their birth and capture years.

There is a model of the Warsaw Ghetto and a reconstruction of the façade of a concentration camp barracks when you descend the stairs to the crypt. The largest, black marble Star of David in the crypt is holding an Eternal Flame, and it is the most stirring piece. This is a powerful metaphor for the unburied victims' tombs. On February 24, 1957, Chief Rabbi Jacob Kaplan buried the ashes of victims from the Warsaw Ghetto and the death camps on soil that he had brought from Israel.

The history of Jews in France, the years of Jewish persecution during World War II, the history of anti-Semitism in Europe, narratives of Jewish resistance, and more are all covered in exhibits past the crypt. These exhibitions include newspapers, documents, diaries, picture exhibits, texts, and videos.

A Memorial of the Children Killed in the Shoah is also on display.

The Center of Contemporary Jewish Documentation is situated inside the Memorial to the Shoah. A bookstore, a café, a multimedia learning center, meeting spaces, temporary and permanent exhibits, and reading rooms are all located here. In another room, from 1941 to 1944, the Vichy Government police files on Jews are kept. Experiences at the Memorial to the Shoah are potent and deeply moving. It is a location to remember and learn.

Once more passing through a set of double locking security doors is required to exit the Memorial. The majority of those who were detained in concentration camps never had the feeling of being released or set free. The Memorial is open from Monday through Sunday from 10 a.m. to 6 p.m. and on Thursday until 10 p.m. It is closed on Saturday and on Jewish and national holidays.

- There is no admission fee. Appropriate attire is requested.

Memorial to the Martyrs of the Deportation

At the eastern end of Ile de la Cité, in a peaceful landscape known as the Square d'Ile de France, is the Memorial to the Martyrs of the Deportation. It is situated on the Square Jean XXIII, which is directly behind the Cathedral of Notre Dame's park, and across the street from Quai de l'Archevéché. On the southeast side of the garden, there is a straightforward staircase that leads to the entrance. An adjacent modest wall made of white stone marks the Square's perimeter. These words are written in red letters on this small wall: (1940 aux deux cent mille morts dans les camps martyrs francais de la deportation 1945)

1940 in English To the 200,000 French Martyrs of the Deportation in 1945 Who Died in the Camps. President Charles de Gaulle dedicated this monument on April 12, 1962, which was created by architect Georges Henri Pingusson. It honors the memory of the 160,000 persons, 85,000 of them were political activists, resistance fighters, homosexuals, and gypsies, who were transported from France to concentration camps between 1940 and 1945.

Of them, 76,000 including 11,000 kids were Jews. Of those deported, only 2,500 people survived. It honors the memory of the 160,000 persons, 85,000 of them were political activists, resistance fighters, homosexuals, and gypsies, who were transported from

France to concentration camps between 1940 and 1945. Of them, 76,000 including 11,000 kids were Jews. Of those deported, only 2,500 people survived.

The victims' ashes and earth are kept in the black triangles carved with the names of the execution camps and set into the walls. There are 160,000 stones lining the Hall of Remembrance. It symbolizes the Jewish custom of laying a stone on a loved one's grave.

Memorial to the Deportation Hours Martyrs

During the months of April through September, the Memorial to the Martyrs of the Deportation is open daily from 10 a.m. to noon and again from 2 p.m. to 7 p.m. The Memorial shuts down at 5 p.m. the rest of the year. There is no entrance charge. Please wear appropriate clothing and switch off your cell phone.

Notre Dame de Paris

A Roman Temple to Jupiter was the first structure to be erected on the site of Notre Dame. The earliest Christian church, built in the fifth and sixth century and dedicated to Saint Etienne and Saint Stephen, came next. With the numerous Norman invasions, this was destroyed. A church honoring Notre Dame, Our Lady, was built in the seventh century. The entrance to the Notre Dame Crypt, a priceless archaeological find, is located on the western side of the square in front of the cathedral. The ruins and foundations of these original churches can be seen here. Under the direction of Maurice de Sully, the bishop of Paris, work on the Notre Dame de Paris began in 1163, during the reign of Louis VII. It was constructed in a design that has come to be regarded as "gothic." The basilica of Saint Denis, located in the town of St. Denis just north of Paris, is the first church constructed in this style.

Several different architects worked on the cathedral of Notre Dame, though none were specifically linked by name. One of them would be Pierre de Montreuil, who is also said to have designed Sainte Chapelle, which was finished in 1248. Pierre de Chelles and Jean Ravy are also referenced in relation to the later years of building. The earliest glass in the structure is found in the North Rose Window, which was finished in 1250 and still has 85% of its original glass. The Old Testament is symbolized by it. The New Testament is depicted in the South Rose Window, which was finished in 1260. The last time it was modified was in 1860 when it was rotated a small amount to increase its vertical strength.

The cathedral's first rose window was the West Rose Window, which is a tribute to the Virgin Mary. Its construction started in 1220 but wasn't finished until 1270. There is hardly much of the original glass left. The Great Organ, one of the biggest organs in the world, erected in 1730, has pipes that partially cover The Window. The towers were finished in 1250 after a 25-year construction period. During 12961330, the ambulatory chapels and "flying buttresses" were added. Many of the cathedral's valuables were lost or destroyed during the French Revolution. The cathedral was converted into a warehouse, saving the large bells from being melted down.

A restoration project was started in 1845 under the direction of architects Jean Baptiste Antoine Lassus and Eugene Violletle-Duc, in part due to the popularity of Victor Hugo's book "The Hunchback of Notre Dame." The spire was rebuilt as part of the restoration, which took 23 years. The rule separating church and state was approved in 1911; as with all cathedrals, Notre Dame is still state property, but the Roman Catholic Church is allowed to utilize it.

A significant repair and restoration work that was started in 1991 and was supposed to run for ten years is still ongoing. The church's front door has been renovated, and the results are truly spectacular. When viewed from the Parvis, the Square in front of the church, the detail of the carvings and statuary stands out beautifully. Particularly intriguing is the cathedral's eastern external side. The flying buttresses are clearly visible from the nearby garden at the Jean XXIII Square. The cathedral's two 69-meter square towers on its west face are arguably its most distinctive feature (228 feet).

The cathedral's renowned bell, "Emmanuel," is housed in the South Tower. The bell's clapper alone weighs 500 kilograms, making its total weight 13 metric tons (more than 28,000 pounds). The bell was refurbished in 1631, making it the oldest bell at Notre Dame. The fabled gargoyles (not chimères) of the cathedral are located in the Galerie des Chimères, which connects the two towers. These gargoyles are the fixtures that protrude horizontally from the building and are actually an essential component of the drainage system.

The Chimera, mythical hybrid animals that are perched on the edges of the towers, are the other creatures there. They serve as a barrier against malevolent spirits. There is a statue of the Virgin Mary holding the Baby Jesus in front of the West Rose Window. Viollet le Duc recreated the 28 Kings of Judah statues that make up the Gallery of Kings to replace those that were destroyed during the French Revolution. These statues were beheaded by the revolutionaries who thought them to be representations of the French rulers. These statues' heads were found in 1977, and they are presently on display in the Middle Ages Museum. The three entrance Portals on the west facade show scenes from Mary's life in the Virgin Portal, Christ seated and judging the living and the dead in the Last Judgment Portal, and scenes from Mary's mother's life in the Saint Anne Portal. A plaque installed in the piazza in front of the cathedral designates France's "kilometer zero," the starting point for distance measurements along the roadways departing from Paris.

Significant Events at Notre Dame:

- Napoleon Bonaparte was crowned Emperor at Notre Dame on December 2, 1804.
- The Te Deum Mass took place on August 26, 1944 in the cathedral to celebrate the liberation of Paris from the German Occupation of WWII.
- The Requiem Mass of General Charles de Gaulle took place in the cathedral on November 12, 1970.

Generally, French Catholic religious events of national significance take place in Notre Dame.

Notre Dame de Paris Hours and Admissions

- The Cathedral Notre Dame de Paris is open every day from 7:45 a.m.7:00 p.m. Admission is free.
- The Towers are open every day except for January 1, May 1 and December 25. The hours are from 10 a.m. 5:30 p.m. during the Fall and Winter months and until 6:30 p.m. during the Spring and Summer months. The last entrance is 45 minutes before closing.

Admissions for the Towers are:

- 7.50 euros for adults; 4.80 for those under 26 years of age and free for those under 18 years of age. Groups of more than 20 persons are 5.70 euros each.

Panthéon

Under the direction of architect Jacques Germain Soufflot, work on the Pantheon began in 1758. (17131780). On the same site as the St. Genevieve Abbey, which was still existing but in ruins at the time, a church was constructed in her honor. St. Genevieve is the patron saint of Paris. Louis XV gave the go-ahead for its construction after he recovered from a nearly deadly sickness in 1744. One of Paris' more notable landmarks, the Pantheon is located atop Mont Sainte Geneviève in the Latin Quarter. It is situated next to Saint Etienne du Mont's church. After Sufflot passed away, Jean Baptiste Rondelet finished the structure in 1789.

The structure was used as a mausoleum for the interment of notable Frenchmen after the French Revolution, when it ceased to serve as a church. (In actuality, two women are also interred here: Marie Curie, who was interred in 1995, and Sophie Berthelet, who was interred in 1907 with her husband, Marcellin.) "Aux Grandes Hommes La Patrie Reconnaisante," or "To Its Great Men The Grateful Homeland," is written over the door. Additionally, there is a bas-relief sculpture by David d'Anger. It was constructed in the first Parisian Neoclassical style, which departs from the rococo and baroque aesthetics and emphasizes grandeur and simplicity. It established the bar for later structures constructed in a similar style, including the Arc de Triomphe and the church La Madeleine.

The Pantheon in Paris is shaped like a Greek Cross and is based on both the Pantheon in Rome and St. Paul's Cathedral in London. Its Greek temple-style façade is highlighted by 18 Corinthian columns. The building itself is 83 meters high, 84 meters wide, and 110 meters long (350 feet) (270 feet). "Assumption of St. Genevieve" is a fresco that adorns the interior of the dome (1811). Puvis de Chavannes painted frescoes on the walls that depicted Charlemagne, Louis IX, Joan of Arc, and the life of Sainte Geneviève. Napoleon returned the structure to the Church in 1806. It was once again State property from 1831 until 1852. After afterwards, it served as a house of worship once more before eventually returning as a public structure in 1885.

In the Observatoire de Paris, Leon Foucault first displayed his now-famous Foucault Pendulum on February 3, 1851. On March 26, 1851, the future Napoleon III, Prince Louis Napoleon, requested another performance to be held in the Pantheon. The evidence that the earth does, in fact, revolve on its axis was presented by this ground-breaking demonstration, and it continues to be so today. In the Conservatoire des Arts et Métiers, Foucault's Pendulum has been hanging and swinging since 1855. The 67-meter Pendulum resided temporarily in the Pantheon while this structure was being renovated. Since then, it has been brought back to the Musée des Arts et Métiers, where it is on display. Alexandre Dumas was buried in the Pantheon for the first time most recently (18021870). The incident happened on November 30, 2002. His remains had been removed from his original French cemetery in Aisne.

Pantheon Hours and Admissions

- The Panthéon is open every day from 10 a.m.6:30 p.m. The last entrance is at 5:45 p.m. The last entrance for the Upper Level is 5:15 p.m. The last entrance for the Crypt is 6:10 p.m.
- Admission Fees are:7.50 euros for adults; 4.80 euros for those between 1825 years of age; free for those under 18 years of age.
- There are 206 steps to climb to the Upper Level, making an elevation change of 35 meters.

6eme Arrondissement

Palais et Jardin du Luxembourg

The Palais du Luxembourg et Jardin, often known as the Luxembourg Palace and Garden, was formerly the site of a Roman camp. Here, a convent was erected in 1257. Between 1615 and

1627, the Luxembourg Palace was constructed. Following Henri IV's murder, his widow, Marie de Medici, made the decision to construct an opulent mansion for herself in Paris's Luxembourg neighborhood. She acquired the Hôtel Flanco de Luxembourg, its 18 hectares, as well as a few adjacent properties to make a total of 20 hectares. She then commissioned Salomon de Brosse, an architect, to recreate her childhood home, Florence's Pitti Palaco, into a palace for her. Salomon de Brosse, with the assistance of designers Jacques Le Mercier and Alphonse de Gisors, created the new palace in a French, not an Italian, style.

The "Marie de Medici Cycle," which consists of 24 pieces, was commissioned by Marie de Medici in 1621 and was completed by Antwerp-based painter Peter Paul Rubens. The majority of the paintings at the Louvre now show her marital life to Henri IV. The Queen commissioned Thomas Francino to create the terraces and fountains for the Garden and Boyceau de la Barnuderie to create the flowerbeds. Marie de Médici only spent a brief period of time here before her son Louis XIII banished her in 1631. 1642 saw her passing in Cologne. The French nobility were then housed in turn at the Palais du Luxembourg. Revolutionaries seized control of the Palais du Luxembourg in 1792 and turned it into a jail. Josephine de Beauharnais and her murdered husband Alexandre de Beauharnais were among those detained here. Josephine was spared death, nevertheless, and she and her second husband,

Napoleon Bonaparte, returned to the Palace a few years later as Empress.

Revolutionary Camille Desmoulins, Revolutionary commander Georges Danton, Revolutionary writer Thomas Paine, and Revolutionary painter Louis David were all detained here. Napoleon I temporarily seated the Senate in the Palace in 1797. In 1879, the Senate moved back into the Palace, where it is still. The Nazis used the Palais as the Luftwaffe's administrative center during World War II. There are numerous paintings and frescoes inside the Palais du Luxembourg, including works by Eugene Delacroix. The Musée du Luxembourg, located next to the Palais du Luxembourg, formerly had a permanent collection of artwork from the 19th century. It now features transient exhibits organized by the Senate and the Ministry of Culture.

The Jardin du Luxembourg is among Paris's biggest and most stunning parks. There are numerous sculptures dotted around the grounds, including the Fountain des Médicis, statues of the French Queens and Sainte-Genèvieve, the patron saint of Paris, Rodin's bust of Stendhal, Sicard's sculpture of George Sands, a miniature Statue of Liberty (a gift from Bartholdi to the City of Paris), and a great number more. A large children's playground and a carousel are both present in the Garden. Model sailboats are available for rent at the Grand Basin on Wednesday, Saturday, Sunday, and school holidays from 2:00 p.m. to 4:30 p.m. in the winter and until 7:00 p.m. in the summer. For all ages, the Théâtre du Luxembourg offers marionette performances. Wednesday, Saturday, Sunday, and holidays are when performances take place. During the summer, performances take place every day at 2:30, 3:30, and 4:30 p.m.

For the younger kids, Shetland Pony rides are also offered in the Garden. There is a garden of beehives in addition to the 350 000 plants and flowers that are planted each spring, including 150 palm and orange trees. On Wednesdays and frequently on Saturdays, there is a "keeper of the hives," and beehive management classes are available. The Luxembourg Garden also features numerous pétanque (boules or bocce ball) tables, tennis courts, basketball courts, volleyball courts, and basketball courts.

7eme Arrondissement

Assemblée Nationale

The Assemblee Nationale, or National Assembly, was established in 1789 and created a constitution that curtailed the king's authority and gave elected national representatives absolute power. The Assembly had the authority to pass laws, regulate taxes, oversee public finances, ratify agreements, and even declare war. The king continued to have executive authority and had a two-year time limit in which to veto Assembly legislation. Louis XVIII reinstated regal authority in 1814. With the Assembly now split into two Chambers, the king could call meetings and call them to order, giving the Chambers no real governing power. However, a new charter was adopted in 1830, creating a unified sovereignty between the king and elected delegates.

The Assemblee Nationale was split into four assemblies under Napoleon, lessening its influence and enhancing his own. The constitutional statutes of 1875 laid the groundwork for the parliamentary system that would gradually solidify over the following few decades after the fall of the Empire. Parliamentary sovereignty was established under the Constitution of 1946. Once more referred to as the Assemblee Nationale, the elected representatives choose their own meeting time and agenda. Parliamentary powers were more precisely defined in 1958 under de Gaulle, and they have persisted ever since.

The Palais Bourbon is home to the National Assembly. Louise Françoise de Bourbon, the legitimated daughter of Louis XIV and Madame de Montespan, constructed it between 1722 and 1728. The building was started by Hardouin Mansart and Italian architect Giardini. Jacques Gabriel finished the project after Giardini passed away two years later. The prince de Condé expanded and modified the mansion in 1765, working with architect Soufflot.

The marquis de Lassy built the Hôtel de Lassay during this time, which is located just next to the palace. The palace became national property after the Revolution. The Council of the Five Hundred began using it in 1798. Around this time, a gallery connected the Hôtel de Lassay and the Palais Bourbon, and the Hôtel de Lassay started serving as the home of the assembly' presidents. In 1827, the chamber was rebuilt, the hallways and adjacent rooms were reconfigured, and a library was added. Delacroix also designed one of the salons and the library. Most of the earliest parliamentary assemblies have met in this new chamber since its 1832 opening. The exceptions were from 18711879, when it was held in Versailles, and during World War II, when there were so many members that they had to shift to a temporary chamber erected up in the courtyard.

Hôtel des Invalides

It was created by Louis XIV to serve as the first hospital and retirement community for military veterans, and it still does. A number of museums dedicated to France's military history are also located there. The Hôtel des Invalides is home to the Musée de l'Armée, the Army Museum, the Musée de l'Ordre de la Liberation, the Liberation Order Museum, and the Musée des Plans Reliefs, the Relief Maps Museum. On November 30, 1671, work on the Libéral Bruant design, which was chosen by King Louis XIV, began. The first crippled soldier stayed there in October 1674 after the Hotel des Invalides was essentially finished in three years. 6,000 additional soldiers soon after. The complex was expanded in 1676, adding fifteen courtyards, the largest of which, the Cour d'Honneur, was used for military parades.

Military parades, award ceremonies, ceremonies for decorations, and concerts are still held in front of the Cour d'Honneur. 64 meters broad and 102 meters long make up the courtyard. There are two rows of arcades lining it. On the top floor, in a huge arcade, stands a sizable statue of Napoleon I, which Seurre built in 1833 and faces the courtyard. Originally, this statue sat atop the Colonne Vendôme. In 1863, it was imported here. There are three wall sundials in the courtyard. Three are located: one on the east façade, one on the north façade, and one on the west façade. The building that encloses the courtyard has higher levels that serve as a memorial to those who have fought and died in French conflicts since the 19th century.

Walls are covered with plaques recognizing groups like "Les Forces Feminines Françaises," "des Formations Sanitaires," or "For the Foreigners Fought in France, for France," which includes citizens of Poland, Holland, and the United States. The Red Cross, its nurses, and its ambulance drivers are both honored, as is the Resistance of the Swiss Volunteers. Even the deceased people's families are remembered. To Their Fathers, Dead for

France, The Sons of Those Killed, The Parents of Those Killed is how this plaque is roughly translated. Cannons and old transport vehicles are on display in the lower floors of these buildings. In 1679, the veterans' church was finished. The veterans were obligated to attend on a daily basis, and it was known as the Church of St. Louis.

In order for him and the soldiers to attend the same Mass, Louis XIV intended to build a chapel. Of course, the soldiers were unable to enter through the King's entrance. The Church of St. Louis, also known as the Soldier's Church, and the Eglise du Dôme, also known as the Church of the Dome, or the Royal Church, were built as a dual complex to address this issue. The dome was based on St. Peter's Basilica in Rome, according to Jules Mansart. After Mansart passed away in 1708, Robert de Cotte finished the construction that had started in 1706. The Dome is 107 meters, or 350 feet, tall. In 1989, it was re-gilded using 550,000.2 micron-thick gold leaves totaling 12.65 kilos of gold. The Eglise is sometimes cited as Paris' best example of religious architecture from the 17th century. Along with some of his family members and other notable military figures, Napoleon Bonaparte is currently interred in the Eglise du Dôme. Napoleon I was initially interred on the island of Saint Helena, where he passed away on May 5, 1821, while living in exile. King Louis Philippe ordered the transport of his bones to Paris in 1840, and on April 3, 1861, he was interred in the Eglise du Dôme.

A list of those entombed at the Eglise du Dôme:

- Joseph Bonaparte (17681845) Napoleon's eldest brother
- Jerome Bonaparte (17851851) Napoleon's youngest brother
- Napoleon II, Francis Bonaparte (18121833) son of Napoleon
- Geraud Duroc (17741814) Officer who fought with Napoleon
- Claude Joseph Rouget de Lisle (17601836) Army captain and the author of France's national anthem, La Marseillaise
- Ferdinand Foch (18511929) Commander of the Allies during WWI
- Henri de la Tour d'Auvergne (16111675) Marshal of France under Louis XIV.

The church's dome dominates Les Invalides' 200-meter-long façade from the north and appears to be a part of the same structure, but is really divided by the Cour d'Honneur, which is more than 100 meters long. The vast Esplanande des Invalides is located to the north of the Hôtel des Invalides. The Pont Alexander III bridge is located at the northern end of the Esplanade. The Petit

Palais and the Grand Palais are separated by this incredibly elegant bridge.

Hotels of the Invalids hours and entrance fees

Throughout April through September, the Hôtel des Invalides is open daily from 10:00 a.m. to 6:00 p.m. It is open till 9:00 p.m. on Tuesdays and has a lower admission price after 5:00 p.m. In the months of July and August, The Dome is open until 7:00 p.m. The Invalides shuts at 5:00 p.m. the remainder of the year.

The first Monday of every month, as well as January 1, May 1, November 1, and December 25 are all holidays. The Musée de l'Armée, the Museum of the Army, all other museums, Le Tombeau de Napoléon, the Tomb of Napoleon, and the Eglise du Dôme all require a combination ticket for admission. Tickets cost 9 euros as of April 1, 2010, and anyone under the age of 18 is admitted free. The cost is 7 euros starting at 5:00 p.m. on Tuesday. From April through September, the Museums are open on Tuesdays until 9:00 p.m.

Both the grounds and the courtyards are free to enter.

The Jardin de l'Intendant, or Garden of the Steward, is located in the southwest corner of the grounds of the Hotel des Invalides and borders the Eglise du Dôme.

Tour Eiffel; Eiffel Tower

Few buildings are as instantly recognized as the Eiffel Tower, often known as La Tour Eiffel. The tower, a Paris landmark, was started in 1887 and completed in time for the inauguration of the Universal Exposition in 1889, the year of the French Revolution's 100th anniversary. The structure served as the Exposition's entrance arch. Its conception and construction are fascinating in and of themselves, and its following history is rife with fascinating anecdotes. The Tower has evolved into one of the most popular tourist destinations in the world despite receiving harsh criticism when it first opened. It was one of the most amazing structures ever designed, and it was an engineering marvel in its time. The Tower can be reached in a variety of ways. The Seine River approach from the Palais de Chaillot provides a stunning vista.

History of the Eiffel Tower

Gustave Eiffel (18321923) created the Tower after receiving over 700 entries in a design contest. An inventor, Gustave Eiffel was a French architect and engineer from Dijon who created a number of beautiful structures during his lifetime. The Tower is 7300 tons and 318 meters (1043 ft) tall. With decking, elevators, railings, and paint, the whole weight is 10,100 tons. For forty years, it was the highest building in the entire globe. The tower's official website states that there are 1,665 steps needed to get to the peak. The 18,000 pieces of iron that make up the Eiffel Tower are fastened together with 2.5 million rivets. There are eight elevators in it.

The Tower only sways a maximum of seven centimeters on windy days. It may bend up to 18 cm on a hot day as a result of the sun's heat expanding the metal. The Tower must be painted with fifty tons of paint, which is done every seven years. The paint's hue is occasionally altered. It is now painted a brownish color. Interactive consoles where you can choose a future color are located on the first floor of the Tower. Originally, Gustave Eiffel received permission to leave the Tower standing for 20 years, more than covering his costs. However, because it proved useful for communications, the permission to keep it standing was extended. The Eiffel Tower has been utilized for transmission since the turn of the 20th century. A triangle aerial, made up of multiple wires, ran from the top to anchor points in the Champ de Mars, the park where the Tower is located, until the 1950s. On the Champ de Mars, there were a few small housings housing longwave transmitters that supplied this aerial. The Eiffel Tower features an aerial on top since it has served as a transmission tower for FM and TV since 1957.

Eiffel Tower Admission Prices and Hours

- The Tower is open every day from 9:00 a.m. to midnight from the middle of June to early September. The remainder of the year hours are 9:30am to 11:00 pm
- Hours are subject to change depending on the crowds of people, the weather and the event of strikes.
- The prices for taking the elevator for adults are: 2nd Level: 9 euros, Top Level: 15 euros
- For those between 1224 years old the elevator prices are: 2nd Level: 7 euros, Top Level: 13.50 euros
- For those between 411 years old the elevator prices are 2nd Level: 4.50 euros, Top Level: 11 euros
- Those under 4 years of age are admitted free.
- The price for taking the stairs to the 2nd Level for adults is 5 euros
- For those between 1224 years old, 4 euros
- For those between 411 years old, 3.50 euros
- The Top Level is no longer accessible by stairs.

Interesting Events in the Life of the Tower

- Father Theodor Wulf, in 1910, took observations of radiant energy from the top and the bottom of the Eiffel Tower and was the first to detect what are today known as cosmic rays.

- In 1925, a con artist Victor Lustig, "sold" the Eiffel Tower for scrap. He did this not once, but twice.
- In 1930, the Tower lost the title of the World's Tallest Structure. That honor then passed to the Chrysler Building in New York City.
- From 1925 to 1936, the Citroën automobile company installed neon signs on three of the tower's four sides, making it the tallest billboard in the world.
- When Adolf Hitler visited occupied Paris in 1940, the elevator cables were cut by the French so that he would have to climb the 1,665 steps to the summit. Hitler chose to stay on the ground. The parts to repair the elevators were, supposedly, impossible to obtain at that time due to war shortages. However, they were working again within hours of the Liberation of Paris.
- A Frenchman scaled the Tower, during the German Occupation, to hang the French flag.
- On January 3, 1956, a fire damaged the top of the tower.
- In 1959, the present radio antenna was added to the top.
- In the 1980s, an old restaurant and its supporting iron scaffolding midway up the Tower, was dismantled. It was purchased and reconstructed in New Orleans, Louisiana,

originally as the Tour Eiffel Restaurant, more recently known as the Red Room.

- For the celebration of the Millennium, 30,000 small lights were placed all over the Tower, set to blink on the hour for 10 minutes. Due to the popularity and beauty of the spectacle, the lights were permanently installed in 2003. However, in 2009, the duration of the light show was reduced to five minutes.
- The Tower received its 200,000,000th guest on November 28, 2002.
- At 7:20 p.m., on July 22, 2003, a fire occurred at the top of the Tower, in the broadcasting equipment room. The Tower was evacuated. The fire was extinguished in forty minutes and there were no reports of injuries.

Eiffel Tower Appearances in Film

- In the film "Van Helsing", the Eiffel Tower is under construction.
- In "Rugrats in Paris: The Movie", the babies are atop the Tower while using the giant Reptar invention.
- In "Team America: World Police", a rocket blows the tower up, then the Tower falls on the Arc de Triomphe.

- The James Bond film, "A View to a Kill", has a scene in the Eiffel Tower, including scenes in a fictional restaurant there.
- The Tower is shown in the 1970 animated film "The Aristocats".
- The Tower is destroyed in "Armageddon".
- The Tower flies and moves around Paris in the puppet version of "Without a Paddle". That scene starts after the moviecredits end.
- The Tower (and the rest of Paris) were almost blown up by a terrorist nuclear bomb and Lois Lane almost plunged to her death under its elevator in "Superman II".
- In "Mars Attacks!", the Eiffel Tower is destroyed by Martians.
- In "Godzilla: Final Wars", Kamacuras attacks the Tower.
- The Eiffel Tower can be seen on TV in "Independence Day".
- The Tower is seen in "Eurotrip".
- At the end of "The War of the Worlds", the Tower is seen destroyed.
- Condorman attempts to fly off of the Tower in the movie by the same name.

- At the end of the 1965 Blake Edwards movie, "The Great Race", the Tower is blown up by a misfired cannon shot from Professor Fate's car.
- In "The Real World", a Parisian television program, shown on the US MTV network, the Tower is seen in most episodes.

8eme Arrondissement

Arc de Triomphe

You will come home through arches of triumph! Napoleon promised his Grand Army following his biggest victory in 1805 at the Battle of Austerlitz in what is now the Czech Republic. Napoleon gave Jean Françoise Chalgrin the commission in 1806 to create what is now recognized as the largest triumphal arch in history. Napoleon only once traveled through this arch, on December 15, 1840, when his ashes were brought back from the island of Saint Helena, where he had spent the final six years of his life in exile. This arch was finished in 1836, fifteen years after his death. The Eglise du Dome was eventually converted into a mausoleum, where he was buried after being kept in Les Invalides until 1861.

Millions of tourists have, however, gone through the Arc since it was finished, making it a "must do" on your list of things to do in Paris. The Arc is 50 meters (164 feet) high, 45 meters (148 feet) wide, and 22 meters deep (72 feet). There are sculptures on each of its four pillars. The Arc is 50 meters (164 feet) high, 45 meters (148 feet) wide, and 22 meters deep (72 feet). There are sculptures on each of its four pillars. The most well-known of these sculptures, "The Departure of the Volunteers," or more formally "La Marseillaise," created by Francois Rude, is located on the northeast pillar. The Cortot-designed "Triumph of 1810" is located on the southeast pillar. Both sculptures, "The Resistance of 1814" on the southwest side and "The Peace of 1815" on the northwest pillar, were created by Etex.

The names of Napoleon's smaller victories are written on the internal walls of the main arch. Along the roofline of the arch are inscriptions listing the significant triumphs. The 558 names of Napoleon's generals are engraved on the interior walls of the two smaller arches, one on either side of the main arch. Those who lost their lives in combat are highlighted. The numerous other bas-relief sculptures on the Arc depict significant moments in numerous battles. The World War I Unknown Soldier was interred at the base of the Arc de Triomphe on November 11, 1920, which is also known as Armistice Day. Since then, the French President has placed a wreath at this tomb on Armistice Day. The Eternal Flame was ignited in 1923. Plaques honoring the deaths lost in various wars, such as those in Indochina, Tunisia, Morocco, Korea, and World Wars I and II, are buried in the cement beneath the arch.

Additionally, there are plaques honoring the Proclamation of the Republic as well as the return of the Lorraine and Alsace areas to France on November 11, 1918. Here, the general's radio address from June 18, 1940, delivered while he was in exile, is also cast in bronze. The little hill Chaillot's summit is occupied by the Arc de Triomphe. The gold-tipped Obelisk of Luxor, which marks the Place de la Concorde, is visible from the ground level as one looks down the Avenue des Champs-Elysées. The Louvre Palace and the Arc de Triomphe du Carrousel are located further on. The Grande Arche de La Défense may be seen if one turns around and faces west along Avenue de la Grande Armée. Ten more streets radiate out in a star configuration, giving this traffic circle one of the biggest in the world its name, Place de l'Etoile [Star Plaza]. From atop the Arc, all of this is seen in a more dramatic light.

There are two tunnels that pass below the congested traffic roundabout that are the only methods to reach the Arc de Triomphe. On the northeast corner of the Avenue des Champs-Elysées is where the tunnel entrance is most frequently used. A sign saying that it leads to the Arc de Triomphe sets it apart from the Metro station entrance, which is also on this corner. On the north corner of Avenue de la Grande Armée, on the northwest side of the Arc, is where you can reach the other tunnel. Every night, these tunnels stay open until 10:30 p.m. A ticket must be purchased in order to utilize the elevator offered for those unable to use the steps or to ascend the stairs to the top of the Arc. The ticket window for these tickets is situated at the stairs leading up to the Arc in the entrance tunnel. More than 600,000 people every year visit the Arc de Triomphe's summit.

Arc de Triomphe Hours and Admissions:

- The top of the Arc is open from 10 a.m.10:30 p.m. during winter months and until 11 p.m. during the summer, with the last entry being 30 minutes prior to closing.
- Tickets are 9.50 euros for adults, 6 euros for ages 1825, and free for those 17 and under when in company with their family, free for EU citizens under 26 years old and for disabled persons and a companion.

Chapelle Expiatoire

Beginning in 1720, the garden area of Chapelle Expiatoire served as the new cemetery for the parish of La Sainte Madeleine, whose cemetery had outlived its usefulness for the expanding parish. Over the subsequent eighty years, it saw widespread use. It was used in 1770 to bury the 133 victims of a fire and stampede that happened at a fireworks show during the marriage of Louis, the dauphin who would become Louis XVI, and his bride, Marie

Antoinette. The role it played in this King and Queen's existence as well as the occasions that led to the French Revolution was not its final one. More than 300 Swiss Guards were killed on August 10, 1792, while they bravely defended the Tuileries Palace from a crowd. The King and Queen were able to flee to Versailles thanks to their stand. The guards' remains were interred in this cemetery on what would eventually become the Chapelle Expiatoire grounds.

Done 3,000 people from every socioeconomic class in French society were scheduled to be buried here before the Revolution was over. The remains of King Louis XVI was unceremoniously dropped into a pit here in January 1793 following his guillotine death. The body of his wife Marie Antoinette was handled similarly a few months later, in October. A Royalist named Pierre Descloceaux made note of the location of the graves, purchased the garden, and built walls around it to secure the area. Louis XVIII started looking for his older brother's remains during the Restoration of the monarchy in 1814. The location of the King and Queen's bodies was revealed by Pierre Descloceaux, who also gave Louis XVIII the address. The unearthed bodies were taken to the Basilica of St. Denis, where French kings have historically been interred.

Chapelle Expiatoire

In order to seek forgiveness for the Revolution's atrocities, build a chapel there, and honor his late brother and queen, Louis XVIII hired French architect Pierre Fontaine. It took more than two years to prepare the site for construction, but Fontaine finished it, and Chapelle Expiatoire opened its doors in 1826. Charles Percier, an architect, designed the chapel's dome. The Chapel's final service took place there in 1882. Square Louis XVI, a magnificent and welcoming area, surrounds the Chapelle Expiatoire. It is a serene and well-liked refuge with park seats, expanses of grass, floral shrub plantings, and rose beds. The garden's diverse tree species were planted as a memorial to the various social groups represented among the Revolutionary War dead.

Three storeys make up the Chapelle Expiatoire complex. There is a foyer that opens up to a gated courtyard that is designed to look like a cemetery. Simple in design, the courtyard has rose bushes and gravestones on either side to honor the deceased. By ascending a flight of twelve stairs and passing through a facade supported by basic Doric columns, one can access the chapel itself. The building's clean lines and simplicity give the entire complex a solemn and reverent atmosphere. The treatment is significantly more elegant inside the chapel. Four columns support the dome itself. They stand in for the Paschal Lamb, the Blessed Sacrament, the Law of Moses, and the Trinity. A bas-relief sculpture commemorating the exhumation and procession of Louis XVI and

Marie Antionette's remains to the Basilica of St. Denis is located above the entryway. Gerard, who also worked on the Arc de Triomphe, created the interior carvings and basreliefs.

At the back wall's center lies the altar. The interior's ornamentation is completed with two marble statues. Marie Antoinette is depicted in a marble statue on the left as you enter. Religion-based support. Jean Pierre Cortot is the author of it. The one on the right, which is Françoise Bosio's creation, shows Louis XVI being carried up into heaven by an angel. The two pieces are 19th-century masterpieces. A staircase behind each statue goes to the sacristy, which is not accessible to the public, as well as the crypt, which is. A round, vividly colored stained glass window is placed just behind the altar in the plainly designed crypt. One of Paris's lesser-known beauties is the Chapelle Expiatoire. It combines history, art, and architecture and provides a haven of peace away from the bustle of the nearby metropolis.

9eme Arrondissement

Opéra National de Paris Garnier

At the northern end of the Avenue de l'Opéra, the Opera Garnier is a significant landmark. It is regarded as one of the greatest pieces of architecture ever created. It is the thirteenth theater to hold the Paris Opera since it was established by Louis

XIV in 1669, and it was constructed in the Neo-Baroque style. Originally known as the Paris Opéra, it has been known as the Opera Garnier since the construction of the Opéra Bastille in 1989. It was built as a part of the city's rebuilding by Napoleon III and his engineer, Baron Haussmann, and is also known as the Palais Garnier. After a competition, Charles Garnier, a 35-year-old architect, was chosen to design the opera (18251898). Later, he would construct Monaco's Opéra Garnier de Monte-Carlo. The Franco-Prussian War, the collapse of the Second Empire, and the Paris Commune Uprising all delayed the start of construction, which had started in 1857. The discovery of an underground lake beneath the construction site presented another issue.

This necessitated the construction of an underground reservoir underneath the structure. The infamous "The Phantom of the Opera" was later to be inspired by this episode. The Palais Garnier was formally inaugurated on January 15, 1875, after it was finished in 1874. This enormous structure is 11,000 square meters (118,404 square feet) in size and includes a big stage that can hold up to 450 performers. It is a luxurious structure in a monumental style that is ornately embellished with intricate multicolored marble friezes, columns, and priceless statues. Cherubs, nymphs, velvet, and gold leaf are abundant inside. The main chandelier in the auditorium is almost six tons in weight. Marc Chagall painted the ceiling in 1964. Ballet performances are typically held at the Opera Garnier. The Opéra Bastille is now the main opera theatre in Paris.

Tours of the Opera Garnier:

- Visits without guides are available every day during school vacation time from 10 a.m.4:30 p.m., or until 1 p.m. in the case of a matinee performance. The rest of the year, the building is open during the same hours on Wednesday, Saturday and Sunday.
- Fees are 7 euros for adults and 4 euros for students.
- Guided tours in English are available on the same days as above at 11:30 a.m. and 2:30 p.m.
- Fees are 11 euros for adults, 9 euros for students and seniors, 6 euros for those under 12 years of age.
- Tickets need to be purchased 1/2 hour before the tour begins.

12eme Arrondissement

Opéra Bastille

President François Mitterrand established l'Établissement Public Opéra Bastille (the Opera Bastille Public Establishment) in 1982 with the goal of establishing a new opera theater that would offer affordable performances, or a "people's opera house." The

Establishment held a global architecture competition in 1983. Carlos Ott, a Canadian-Uruguayan, was selected as the winning architect on November 10, 1984, out of 1,700 candidates. The Place de la Bastille was chosen as the location for the new opera house. The 1859 Bastille train station, which had been vacant since December 14, 1969 and had been used as a temporary art exhibition hall since then, had to be destroyed in order to start rebuilding in 1984. The National Opera of Paris is housed in the enormous, curved, glass-exterior Opera Bastille, which is 80 meters high above street level and another 30 meters below. There are 22,000 square meters on each level.

Each seat in the 1,200 square meter main auditorium provides a clear view of the stage and can accommodate 2,700 people. The main auditorium has a glass ceiling and is 20 meters in height, 32 meters in depth, and 40 meters in width. The orchestra pit can be covered and is moveable and flexible. It has a maximum capacity of 130 musicians. 30 meters wide by 25 meters deep, the main stage is 45 meters high. It contains nine elevators, allowing for the creation of several storeys. The stage's three major elevators are used to raise the scenery. The opera can produce two shows at once thanks to the four storage chambers that are utilized for rehearsals and have the same size as the stage. The backstage area also contains a scenery turntable. Additionally, the structure houses workshop spaces that are used for both productions at the Opéra

Garnier and here. Large-scale operas are typically performed at the Opera Bastille. Although the Opéra Garnier is now the primary ballet stage, it still presents ballets on occasion. The Opéra Bastille has two smaller performance stages for smaller events like chamber music and recitals. The Amphitheatre has a seating capacity of 450 people and measures 700 square meters in area and 21 meters in depth.

The Studio is 280 square meters in size, with a depth of 19 square meters, and can accommodate 237 seats. For both individuals and organizations, there are guided tours of the Opera Bastille available. The tour includes stops at the main auditorium, the open foyers, and the backstage areas. It is presented practically every day for roughly 75 minutes, usually at 1 p.m. or 5 p.m. Although English tours can be arranged, the tours are in French. Adult tickets cost 10 euros; tickets for those 60 and over cost 8 euros; tickets for students and those under 26 cost 5 euros. Tickets are available at the Opéra Bastille box office 10 minutes prior to the tour. However, the Opéra Bastille trips are not offered during the summer.

13eme Arrondissement

Bibliotehèque NationaleTolbiac

The new French National Library at Tolbiac, the Bibliotheque Nationale de France, was the final of François Mitterand's "great projects." 7.5 hectares in size, Dominique Perrault's design is made up of four glass and steel towers that are each 24 floors and 80 meters high and shaped to resemble open books. The Bibliotheque Nationale de France's towers have names. They stand as the tower of Time, Letters, Numbers, and Laws. At a cost of 8 billion francs, construction on the Library started at the end of 1990 and was finished in March 1995. (5.2 billion euros). 1,600 people can sit in the 1,600 public seats, many of whom have a view of a two-level courtyard designed in the style of a garden. There are 2,000 seats in the library's research section. In December 1996, the public reading room was inaugurated. Although there were many issues when it originally opened (a librarian strike, computer problems, leaking ceilings, and bookshelves that were exposed to the sun) it is now regarded as one of Europe's most user-friendly academic buildings.

Ironically, many of the library's structural and technical issues were fixed during the strike. The Bibliotheque Nationale de France's contemporary capabilities place a strong emphasis on microfilm and electronic documentation. 260,000 books are available to the general public. Of the library's 11 million books, researchers can access 550,000 of them, including 200,000 rare books, 350,000 periodicals, 76 000 microfilms, 950,000 microfiches, 100,000 digitalized texts, 50,000 multimedia materials, 900,000 sound recordings, 90,000 videograms, and 400 kilometers of shelves.

The collections of books and periodicals are divided into four departments:

- philosophy, history and humanities;
- law, economics and politics;
- science and technology;
- and literature and art.

Additionally, there are divisions for audiovisual materials and bibliographic research. Tuesday through Saturday from 10 a.m. to 8 p.m., and on Sunday from 12 noon to 7 p.m. On Mondays and during holidays, the Bibliotheque Nationale de France is closed. The cost of using the reading rooms is 3.50 euros for an admission card.

The library does not allow anyone younger than 16 to enter.

The research library is open from 9 a.m. to 8 p.m. on Tuesday through Saturday and from 2 p.m. to 8 p.m. on Mondays. No one under the age of 18 is allowed in the library. The Rare

Books Room is open Tuesday through Saturday from 9 a.m. to 6 p.m. and on Monday from 2 to 6 p.m..

14eme Arrondissement

Observatory of Paris

The oldest continuously running observatory in the world is the National Astronomical Observatory of Paris. Jean-Baptiste Colbert pushed Louis XIV to establish the Paris Observatory because he thought it would enhance France's capacity for maritime exploration and promote trade. Architect Claude Perrault started building the Observatoire de Paris in 1667, and it was finished in 1671. The structure is pointed toward the four cardinal directions. The center of the structure corresponds to the Paris meridian. The Colonnade entrance on the eastern side of the Louvre was also created by Claude Perrault. In 1730, 1810, 1834, 1850, and 1951, the Observatory of Paris had renovations and additions. The Meridian Room, created by Jean Prouvé, is the most recent addition. One of the top locations for astronomical research is still the Observatory of Paris. Gian Domenico Cassini was the first of his family's four generations to serve as the Observatory's director.

In the Observatoire de Paris, Leon Foucault first displayed his now-famous Foucault Pendulum on February 3, 1851. On March 26, 1851, the future Napoleon III, Prince Louis Napoleon, requested another performance to be held in the Pantheon. The evidence that the earth does, in fact, revolve on its axis was presented by this ground-breaking demonstration, and it continues to be so today. In the Musée des Arts et Métiers since 1855, Foucault's Pendulum has been hanging and swinging. The 67-meter Pendulum resided temporarily in the Pantheon while this structure was being renovated. Since then, it has been brought back to the museum for viewing. Since 1960, light pollution at the Observatory has precluded it from being utilized for astronomical observations due to its placement in the heart of the city. The Observatory of Paris still continues to examine astronomical data obtained from all around the world and to carry out astronomical and astrophysical research. Four graduate programs in astronomy and astrophysics are also offered by the Observatory. On the first Sunday of every month, starting at 2:30 p.m., the general public is welcome to attend on a reservation basis, with the exception of August. It takes the tour two hours.

Reservation requests are accepted by mail, with a stamped, self-addressed envelope, at:

l'Observatoire de Paris

Service de la Communication (Service des visites)

61 Avenue de l'Observatoire de Paris

75014 Paris

Adult admission is 5 euros, 2.50 euros for students, seniors over 60, and 120 euros for groups. Group visits are possible on Tuesdays and Wednesdays at 2 p.m., with a limit of thirty individuals. On these excursions, astronomical observational tools can be seen, including the telescopes that were initially employed at the Observatory. These tours include cover the first "speaking clock," developed by E. Esclangon in 1933, as well as the atomic clocks that the Bureau International de l'Heure, or International Time Bureau, uses to determine the world's standard time. The tour includes a stop at the Cassini Room. The north-south meridian line runs through this room in brass. The tour also includes the Arago Coupola, which has a telescope on display. With 135 bronze medallions measuring 12 cm in diameter, Dutch artist Jean Dibbets etched out the north-south meridian line that passes through Paris in 1995 to honor François Arago, who served as director of the Observatory of Paris from 1834 until 1853. However, several of these medals have been taken following the publication of a well-liked book and movie.

Under locations like the Louvre, the Palais Royal, and the Garden of the Luxembourg Palace, they are buried in the earth. The words "Arago" and the letters "N" and "S," which stand for north and south, are inscribed on them. You will be 100 meters away from the Church of Saint Sulpice and the Inverted Pyramid of the Louvre Museum if you follow these medallions to find them. This book is not a reliable source for details on astronomy, theology, or how to get around Paris by car. Neither the Zero Meridian nor the alleged "Rose Line" are represented by the brass line that runs across the floor of the Church of Saint Sulpice. What has been wrongly referred to is an indicator line that is a component of the gnomon, a measuring device that was put in place here in 1727 and used to determine Easter, which is the first Sunday following the first full moon following the vernal, or Spring, equinox.

For many years, the time standard and placements of naval warships were determined using the Paris Zero Meridian line, which was established in 1667. A new global standard was created in 1884, locating the Zero Meridian at Greenwich, England. The new meridian wasn't acknowledged in France until 1911, when Greenwich Mean Time (GMT) became the accepted time zone. Currently, Paris' meridian is located at longitude 2°20'14.025" east.

15eme Arrondissement

Memorial of the Liberation of Paris

The Jardin Atlantique and the Memorial of the Liberation of Paris are situated side by side on the roof of the Gare Montparnasse train station in Montparnasse, France. Le Mémorial du Maréchal Leclerc de Hauteclocque et de la Libération de Paris Musée Jean Moulin is another name for the Memorial. On August

24, 1994, on the occasion of the 50th anniversary of Paris' liberation from German occupation during World War II, the Mayor of Paris, Jacques Chirac, officially opened the Mémorial du Maréchal Leclerc de Hauteclocque et de la Libération de Paris Musée Jean Moulin. French commander General Maréchal Leclerc (1902–1947) fought in North Africa. Upon his return to France, he commanded the 2nd Armored Division in the liberation of Paris from German occupation in August 1944, with the assistance of the 4th Division of the American Infantry. The Memorial of the Liberation of Paris serves as a hub for information sharing, documentation, reflection, and study. The general public, as well as organizations, associations, researchers, teachers, and schools, may access it.

A council of historians and Second World War experts oversaw the design of the Memorial to the Liberation of Paris. Some of General Leclerc's personal belongings are on exhibit in the Memorial of the Liberation of Paris, including jackets he wore in Africa and Indochina, a tropical helmet, and walking sticks. Drafts of coded messages, documents, photographs, records of Leclerc and the 2nd Armored Division under his command, and propaganda posters from Vichy and the Allies are all there. Additionally, there are reproductions of historical leaflets and underground newspapers. Testimonies and visuals of combat are presented in audiovisual exhibitions. The visitor can watch the development of the war using a variety of charts. The Memorial relocated within a structure with an elliptical interior wall. This wall has been transformed into fourteen moving picture screens. These screens transport the viewer to the powerful cinematic presentation Occupied Paris, the Resistance of Paris, and the Liberation of Paris. The Musée Jean Moulin is also housed in this structure. The Jean Moulin Museum keeps a record of Jean Moulin's life and career as the acknowledged head of the Resistance Movement.

In 1939, Jean Moulin (1899–1943) was chosen to serve as the region's prefect. When the German Army invaded France in June 1940, he refused to assist them, especially by refusing to sign a German paper that falsely accused the French Senegalese Army of killing civilians. The German Army detained him for it, and while he was imprisoned, he was tortured. He used a piece of glass to try to slit his throat in this effort. Soon later, he was freed from jail. The Vichy Government ordered all prefects to oust communist mayors in November 1940. When Moulin refused, the Vichy Government had him removed from his position. Soon after, Moulin began gathering with other individuals who were opposing the Vichy regime and seeking to drive the Germans out of France. One of them was Henry Frenay, who had put together "Combat," the most significant of the early Resistance units. Under the guise of Joseph Jean Mercier, Jean Moulin traveled to London in

September 1941 to meet with Charles de Gaulle, the commander of the Free French forces in exile. Moulin was given the job of leading the Resistance by De Gaulle.

Moulin returned to France via parachute on January 1st, 1942.

The Resistance was unified by Jean Moulin. He was successful in concentrating the Movement's anti-German efforts. Because of Jean Moulin's efforts, France was spared the civil wars that Greece, Poland, and Yugoslavia went through during the war. While having a meeting with many of the leaders of the Resistance on June 21, 1943, Moulin was taken into custody by the Germans at Caluireet Cuire, in the Rhône region, at the home of Dr. Frédéric Dugoujon. He was brought to Lyon and questioned there. The Gestapo chief Klaus Barbie then transported him to Paris for questioning. Nothing was ever divulged by Jean Moulin. On July 8, 1943, Jean Moulin passed away from torture-related wounds while he was riding the train to the concentration camp. In Paris' Père Lachaise Cemetery, Jean Moulin was laid to rest. The Panthéon received his ashes on December 19, 1964.

- The Memorial of the Liberation of Paris also presents temporary exhibitions.
- Admission to the permanent exhibit of the Memorial of the Liberation of Paris is free.

The temporary exhibits have admission fees which are 4 euros for adults and 2 euros for those under 26 years old. It is free for those under 13 years old. The Memorial of the Liberation of Paris is open Tuesday - Sunday from 10 a.m.6 p.m. It is closed on Monday and on holidays.

- A Document Center is available by appointment and is open from 10 a.m.5 p.m.

Overlooking the Montparnasse railway station's tracks lies the Memorial to the Liberation of Paris. The Memorial can be reached in a number of ways. The Gare Montparnasse serves as one entry. A staircase leading to the Atlantic Garden on the roof, which the Memorial borders on the north end, is located in the far left, eastern corner of the station's second level.

Two elevators with glass sides are also available for accessing the rooftop Garden. One is situated on the northeastern side of Gare Montparnasse, in front of 4 Rue du Cdt. René Mouchette. The other is on the northwest side of the train station, in front of 25 Boulevard de Vaugirard. These elevators do not, however, always run. A staircase leading to the Memorial of the Liberation of Paris is located in the building across from the elevator on Boulevard de Vaugriard. There isn't a stairway that can be used instead of the elevator on Rue René Mouchette.

Montparnasse Tower

The Tower of Montparnasse is the tallest building in Paris, measuring at 290 meters (690 feet). It is 32 meters wide. The tallest structure in Paris is the Eiffel Tower, at 318 meters tall. As the business center of La Defenseis located outside of the Paris city limits, the Montparnasse Tower stands as the only skyscraper within Paris city limits. It is equipped with the fastest elevator in Europe, traveling from the ground to the 56th floor in just under 38 seconds.

On the 56th floor is a restaurant, a café, gift shops and a theater presenting movies of Paris taken from the air. Two stories above is the outside viewing terrace affording 360 degree vistas. On a clear day you can see nearly 25 miles. Quite the site for those who enjoy being above it all. At the time of its completion, in 1973, it was the tallest building in Europe.

- Hours for the Tower are 9:30am11:30pm.
- The ticket prices for ascending to the Observation Terrace are 8.50 euros for adults, 7.50 euros for students between the ages of 1418 and 5.80 euros for children under 14 years old.

16eme Arrondissement

Palais de Chaillot

In the 16th century, Catherine de Medici constructed a "country hamlet" for herself atop the 65 meters (230 feet) Chaillot Hill. England's Queen Henrietta bought this farm house in 1651, and it was there that she started the Convent of Visitation. Napoleon I ordered the destruction of this monastery at the beginning of the 19th century so that his son may have a mansion there.

This palace never was constructed.

Gabriel Davioud's Moorish-inspired Trocadéro Palace was constructed for the 1878 International Exposition. The Trocadero Gardens were also established about this time. The Palais de Chaillot, which is still present there now, took the place of the Trocadero Palace in 1937. The architects Léon Azéma, Jacques Carlu, and Louis Hippolyte Boileau created the Palace. It was constructed for the 1937 Universal Exposition. At the same period, the Trocadero Gardens underwent renovation. The Palais de Chaillot is made up of two sizable, curved structures that are divided by a grand, magnificent plaza covered in marble. With columns and statues inlaid with gold, the two buildings adorn the plaza. The plaza was ceremoniously awarded an engraved marble plaque in April 2005 to mark the 60th anniversary of the liberation of the WWII concentration camps. This plaque designates the plaza as the "Place of the Liberties and the Rights of Mankind," as declared by President François Mitterand on May 30, 1985.

The Thêatre National de Chaillot is housed in the structure to the east. It once housed several buildings that are no longer there, including the Musée National des Monuments Francais and the Musée de Cinéma Henri Langlois. The Musée du Cinéma moved to 51 rue de Bercy, next to Bercy metro station, and inaugurated in the fall of 2005. The City of Architecture and Heritage, or Cité de l'Architecture et du Patrimoine, was very recently inaugurated in September 2007 in this east wing of the Palace. The Museum of Mankind and the Maritime Museum are housed in the structure to the west of the building. Place du Trocadéro is where the Palace of Chaillot is located, and the Trocadéro metro station is where lines 9 and 6 originate.

20eme Arrondissement

Pere Lachaise Cemetery

When Pere Lachaise Cemetery first opened on May 21, 1804, it was known as "The East Cemetery." Because it was perceived as being too far away and in a "unfavorable" area, it saw little use.

It only had 60 burials in the first three years.

Father François de Lachaise d'Aix, a Jesuit, served as Louis XIV's confidant as Pere Lachaise. He erected a Jesuit Rest House on this hill in 1682, which later served as his home. Cimetiere du Pere Lachaise, or Cemetery of Pere Lachaise, was a well-known name because it had been used to refer to the land for about 120 years. Officials started reinterring famous people from other cemeteries in order to promote the purchase of grave plots here, starting with playwright Molière, poet La Fontaine, and the ancient remains of Abelard and Heloise, whose sad love story from the 12th century is legendary among Parisians. It was a good concept. At Pere Lachaise Cemetery, 33,000 tomb spaces had been acquired by 1830. For a weekly publication, Honore de Balzac, who is also buried here, composed a collection of short stories in which the characters who passed away were interred in Cimetiere du Pere Lachaise. The cemetery gained some reputation and public attention as a result of this. In quest of such imaginary graves, people started to come to this Paris Cemetery. Since then, it has grown to be both Paris's most prominent and largest cemetery, spanning more than 100 acres and housing more than 70,000 tombs for more than one million people.

Families occupy the majority of the graves. There are multiple bodies in each cemetery because when a family member dies, the family grave is opened and the freshly deceased is buried there. The grave site belongs to the family, and it is their duty to keep it up. Some people have done a greater job than others at it. The Pere Lachaise cemetery now offers 30-year grave plot leases as a result. The family's tenants are evacuated and the grave is liberated, pardon the pun, if they decide not to renew their lease. This hill was primarily covered with vines during the 12th century and was referred to as "The Bishop's Field." The hill itself is now referred to as Mont Louis. At the age of fourteen, Louis XIV traveled there to witness the fights of the Fronde revolt taking place in Saint Antoine's environs. This royal visit is how the hill received its name. According to a different legend, Louis XIV paid a visit to the Jesuit Rest Home, for which reason they called the hill in his honor.

Hippolyte Godde, an architect, constructed a Chapel on the site of the Jesuit Rest house in 1823. He built the cemetery's main entrance's gates in the year 1825. Pere Lachaise Cemetery was as the scene of one of the final clashes of the Communard Uprising of 1871. 147 combatants were executed on May 28, 1871, close to a cemetery wall that is now known as the "Wall of the Federates" or "Mur des Fédérés." They were interred beside another 690 of their deceased teammates in a shared burial along this wall. Over 5,000 trees, including oaks, maples, ash, planes, accacias, and hazelnuts, can be found at the Pere Lachaise Cemetery. These trees range in age from 100 years and older. Visitors can more easily find a specific burial on the grounds because they are divided and labelled into 97 sections. Since 1986, a "Garden of Remembrances" has been along the cemetery's east wall. It is a location where the cremated remains of those who were not maintained by the family or in the crematorium are spread.

The chapel and entrance gate of Hippolyte, the sculpture "Monument to the Dead" by Bartholome, and the graves of Molière, La Fontaine, Abelard, and Heloise are among the buildings and tombs that have been designated Historical Monuments in this area. There are memorials at Pere Lachaise Cemetery for victims of the Holocaust, World War I, and other wars, as well as for civic leaders and tragedies such aircraft mishaps. More than 100 famous people are buried here, including Felix Faure, the President of France from 1895 to 1899, as well as other world leaders, writers like Marcel Proust, Oscar Wilde, and Apollinaire, painters like Louis David, Eugene Delacroix, and Theodore Gericault, musicians like Fredrick Chopin, Georges Bizet, Edith Piaf, and Jim Morrison, and writers like Oscar Wilde, Oscar Wilde, and Apollinaire.

Pere Lachaise Cemetery Hours and Admissions

- All municipal Paris cemeteries are open every day and there are no admission fees.
- The hours for Pere Lachaise Cemetery are from 8:00 a.m.6:00 p.m. during the summer months and until 5:30

p.m. during the winter. It opens at 8:30 a.m. on Saturday and at 9:00 a.m. on Sunday and holidays.

- Free maps and information are available at the Conservatory Office located just north, left, of the main entrance on Boulevard de Menilmontant.
- Office hours are from 8:30 a.m.12:30 p.m. and from 2:00 p.m.5:00 p.m. It is closed on weekends.
- The main entrance of Pere Lachaise cemetery is used primarily by cars.
- Pedestrians generally use the smaller entrances located near the Metro stations:
  Pere Lachaise station on lines 2 and 3;
  Phillipe Auguste station on line 2;
  Gambetta station on line 3, with its entrance at the top of the hill allowing for a downhill visit of the cemetery and not uphill as from the other stations.
- At each entrance is a map of the cemetery marking the locations of the famous.
- Toilets are found just to the left of the main entrance, in the Conservatory office building, near the Philippe Auguste metro station entrance and and at the Gambetta entrance.
- Bring an umbrella. Being that it's a cemetery, in Paris, it may be raining.

- Ravens fly amongst the trees here and black cats have been seen sneaking around the graves of Pere Lachaise cemetery.

Outside Paris

The Grand Arch of La Défense

Just west of the Paris city limits, in the ultra-modern La Défense business district, is where you can find the Grande Arche. But you can get there by bus, RER, and metro. Otto von Spreckelsen, a Danish architect, created the Grand Arche of La Defense, which was built between 1982 and 1989. White marble is used to build an almost perfect cube that is 108 meters deep, 110 meters high, and 112 meters wide. The Arc de Triomphe is roughly three times smaller than this structure. In July 1989, the Grande Arche was officially opened to commemorate the 200th anniversary of the French Revolution.

The metro, the RER, and a road are all located beneath the Arche.

There are exhibition rooms, a scale model of the Arche, videos on its construction, art displays, a cafeteria, and a bookstore inside the Grands Arche of La Defense. The summit of the Arche can be reached by elevator. Because it was erected as a freestanding elevator practically directly beneath the center of the Arche, the elevator provides panoramic vistas.

<u>The Grande Arche of La Defense Hours and Admissions</u>

The elevators run every day, from 10 a.m.7:00 p.m., with the last one going up at 6:30 p.m. Admission is 7.50 euros for adults, 6 euros for ages 617, and free for those under 6 years old. Family rates are: 2 adults, one child is 19 euros; 2 adults 2 children is 22 euros; 2 adults with 3 children is 25 euros. Groups of 10 or more people is 6 euros per person.

Gardens in Paris Organized by Arrondissement

With more than 400 public "green spaces," there is always a garden nearby in Paris, providing a tranquil respite from the busy city. Paris is such a pleasant city to live in and visit because of these gardens and parks. Paris is the greenest city in Europe, with parks, gardens, and woods occupying more than one-fourth of its entire area. Paris has a wide variety of parks and green spaces, from the formal and opulent Tuileries and Luxembourg to the expansive Champ de Mars and Les Invalides, as well as the smaller ones that just seem to spring up all over the city, like the Square Georges Cain.

The large woodlands, or bois, are located at the eastern and western boundaries of Paris (bwaa). The Bois de Boulogne is on the west, and the Bois de Vincennes is to the east. For the flowers and bushes that it plants in the numerous little and big parks located across the city, the City of Paris has a 2.5 million euro budget. Traditionally, lawns were not for sitting on, which was thought to be extremely unaristocratic. Instead, they were for admiring. All parks with lawns larger than a particular size are now open to the public. You may occasionally come across signs that read "Pelouse Interdite" or "Pelouse au Repose," which translate to "Lawn Not Allowed" or "Lawn at Rest," or simply "Keep off the Grass." Here is a list of a few of the most noteworthy Parisian parks and gardens.

1er Arrondissement

Garden of Les Halles

The original Parisian central market, immortalized in Emile Zola's book "Le Ventre de Paris," located where the Jardin Les Halles now stands ("The Belly of Paris"). The area has been transformed into a sizable park with walking trails, a large-scale trellis, sculptures, and fountains by Louis Arretche and François Xavier Lalanne. Our self-guided walking tour from the Palais Royal to the Hotel de Ville includes a stop at Le Jardin des Halles, also known as the Garden of Les Halles. Without sacrificing the great, overall perspective, the Garden of Les Halles is artistically split into smaller areas, each with its own ambiance and unique features.

All of it is situated in front of St. Eustache's beautiful church.

A huge, seventy-ton sandstone sculpture of a head resting on a hand is positioned here at Place René Cassin in front of St. Eustache. Henri de Miller produced "Ecoute" ("Listen"), which was installed there in 1986. The 13th-century St. Eustache Cathedral lies just in front of "Ecoute," which offers a spectacular example of the city's signature juxtaposition between old and new. Henri de Miller constructed the "Cadran" (also known as the "Sundial") in Place René Cassin, realizing mathematician Dandrel's invention. Sundials often use a shadow's movement to indicate the passing of time. This one makes use of the sun's rays, which pass through slits in the sundial eight feet above the ground. Light is directed to a dial on a low wall where it registers the time when it strikes a horizontal fiber optic inside the sculpture. There is a network of small waterfalls on the side of Place René Cassin that faces St. Eustache. A recessed tropical greenhouse with four glass pyramids over it may be found close to the circular Commercial Exchange (Bourse du Commerce) structure.

It was constructed in 1988 and embellishes one side of a 50-meter indoor pool. Due to the fact that it was made to be observed from the outside, the greenhouse is not open to guests. It holds about 30 different plant types and has a 500 square meter surface area. The Jardin des Enfants des Halles (the Children's Garden), which is a part of the Garden of Les Halles, is situated at 105 rue

Rambeteau, just across from one of the Metro entrances to the Les Halles station and just to the east of St. Eustache. There are six "worlds" on the playground. There is a world of geometry and music, a soft world, a volcanic world, an island world, and a tropical forest world with a monkey bridge, a tiger trap, a canyon, huts, and bamboo forest. There is also an ancient world with mazes and columns.

There are many different activities available, such as a climbing wall, many slides, a maze, and more traditional playground equipment. Children under the age of 715 are welcome at the Jardin des Enfants. We apologize, but adults are not permitted in the Garden. Children pay 40 centimes per hour, which entitles them to one hour of admittance. Parents are instructed to pick them up later. To ensure that parents don't miss out on the excitement, there are observation decks. Tuesday, Thursday, and Friday from 9 a.m. noon and 2 p.m. 6 p.m., Wednesday and Saturday from 10 a.m. 6 p.m., and Sunday and public holidays from 1 p.m. 6 p.m. In case of rain and on Mondays, the Garden is closed. The Saturday hours of 10 a.m. to 2 p.m., when the playground is open to kids of all ages and their parents, are an exception to the "no adults" restriction. The Garden of Les Halles has a lot of lawns where you may have a picnic and catch some rays. Another well-liked activity in the Garden of Les Halles is playing boules, a French national game that mixes bowling and shuffleboard.

Garden of Palais Royal

Le Jardin du Palais Regal, sometimes known as the Royal Garden, has a long history, both royal and not so royal. It is not a noticeable garden from a distance because it is surrounded by the Palais Royal, a courtyard, and arcades. Cardinal de Richelieu acquired the former Hôtel Rambouillet and the adjacent lands in 1624. These structures were demolished so that the Palais Cardinal and a sizable adjacent garden could be constructed. This property was handed to the crown by Cardinal de Richelieu when he passed away on December 4th, 1642. The family of Orleans resided here until the Revolution, after Louis XIV officially transferred the property and possession to his brother. The Parc Monceau was also owned by the Duc d'Orléans, subsequently Philippe Egalitié, who hired architect Victor Louis in 1781 to enlarge the palace and reduce the park so that homes with standard arcaded facades could be built on three of the garden's sides.

In 1784, the building project was completed. The duc d'Orléans constructed boutiques beneath the arcades and rented them out to pay for the reconstruction. Philippe Egalité allowed the public access to the Jardin du Palais Royal but forbade the police from using it. As a result, it developed into a haven of freedom unmatched in all of Paris and a hub for thinkers and creatives. There were stores, cafes, gambling establishments, and the first House of Wax lining the arcades. What had grown to be Paris's most well-liked gathering spot attracted large crowds. As they are now, there were two theaters at either end of the Jardin du Palais Royal. The Comédie Française still occupies the southwest corner now as it did then. Around 1641, Cardinal Richelieu ordered it, and Lemercier created the design. From 1660 through 1673, Molière performed his plays there. The theater then hosted operas. The Théâtre du Palais Royal is the second theater in the garden, located in its northwest corner. The Jardin du Palais Royal was the busiest area in Paris in 1789. People come here to learn about the most recent political rumors and news. Speeches, conversations, drinking, and games took place there.

On July 12, 1789, a young lawyer named Camille Desmoulins leaped onto a table in the Café de Foy and said that Jacques Necker, the well-liked Minister of State, had been forced to retire. Desmoulins shouted, "To the arms, citizens!" "To arms, fellow citizens!" The Bastille was captured two days later. The Palais Royal and Garden became part of the National Domain after Philippe Egalitié's execution in 1793. The government shut down gambling establishments in 1836. Invasion and looting of the Palace took place during the 1848 Worker's Revolution. Buildings caught fire during the Commune of 1872, and they weren't repaired until 1876. Soon after, the Conseil d'Etat, the State Council, and the Secrétariat d'Etat aux Beaux Arts, the Secretary of State for the Arts, shared the Palais Royal. In 1958, the Constitutional Council arrived, and André Malraux established the Ministry of Cultural Affairs. The Court of Honor is located on the south side of the Garden of the Palais Royal, which still retains colonnaded arcades on three of its sides. The 180 hanging electric lighting and the mosaic walkways are still present.

Women's apparel, jewelry, vintage trinkets, historical figurines, and even high-end gardening tools are available in stores. Under the arcades, there are two cafés, three restaurants, including the Restaurant Vefour, the only business from the Garden's Pre-Revolutionary era still in operation. Although the State had attempted to retract the contract with the designer, David Buren, during its construction, the Court of Honor was renovated with stripped black and white poles, both short and tall, in the middle of the 1980s. Here, in the Gallery d'Orléans that divides the courtyard from the garden, are the Fountains of Pol Bury. Every day since 1990, the customary nooncannon has sounded. The Garden's doublerow of trees, which extends down both sides of the space, offers the coolest outdoor cover available in August. Between these rows of trees, there are two sections of walled turf that are enclosed by flowerbeds. There are enclosed, bench-filled seating areas on both ends of each grass. A weathered statue of a goatboy and a lively youngster are each placed in front of one of these seating spaces.

There is a circular pond with a fountain situated between the two lawns. It's a beautiful spot to take in the sunshine and the sound of water splashing. A sandbox for kids and their parents is located on the north end of the north lawn. The Jardin du Palais Royal frequently hosts transient outdoor sculpture exhibitions. And now for the good news: The Jardin du Palais Royal does not permit dogs. One of the few open areas in Paris where you can walk about without worrying about what you might tread in.

Garden of the Tuileries

The guarded entrance to Le Jardin des Tuileries, the Tuileries Garden, the oldest park in Paris, is located on the east side of the Place de la Concorde. The statues by Antoine Coysevox known as the "Chevaux Ailée," or "Winged Horses," are perched on either side of the gate.

They are replicas. The Louvre Museum houses the originals.

A bookstore that caters to various gardening interests may be found on the left (north) side after entering the Garden through the gates. A public restroom is located on the right (south) side and costs 40 centimes (pronounce it "sahnteem") to use. Direct entry into the Tuileries Garden will lead you to a sizable pond and fountain that are surrounded by statues of mythological characters and events. You'll note that the harmful effects of "acidrain" have disfigured these sculptures. The enormous "Les Nymphéas" by Monet is housed in the Musée de l'Orangerie, which is the structure to the south (Water Lilies). After substantial restorations lasting several years, it reopened in May 2006. The Jeu de Paume, which was formerly an indoor tennis court, is to the north. Temporary art exhibitions are now housed there. The Impressionist painting collection was kept at the Jeu de Paume until 1986. After thereafter, this collection was transferred to the magnificent Musée d'Orsay.

Two cafés that are located on either side of the main path farther into the Garden offer salads, sandwiches, snacks, and drinks. The park is filled with benches and garden chairs that are located in both sunny and shaded areas and are perfect for watching the procession of onlookers go by. There are chairs with sunken seating in the Tuileries Garden that encourage reclining while seated. They are suggested. The number of sculptures throughout the park is too great to list them all here. One of the more peculiar ones, though, may be discovered where the southern trail diverges from the main path after passing the pond. A fallen and uprooted bronze tree is lying in this undergrowth. This route can be followed until it reaches the Solferino Bridge, a pedestrian bridge across the Seine that connects to the Musée d'Orsay. A staircase on the left just before the Solferino Bridge leads to an elevated deck with a view of the Tuileries Garden. A menacing sculpture titled "Cain and His Sons" can be found at the eastern end of this promenade.

You may reach another sizable pond that is ringed by mythological statues by strolling down the Tuileries Garden's main road. Rentable wooden toysail boats are offered on the weekends for cruising this pond. The Tuileries Garden's floral part, which is always stunning, is located here. The gated eastern end of the Tuileries Garden is located beyond this pond and up some stairs. The outdoor sculpture garden at Maillol officially starts here. Here you may find a lot of Maillol's works. You are welcome to wander the grounds, navigate the hedge mazes, and take in the sculptures and open space from every viewpoint. You may reach the marbled Arc de Triomphe du Carrousel by passing through this area. It was designed and built between 1806 and 1808 under Napoleon's commission to honor his triumphs in 1805. Charles Percier and Pierre Fontaine were responsible for its creation. After the original horse statues were brought back to Venice in 1815, Baron Bosio constructed the chariot and horses atop the Arc in 1828.

Turning left (north) at this point will allow you to leave the park and visit the gilded statue of Jeanne d'Arc on Rue de Rivoli. Stairways leading to the Carrousel du Louvre, an extravagant shopping mall with marbled floors and walls, an entrance to the Louvre Museum, and the inverted glass pyramid are located on either side of the Arc de Triomphe du Carrousel. To get to the Place du Palais Royal, where the Palais Royal Musée du Louvre metro station on lines 1 and 7 is located, turn left (north) and cross Rue de Rivoli. Watch out for rollerbladers and appreciate their acrobatics as they frequently whizz and bounce around this Place. You may reach the Seine river and the Bridge du Carrousel by turning right (south) at Place du Carrousel. Following Place du Carrousel straight (east), you will arrive at the Cour Napoleon, the Louvre's central courtyard. A 21-meter-high glass pyramid serves as the Louvre Museum's primary entrance. It is in plain sight.

Tuesdays when the Louvre is closed are actually a fantastic time to explore this courtyard as there won't be many people around. The courtyard is beautifully illuminated at night, highlighting the sixty-six sculptures of illustrious Frenchmen who stand overhead on the first story rooftop, making it a lovely time to visit. The Richelieu archway is located in the left (north) wing of the Louvre. This leads to a different entry to the Louvre that is only accessible to individuals with tickets in hand, tour groups, staff members, and holders of Friends of the Louvre membership cards. This passageway provides views of the museum through large glass windows, including the Cour Marly on the west side, which houses the original Marly Horse sculptures made by Guillaume Cousteau in 1745 and once stood at the eastern end of the Avenue des Champs-Elysées, and the Cour Puget on the east side, which houses the "Chevaux Ailée," or "Winged Horses," made by Antoine Coysevox and once adorned the western entrance to the Jardin des

Tuileries. These original statues were duplicates that are now seen there.

Louis XIV ordered these sculptures for his Château Marly, which was destroyed during the French Revolution. Following the passage will lead you to the Place du Palais Royal and the rue de Rivoli, which are both home to the metro stations for lines 1 and 7. You can enter the smaller, older courtyard known as the Cour Carrée, or the Square Courtyard, by passing through the Sully corridor after you have passed through the Cour Napoleon. A fountain and circular pond are located here. You may go to the Pont des Arts bridge and the French Institute across the river by taking the right (south) exit from this fountain. The rue de Rivoli is reached by using the left (north) exit. You can access rue de la Amiral de Coligny by passing straight through the courtyard. The Saint Germain l'Auxerrois church is located directly across this street. Here are the graves of numerous painters who contributed to the construction of the Palais du Louvre in the 17th and 18th century. You may reach rue de Rivoli and the Louvre by turning left (north) on Rue de la Amiral de Coligny. Line 1 metro station in Rivoli.

3eme Arrondissement

Square du Temple

Public access to the 7,965 square meter Square du Temple began in 1857. The palace of the abbey of the Templiers and its garden, which were there in the 16th century, are now partially covered by the square. From 1792 to 1808, this palace was converted into a jail. It put Louis XVI and Marie Antoinette in prison in 1792. Their son, the Dauphin, was similarly detained in the tower until his enigmatic disappearance in 1795. A large portion of the palace was destroyed in 1809. The Tower of the Temple was demolished in 1811 by Napoleon's order, which was dated March 16, 1808. This indicated that the entire historic templar monastery had been demolished, with the exception of the Great Prior's mansion.

However, the Palace of the Grand Prior was destroyed in 1853 as part of Baron Haussmann's extensive citywide repairs under Napoleon III to create place for the current area. On 1867, Alphand created the English garden-inspired Garden in the Square du Temple. There is a sizable pond with boulders from Fountainbleu lining a little waterfall. Green, flowering plants and a few unusual tree kinds line the pond's perimeter. Davioud created the ornate front gate, and there is a gazebo for afternoon performances close to a playground for kids. On a warm day, people like to picnic and have lunch on the vast grassy area, which has both shaded and sunny benches available. A stone bust of the cabaret singer and poet Béranger, sculpted by Lagriffoul, can also be discovered beneath the shade, immediately to the left (north) as one enters the Square from the main entrance.

4eme Arrondissement

Square Jean XXIII

The Cathedral of Notre Dame has the Square Jean XXIII on its southern and eastern sides, along its riverfront, and behind it. The Archbishop's Palace and garden have been located here since the 17th century. The palace was destroyed after being looted and vandalized by rioters in 1831. The current Square was designed and constructed in 1844 by the Prefect of Paris, Claude Philibert Barthelot, Comte de Rambuteau. The Arc de Triomphe was finished during his presidency as well. Pope John XXIII, who presided as pope from 1958 to 1963, is remembered by the name of the Square. The Gothic-style Fountain of the Virgin is located in this Square, behind the cathedral. From an architect Vigoureux design, Merlieux created the sculpture in 1845. Additionally, Eduardo Fortini sculpted a bust of Goldini. A dramatist from Venice named Goldini passed away in Paris in 1793. On his birth anniversary's bicentennial in 1907, the bust was erected in the Square.

Behind the cathedral, the main area of the Square is shaded by several lime and elm trees as well as Japanese cherry trees. A wonderful view of the flying buttresses that support Notre Dame's walls and roof may be found in Square Jean XXIII. Here, you can sit on any of the many shady benches and take in the sights of the cathedral, the Seine River, and its bridges.

Square Louis XIII (Place des Vosges)

The Place des Vosges is one of Paris's oldest and, according to some, most attractive squares. This was the location of Hotel des Tournelles from the late 1300s to the mid-1500s. While competing in a jousting match there in 1559, King Henri II was injured and quickly passed away as a result of the injuries. The Hotel des Tournelles and its grounds were later destroyed by his widow, Catherine de Medici. Henri IV constructed the Place des Vosges, also known as Place Royale, between 1605 and 1612; it is a real square (140 meters x 140 meters). Since Henri IV was slain in 1610, Louis XIII, who was just 8 years old when he assumed the throne, was in charge when the Place was finished.

The first initiative in royal city planning was Place Royale.

King Henri IV oversaw a number of construction initiatives for Paris. He also built the Pont Neuf (New Bridge), the Hôpital Saint Louis, the Place Dauphin, and additions to the Palais du Louvre.

Residential squares in several European cities were modeled after Place Royale. Place Royale was not truly home to any royalty despite its name. However, Cardinal Richelieu was only a temporary residence before he was made a cardinal. Victor Hugo, a writer, may have been its most well-known occupant. Victor Hugo lived at 6 from 1832 until 1848; it is now the free museum Maison de Victor Hugo. His First Minister, Cardinal Richelieu, commissioned a bronze statue of Louis XIII riding a horse in the middle of the Place. During the Revolution, however, this statue was destroyed by fire. The current version, which is still there now, was put in its place in 1818. When the Vosges department became the first to pay national taxes to Napoleon in 1800, the place was renamed. It is now a very popular and festive location to take in the atmosphere of Old Paris.

5eme Arrondissement

Arena de Lutece and Square Rene Capitan

The only intact building from the Roman era is the Arena of Lutece, together with the Thermes de Cluny and the foundation stones in the Crypt of Notre Dame. It is noteworthy for being Paris's oldest monument. The oldest structure in Paris is the Obelisk of Luxor on the Place de la Concorde. The Arena (Lutece is the Roman name for the city) was constructed at the close of the first century and served as a venue for both theater and athletic events.

The Arena had a capacity of about 15,000 people and had a floor surface of about 13,000 square meters. The Arena and the Thermal Baths of Cluny together up Roman Paris's cultural center. The Arena was abandoned, filled in throughout the years, and in some areas, it was submerged to a depth of 60 feet. Eventually, homes were constructed over the area. The Arena was rediscovered and later repaired during Napoleon III's rule and the urban redevelopment of Paris under the direction of chief city planner George Eugene Haussmann.

Despite the fact that over the years and during its restoration, portions of it were permanently lost or damaged, what is still there is a truly spectacular illustration of Paris' Roman heritage. The Arena is a fantastic park and a highly well-liked hangout for the neighborhood schools. It provides a stimulating environment for pupils to learn about Paris's Roman heritage. The gladiator battles and track and field competitions that took place in this stadium are easily visualized. The actual field is now a free-flowing area where anyone may stroll and work on their soccer skills. The extensive collection of Roman antiquities in the Louvre aids in putting the Arena of Lutece in its proper historical context. Stone benches and stairways leading to the gardens around the Arena and the Square Rene Capitan, which it borders, encircle the field. Square An enormous stone stairway leads to Rene Capitan. It has a playground that is a favorite of the young children and their parents who reside in this gorgeous neighborhood, as well as a lovely flowerbed that runs the entire length of the Square. It is open all year round, from 8 a.m. to 5:30 p.m. in the winter and from 8 a.m. to 10 p.m. in the summer.

Jardin des Plantes

The principal botanical garden in France is called Jardin des Plantes, or Garden of Plants. It spans over 24 hectares, or 235,000 square meters, and is located in the 5th arrondissement on the left bank of the Seine. Botanist Jean Hérouard, the king's top physician, proposed the idea of a garden of medicinal plants to Louis XIII in 1626 for usage and research. The garden was started in 1633 by physician Guy de La Brosse. The Garden of the King, or Jardin du Roi, was its previous name.

The public might enter in 1640.

The curator from 1739 until his death in 1788 was the Comte de Buffon. He increased the size of the garden and built the Labyrinth, which is still there today, at the top of a tiny hill. Within the Jardin des Plantes is the Musée National d'Histoire Naturelle, or National Museum of Natural History. The Grand Gallery of Evolution, the Mineralogy Museum, the Paleontology Museum, and the Entomology Museum are its four galleries. There are gardens, an aquarium, and a small zoo in addition to those. To maintain biotic diversity, the Jardin des Plantes runs a botanical school that builds display gardens and trades seeds. On a one hectare, or 10,000 square meter, plot, about 4,500 plants are grouped by family. The Jardin des Plantes has three hectares of horticultural exhibits of ornamental plants, including a lovely Iris Garden. Three thousand species from all over the world are present in an Alpine garden.

Regional flora that are not native to France are shown in specialized structures like the Orangerie and the Mexican and Australian hothouses. Charles Rohault de Fleury constructed the Australian and Mexican greenhouses in the Jardin des Plantes between 1834 and 1836. A true innovation at the time was using glass as a building material. Numerous rose species can be found in the Rose Garden of the Jardin des Plantes. A huge bronze statue of Jean-Baptiste de Monet de Lamarck, built by Léon Fagel in 1908, is located at the Jardin des Plantes' main entrance. To the Founder of the Doctrine of Evolution is written on it. Darwin did not create the evolutionary hypothesis. Darwin provided the theory of natural selection, which describes how evolution happens.

Before Darwin, there had been some discussion of evolution in the scientific community. Lamarck actually introduced his idea of evolution in 1800. The Galeries d'Anatomie Comparée et de Paléontologie are located to the left and to the east of this statue of Lamarck. The Galleries of Compared Anatomy and Paleontology are open from 10 a.m. to 5 p.m., Monday through Friday (closed on Tuesday), and from 6 p.m. on Saturdays and Sundays. The cost of admission is: 6 euros for adults (this ticket provides reduced entrance fees to all other Garden venues for up to 3 months); 4 euros for those under the age of 14; students under the age of 26; groups of 10 or more; and free admission for those under the age of 4 and for people with disabilities and a companion. There are areas of lush gardens behind the Lamrack statue. These lawns have an astounding amount of plants, all of which are tagged and labeled with the species and types of the plants.

A tiny carousel and a snack bar may be found on the left side of the Garden, behind the Gallery of Anatomy and Paleontology. The Botanical Alpine Garden School, or Ecole de Botanique Jardin Alpin, is located directly west of here, across the lawns. The Alpine Garden, which spans 4,000 square meters and has more than 2,000 species of plants from the Alps, Pyrenees, Greenland, and the Himalayas, was established in 1931. The property is gated. On Monday through Friday, the public is welcome from 8 a.m. to 4:50 p.m. There is no entrance fee and it is closed on holidays. The Jardin des Plantes Ménagerie, one of the oldest zoological gardens in the world, is reached by moving further west. Located on 6.5 hectares, this tiny zoo is home to 1,100 mammals, birds, and reptiles, many of which are in danger of going extinct.

- There is also a vivarium of small reptiles, amphibians and insects.
- The Ménagerie is open everyday form 9 a.m.6 p.m. and until 6:30 p.m. on Sunday.
- Admission fees are 7 euros for adults and 5 euros for others. These full and reduced fare tickets have the same conditions as the ones described above.
- There is also a small restaurant just next to the Ménagerie.

Continuing on south from here you will come to the small hill where is found the Labyrinth, a yewhedged maze that leads to a gazebo at the top. From here, to the west, you will pass a gated wild area. This small hill has been closed for over the past ten years. It is an outdoor laboratory for scientific observation. It has been allowed to grow wild to its natural state.

Ten years ago, this area was heavily used, the soil was depleted and erosion was carving into the slope. Now, it is covered with fifty different kinds of plants and shrubs which have replenished the soil and controlled the erosion. The area is now home to insects and birds, of which six different kinds of sparrows have been seen here. Beyond this outdoor laboratory are the Jardin des Plantes Greenhouses, which have been closed as of April 26, 2004, for complete restoration. The large building on this end of the park is the Grand Gallery of Evolution. The entrance to it is on the west side of the building. The Grand Gallery of Evolution was built in 1899 and restored in 1994. The permanent exhibit is concerned with the evolution of Life, the diversity of the living world and the evolution of living organisms in the history of Earth and Man.

- The renovated museum was inaugurated by President François Mitterrand on Tuesday, June 21, 1994.
- The Grande Galerie de l'Evolution is open every day (closed Tuesday and May 1st) from 10 a.m.6 p.m.
- Admission fees are 8 euros for adults and 6 euros for others with the same conditions on these tickets as the others. There is a boutique and café and coatcheck.

Just before you reach the entrance of the Grand Gallery of Evolution you will come to the Galeries de Minéralogie et de Géologie. The Galleries of Mineralogy and Geology are open Monday Friday (closed Tuesday) from 10 a.m.5 p.m. and until 6 p.m. on Saturday and Sunday. The admission fees are 6 euros for adults and 4 euros for others with the same conditions as the other tickets.

The Jardin des Plantes is an expansive garden of beauty and education.

Chapter Four

Paris Guide and Advise

Visiting Paris for the First Time

All first-time tourists should prioritize getting a thorough understanding of Paris and visiting as many famous sites as they can. Fortunately, many of Paris' most well-known landmarks are close to one another, and there are numerous routes to see them, which is crucial for first-time visitors.

Navigating your location while in Paris

Paris' Seine River is viewed nearly like a city "avenue" because it runs through the city. Especially when you are viewing the most famous landmarks, you will most likely be able to either see the Seine (which is only about six city buses wide) or you will be a few blocks away from it. There are several bridges over the Seine, and famous sites can be seen on both sides of the river. Your most significant landmark while you're on foot or studying a map is the Seine. Ask yourself, "Where is the Seine?" while you scan the area or consult a map. This is usually an effective method for determining where you are or where you want to go.

Seeing the Sights via the Seine

The River is close to or can be seen from several of the most well-known tourist attractions. Almost everyone who visits Paris takes a Seine River sightseeing cruise. Did you take a tour on the Seine? will definitely be a question people ask you when you leave Paris. There's a good reason why most tourists in Paris choose to do this: it's simple, the attractions are actually close to the river, and just it's something that practically everyone does.

There are numerous businesses that provide River tours. Some offer a multilingual narration of the sights you will see. Explore your options online. Being in a glass-enclosed boat on the river has a certain fascination to it. It is an excellent option even if it is raining. There is a lot to look at on the River, no poor seats, and no need to worry about becoming seasick because the boats are steady and there is hardly any "tide." When it comes to the announcements that are made regarding each landmark, some companies have better audio than others. The intercom system is not the best, and the audio information is barely OK, sparse, and spoken very fast, but the websites (below) or office handouts offer useful information. Instead, then learning in-depth information about the destinations via the radio, this is a great method to SEE Paris and to be transported to various sites.

Given how close together Paris's sites are, the majority of Seine sightseeing cruises last an hour. Bateaux Mouches is the usual option for Seine River cruises; they provide a one-hour, round-trip (no stops), Seine River sightseeing tour of Paris (during the day and at night), as well as romantic dinner cruises. Although Bateau Mouches is so well-known that the excursions are occasionally referred to using that name, even if other businesses now offer comparable cruises, reviews of the cuisine served on the River trip are mixed, so explore online for suggestions and alternative firms. Something else than a straightforward 1-hour tour may be a more alluring choice.

In order to allow passengers to board and disembark at a variety of stops along the Seine that are close to tourist attractions, Batobus offers day (and multiday) tickets for the same kind of glass-enclosed boat, same route down the Seine, and identical sightseeing announcements. With the opportunity to use it as a water taxi to various areas, you have a similar sightseeing excursion, offering you flexibility and a more beautiful way to travel throughout the day than utilizing the Metro. You can use the boat as a water taxi to get to your location or you can stay on it for the entire tour to see where everything is and then get off if you'd like. You may ride the Batobus to the Eiffel Tower, then walk to another Parisian site where there is a Batobus stop close by, and then ride the Batobus back to your accommodation. This is a fantastic choice, especially if you've been walking a lot.

The Seine cruises only present one "side" of Paris; they do not present the city in its entirety.

The quickest and best method to learn about the city's sights, in the opinion of many, is to take a bus tour of Paris. Opening Tour The most well-known tour bus is perhaps Paris Bus, which provides double-decker vehicles with open tops and the same get-on/get-off options as Batobus. The organization offers a variety of routes that travel throughout Paris. The Paris Grand Trip, which lasts 2 hours and 15 minutes and shuttles tourists around many of the city's most well-known landmarks, including the Louvre Museum, Eiffel Tower, and Arc de Triomphe, is the longest tour and the ideal for first-time visitors. You board the bus (look for the insignia on the sidewalk), pay (the driver accepts credit cards), and receive an audio tour and earbuds.

As soon as the bus starts moving, the audio plays, and you can hear locations being discussed as you go by. You can chose to utilize this as both a tour bus and a means of transit to tourist attractions, or you can use it only as a tour of Paris and never get off. Choose an attraction that is mentioned as a stop. Get off at that location, explore it, then board another bus to continue the loop. Look at the many ticket options to determine which will be the most affordable option for you (often, the 2-day option must be 2 consecutive days), and take your schedule and interests into account. This is one of the most efficient and enjoyable methods to see all the sights in Paris. Although there are other businesses that offer hop-on, hop-off excursions, it seems like the electric green L'Open Tour buses are more common. There is the sense that L'Open Tour buses arrive more frequently when you are waiting for the next bus at your designated location and are prepared to be picked up. A combined ticket with Batobus Seine River trips may also be available through L'Open Tour Bus.

Free stuff

view the Eiffel Tower from the Trocadero (best pictures)

visit parks and gardens such as Tuileries and Luxembourg

stroll around the Marais district

Walk up the Champs Elysées up to the Arc de Triomphe

stroll around the seine banks

visit large department stores like Galeries Lafayettes or Printemps

Visit the Opera House

First-time visitors need to know one thing: Paris is a city where you walk a lot, the reason is that all major landmarks are quite concentrated, that is why walking is simply the best way to discover Paris, and meet some locals at the same time. This can easily be done with Discover Walks free guided walks of Paris which show you Montmartre, the Latin Quarter, The River and the luxurious Right Bank.

After seeing the neighborhoods on the open bus you'll want to return to certain neighborhoods for shopping and walking. A good overview guide for independent travelers that is organized by arrondissement with photos and maps is No Worries Paris.

Paris Family Travel Guide

Paris is a wonderful place for family travel with its attractions, history, and activities. Planning your vacation's activities is crucial. Paris is a thriving metropolis that may get busy with both locals and tourists. How would you move your family through a crowd without anyone getting lost? How do you make sure that your baby gets some walking practice while avoiding a congested city sidewalk? How well can your kids stand a 30- or 90-minute wait in line? Is your kid a toddler, a preschooler, or a baby? Does your kid have a vivid imagination that she can use a spiral notebook and a pencil to amuse herself with? Will he pass the time by reading a book or working on a crossword or maze? Will a tiny plush animal or matchbox car make him (and you) more comfortable while you wait? If you have a child who is constantly "on the go" and could not wait even if Santa Claus was at the end of the line, perhaps packing a frisbee and enjoying it in the large grass park at the base of the Eiffel Tower is not a good idea. Instead, let him take lots of pictures of the Eiffel Tower from below.

Any sort of stroller, even a small umbrella stroller, can be difficult to maneuver in Paris due to the city's many congested locations and hurried pedestrians. Gravel park walks and uneven roadways are both possible. A large portion of Paris has a very urban feel to it; you must move fast when walking because it is congested, and there are numerous stairs instead of elevators or escalators. Things can be difficult if you have a toddler who wants to be independent in the middle of a sidewalk in Paris or New York City. Even the metro (subway) lacks many escalators, so carrying a child or a stroller requires climbing at least two flights of stairs. If you have a youngster who is in the middle of the "I want to walk myself stage," this is not the time to do it. There will often be a swarm of people behind you going up...or down...the same set of stairs at metro stops. You shouldn't assume that an elevator is available at any location. The majority of well-known landmarks, museums, retail establishments, hotels, etc. lack elevators or escalators. There is a designated area on some buses for strollers.

Contrary to the USA, not all department shops and train stations have facilities for changing and nursing infants.

It may seem obvious, but before your vacation, consider the sights your kids will see and give them some background knowledge on those sights. Show them a map, or you might print one for them to take with them. Using Google Images, you can print off pictures of the objects or locations you visit. Any age your child is, the more engaged they are, the more interested they will be in the location.

For young people who enjoy history, Paris may be a lot of fun. In particular for Notre Dame, where Quasimodo or Les Misérables fans will love to see the Cathedral; it is really impressive and funny for children with all the gargoyles and kings, and there are plenty of family walks for them, walking tours offer a fun, engaging way to learn about the sites while taking in the lay of the land and burning off that extra, pastry-fueled energy. The outside of Notre Dame is more beautiful than the interior, and there is no line to wait in, which is great for tired kids. If you want to learn more about it with your kids.

They might love going to Versailles, the Les Invalides military museum, where they can see weapons from Napoleon's era including his hat and sword, as well as the Egyptian area of the Louvre, where kids throng to see mummified cats. Fans of

Quasimodo or Les Misérables will like visiting the Cathedral; with all the gargoyles and kings, it is incredibly magnificent and humorous for kids, and there are lots of family walks for them. If you want to explore it with your kids, go outside of Notre Dame instead than inside because it's more beautiful and there's no line, which is great for tired kids.

The Cité des Sciences et de l'Industrie at La Villette, which hosts several kid-friendly special events and exhibitions, is a must-visit location for science enthusiasts. Young and old will adore L'Argonaute, a decommissioned military submarine, which is a top attraction. The planetarium at the Palais de la Découverte will also excite them. The Pasteur Museum is another great attraction, particularly for teenagers. The museum, which is quaintly located in Pasteur's former home, features an amazing exhibit of some of his most well-known experiments.

Many of the most popular tourist attractions are visible from or beside the Seine River, which runs through Paris. Everyone who visits Paris desires to view the city from Seine sightseeing boats, taking in all the iconic sites from inside glass-enclosed vessels. The novelty of being on the river, the variety of things to see, and the freedom to explore the boat on their own may appeal to kids (you can see them wherever they go and the ride is smooth). The classic option is provided by Bateaux Mouches: a one-hour, round-trip, non-stop Seine River sightseeing tour of Paris (during the day and at night), as well as romantic dinner cruises. Batobus provides a more family-friendly option: a day ticket for the same kind of glass-enclosed boat, the same route along the Seine, and the same sightseeing announcements, but the ticket allows you to board and disembark at eight or so different stops along the Seine that are close to tourist attractions. With the opportunity to use it as a water taxi to various sites, you have a similar tourist journey while maintaining mobility for your kids.

You can use the boat as a water taxi to get to your location or you can stay on it for the entire tour to see where everything is and then get off if you'd like. If your kids are sleepy, you might want to take the batobus to the Eiffel Tower first, then walk around Paris before taking another batobus "stop" back to your hotel. You could ride the boat all day long if you had a daring "sailor"! Look into the various ticket categories. But take note: Batobus doesn't provide evening or supper trips. Whatever route you choose, make sure your child is interested in the "sights" by giving them a map of the route (found on the websites) and perhaps a brief description of each location (possibly done online before leaving home)! Otherwise, the "sights" might just appear to them as drab, old buildings. The oldest and most picturesque zoo in Paris is located at the Jardin des Plantes, where the Batobus stops. little entrance fee.

Check visit the Bois de Boulogne as well; it's a sizable park on Paris' western border that has been dubbed the city's "main lung." The children's area of the park, the Jardin d'Acclimatation, has a zoo, an amusement park, and a small gauge railroad. The renowned Jardins des Tuileries or Tuilerie Gardens are located behind the Louvre Museum. There is a stealth outdoor trampoline park open all year round on the gardens' Rue de Rivoli side. Your kids will jump on the in-ground trampolines while grinning broadly if you spend a few euros on them (no falling). It is a terrific opportunity for kids of all ages to burn off endless energy and a great photo opportunity. It is also entertaining for parents to watch.

A well-known marble and bronze sculptor, Auguste Rodin created "The Kiss" (The Thinker). Near the Metropolitan metro stop, the Rodin Museum and Gardens (Musee Rodin) are housed in a mansion with sizable "grounds" surrounding it that kids 6 and older would enjoy exploring (not running). There are walks, a formal garden in the back, a snack bar, and tables in the very back of the grounds, as well as large sculptures scattered among bushes and garden areas in the side yards. Many families choose to purchase a ticket to visit the grounds simply (rather than the museum), allowing their kids to play in a relaxed setting as they see some of the more famous sculptures dispersed throughout the grounds. There may be a simpler, more subtle method to introduce sculpture to kids than by keeping them inside. One of Paris' deals is a ticket for the Musee Rodin Gardens' grounds only: it costs just 1 Euro per person, with children under 18 entering free! Additionally, one parent could accompany the kids in the garden while the other went to the museum (6 Euros per person, 10 Euros for the family).

The Paris Arts Performing Centres

A rich cultural scene exists in Paris. There are several cinemas, especially in the Grands Boulevard region, but there are also many in the Latin Quarter and around the Louvre. The Latin Quarter is well known for its "Art et essai" movie theaters. Musicals, ballets, operas, dance, and concerts are just a few of the attractions that are available to those who don't know French. The primary theaters for these kind of attractions are listed below:

Musicals and big shows Palais des congrès Porte Maillot 75017 Paris Tel: +33 (0) 1 40 68 00 05 Reservations: +33 (0) 1 40 68 00 05	Ballets, dance and operas Opéra Garnier 8, Rue Scribe 75009 Paris Tel: +33 (0) 1 40 01 17 89 Reservations (from France): 08 92 89 90 90
Opéra Bastille 120, Rue de Lyon 75012 Paris Tel: +33 (0) 1 43 43 96 96 Fax: +33 (0) 1 40 01 16 16 Reservations (from France): 08 36 69 78 68	Théâtre du Châtelet 1, Place du Châtelet 75001 Paris Tel: +33 (0) 1 40 28 28 40
Concerts L'Olympia 28, Boulevard des Capucines 75009 Paris	La Scène 2 bis, Rue des Taillandiers 75011 Paris Tel. : +33 (0) 1 48 06 50 70

Tel: +33 (0) 1 55 27 10 00 Reservations (from France): 08 92 68 33 68	Fax : +33 (0) 1 48 06 57 07 Reservations : +33 (0) 1 48 06 12 13
Le café de la danse 5, Passage Louis Philippe 75011 Paris Tel. : +33 (0) 1 47 00 57 59 Fax : +33 (0) 1 48 05 65 22	Theatres with architectural interest Théâtre des ChampsElysées 15, Avenue Montaigne 75008 Paris Tel. : +33 (0) 1 49 52 50 50 Fax : +33 (0) 1 49 52 07 41 Reservations : +33 (0) 1 49 52 50 50
La comédie Française 2, Rue de Richelieu 75001 Paris Tel. : +33 (0) 1 44 58 15 15 Fax : +33 (0) 1 44 58 15 50	Bouffes du Nord (managed by Peter Brook) 37 bis, bd de la Chapelle 75010 Paris Tel: +33 (0) 1 46 07 34 50

Be a Parisian

Do you wish to fit in seamlessly and avoid cultural misunderstandings in Paris? The most crucial items to keep in mind in order to live in the French capital's jungle are listed below.

How to greet someone in Paris: Unknown individuals should always shake hands, of course. The French prefer kissing to hugging when they are with friends because they find hugging to be too intimate. Oh, what an unexpected surprise! They exchange double kisses for "hi" and "goodbye." So quickly adapt to this. If you go outside of Paris, there are no longer any regulations, so just let your friend go first to prevent any awkwardness. It could be only one, three, or four kisses.

Another thing Parisians enjoy doing is sending one other out with loads of well wishes at the conclusion of a visit or chat. On the streets, complete strangers greet one another by saying "Bonjour," which lifts the atmosphere and is especially welcoming to visitors. It should be noted, though, that French people in general, even those in Paris, are extremely selective about whom they open up to, so it can take you some time to learn everything you need to know while establishing new acquaintances. Even though there are many locations that cater to English speakers, such as the restaurants and theatres, you can also study basic French words and phrases beforehand if you don't speak it to ensure you comprehend simple things.

What to Wear: It should be amazing to observe how well-groomed and elegant the Parisians are! You should wear shades of black, navy blue, or grey because these are popular choices among Parisians and for good reason. On most people, the colors often slender and flatter them. In addition to wearing fitted coats, crossbody bags, scarves, minimal accessories, and minimal cosmetics, Parisians also enjoy wearing sensible yet fashionable shoes. They then dress everything up with attitude! Additionally, the women nearly never wear any attire associated with sports or exercise.

Before visiting Paris, you might want to think about tipping as well. A 15% service fee is always included in your bill at cafes and restaurants in Paris. French law mandates this since tips are counted as income for tax purposes. Along with the VAT tax, the additional 15% service charge is clearly itemized on your check. The phrase "service compris" (tip included) will always be present, suggesting that the tip has already been added to the final amount due. However, a tiny extra tip will be welcomed by your waiter as a particular "Thank you." You should also give tips to the usherettes at opera houses, the restroom workers, the ladies who take care of your coat during classical concerts, the bartenders, and last but not least the tour guides who lead walking excursions throughout Paris. But keep in mind that you are not required to tip anyone. Simply expressing gratitude for the service you received and, of course, your generosity.

Getting the Best of Paris Stay

One of the most romantic cities in the world, Paris is often described as a lovers' paradise. But Paris has another side; it's also a place that welcomes families! Are you traveling with your children? There are many things to amuse the young ones. Here are a few ideas:

In the beginning, there are lots of carousels, pony rides in the Jardin du Luxembourg, and guignols, or marionette shows, all around the city. The carnival at the Tuileries Gardens will be especially enjoyable for children. The big park is open during the summer and has carnival favorites like a ferris wheel, merry-go-round, cotton candy, and games. The playground at Parc Monceau in the 8th arrondissement and the Jardin d'Acclimmatation amusement park in the Bois de Boulogne are both favorites among the younger crowd. There is a sophisticated playground, some amusements, and even a toddler-friendly museum there.

The Eiffel Tower is a perennial favorite among people of all ages. Take the elevator to the top at night for an incredible perspective of the shimmering City of Light if you're in fantastic shape, or hike to the top with the kids on the first day (wonderful exercise). A "scary" excursion is to the underground Catacombs. If the youngsters are claustrophobic, you might want to skip this. The bones of more than six million individuals are neatly arranged in different configurations along the walk you take beneath the streets of Paris. Although there is illumination, you might want to bring a flashlight if your children are a little uneasy in the dark. Consider it a more advanced version of the "ghost story" your family would tell around a campfire at night!

Want to have a good time while learning something new at the same time? Visit the Jardin des Plantes, a fantastic zoo in the 5th arrondissement next to the Seine, the Parc de la Villette and its family-friendly science museum, or the Jardin d'Acclimation, a distinctive and tranquil amusement park in the Bois de Boulogne.

Children and adults alike will enjoy the magnificent Cite de Science in La Villette. After that, you can travel to the Seine by traveling via a 2 km tunnel and six locks on the Canal St. Martin. A long journey, but one that is suitable for an afternoon when energy is waning.

The Museum of Natural History (Musee de Histoire Naturelle) is a collection of museums centered around a botanic garden close to Gare d'Austerlitz. It is a fascinating place to visit with amazing exhibits, like the Hall of Evolution's stunning taxidermy displays, and it is not at all overrun by tourists. The Arene de Lutece, a nearby outdoor arena constructed by the Romans and still used for amateur football (soccer) matches today, is one of the first outdoor arenas in the area. Your kids can brag to their peers about playing in a stadium that was built in 2000! Travel by rail to Parc Asterix, which has thrill rides including Tonnerre de Zeus, Goudurix, and Mehnir Express, or Disneyland Paris and WDW Studios, which include the typical Disney-style rides and food options. One word of caution: arrive early, especially during peak traffic hours, to avoid huge lines at the park.

A city park guide

You might find yourself needing a break from the crowds of tourists along the Champs Elysees, Notre Dame Square, Eiffel

Tower, Sacre Coeur, and Montmarte. Every arrondissement has one or more public parks, several of which offer free wifi. A sign on the fence will serve as the indication. It's common for Parisians to visit the parks for lunch, so planning your visit for an hour before or after that time is a smart move. The majority of parks contain water fountains and restrooms. They sometimes have happy kids and their parents there on the weekends. Visit the marche in the area, pick up some cheese, charcuterie, and baguettes, then sit on a park seat. During your strolls through the city, you will come across a lot of squares and green spaces. Open the gate and proceed to circle the area. You can get a brief history (in French) as you enter.

Park it here:

Jardin du Luxembourg, Rue de Médicis Rue de Vaugirard , Paris 75006 Metro : Odéon

Jardin des Tuileries Place de la Concorde, 75001, Metro : Concorde, Tuileries

Place du Palais Royal , Paris 75001, Metro: Palais Royale

Square du Temple, Rue de Bretagne, 75003, Metro : Temple

Square René Viviani, 2 rue du Fouarre , 75005, Metro : Saint-Michel

Parc Monceau, Boulevard de Courcelles, 75008, Metro : Monceau

Parc de Belleville, 47 rue des Couronnes , 75011, Metro : Couronnes, Pyrénées

Parc de Bercy, 41 rue Paul Belmondo, 75012, Metro : Bercy

Jardin des serres d'Auteuil, 3 avenue de la Porte d'Auteuil, 75016, Metro : Porte d'Auteuil

Jardin du Ranelagh, Avenue du Ranelagh Avenue Ingres avenue Prudhon Avenue Raphaël, 75016, Metro : La Muette

Parc Montsouris, 2 rue Gazan , 75014, Metro : Porte d'Orléans

Jardin des Plantes, Rue Geoffroy Saint Hilaire, 75005, Metro : Gare d'Austerlitz

Parc du Champde Mars, Quai Branly Avenue de la Motte Picquet, 75007, Metro : École Militaire

Clos de Bercy, 41 rue Paul Belmondo, 75012, Metro : Cour Saint Émilion Jardin d'Acclimatation, Bois de Boulogne, 7501, Metro : Les Sablons

General Advise

France's Paris is a fantastic city! The buildings, museums, and monuments are simply breathtaking! Visit some of the countryside and chateaus by taking some excursions outside of Paris. Here are some pointers to assist you:

The scenario in the restroom is somewhat different. Since there aren't many public restrooms, you must enter restaurants and ask to use their facilities (toilette). Although they are supposedly unable to refuse you, some eateries will. Keep a 50 cent piece close by at all times because many of the restrooms had pay toilets. Avoid using public restrooms, which are typically dirtier than those in restaurants. Additionally, it's a good idea to carry some tissue. Versailles is the worst place ever. In order to avoid spending an eternity hunting for restrooms when visiting Versailles, please make a note of where they are when you first arrive. Additionally, be prepared for a 30-minute wait in line and bring your own tpaper!

For around 55E, airport shuttles will pick you up from your Parisian flat or hotel and carry you to the airport, and the opposite is also true. A cab fare may be $65 or less. At Charles de Gaulle airport, there are illegal taxi drivers waiting by the cab door. They are really amiable and typically speak English. Go outside and find a taxi after passing them. When you're not hauling around your baggage, take the bus or train instead! Take the bus, the train, the RER, and the Metro. Even if you don't read or speak French, it's not too difficult to comprehend how the public transportation system works. It is also inexpensive and quick! The buses' large windows allow you to take in the scenery as you go if you are not in a rush.

Before you begin, say "bonjour" to everyone in the room. French people are a little more formal. But don't stare too long in the subway or on the street. It's advisable to keep to yourself in public areas because there are pickpockets and crazy people around. Here are two strategies used by pickpockets: The first is for a young woman carrying a clipboard to approach you and inquire,

"Do you speak English?" While her partner grabs your wallet, she will attempt to get you to join a petition or otherwise divert your attention. The second is for a group of young people (typically girls) to pass you by while pretending to be amused, bump into you "accidentally," and then steal from you. Pickpockets can be treated impolitely. If they start to bother you, try to move along more quickly while firmly telling them "no."

Pay close attention whenever you're in a crowded subway or tourist location. Standing on the subway is riskier than finding a seat. Before you leave, check with your credit card company. It's considerably better to use a card that doesn't have foreign transaction fees than to carry cash. Purchase a pair of walking-specific shoes. Before you travel, make sure they are comfy for around two weeks. In Paris, you'll be walking a lot. Bring bandages just in case your shoes cause you to get blisters. Pack many layers of clothing. During the summer, the temperature can change by more than 30 degrees Fahrenheit in a single week! If taking images is important to you, bring your full frame camera's widest lens. Everything seems large and congested! Learn how to shoot a few photographs with your compact camera and subsequently "stitch" them together in Photoshop if you don't want to carry your bulky equipment. With so many people around, taking pictures is extremely challenging. Take your photos at night or in the early morning if you feel safe doing so. There is so much to see and do in the wonderful city of Paris! Enjoy the journey!

Restaurants in Paris

Granite Restaurant Paris: *6 Rue Bailleul, 75001 Paris*

The young staff at Granite, which is tucked away just around the corner from the Louvre, are sure to earn themselves a few stars in the years to come for the excellent service, stylish décor, and exquisitely created cuisine. Tom Meyer, a 28-year-old chef, is no stranger to multi-Michelin-star perfection. Meyer now has his own spotlight after producing at least 400 incredible dishes for three-star chef Anne Sophie Pic. Meyer heads a group of perfectly dressed young promising talents in the kitchen and three en salle hosting guests. Meyer was chosen by restaurant mogul Stéphane Manigold to revitalize this vacant space that held American chef Daniel Spring's first child in Paris. Granite, a glass fronted eatery with 34 seats, is lined with open grain sculptural wood panels that swerve along the walls. Deep sea blue Danish mid-century style chairs are arranged around stone tables, the raw materials setting the scene for Meyer's cuisine steeped in nature. Granite is not to be confused with the posh Chinese eatery in the south of the city. After being greeted by the chef patissier and directed to their table downstairs by the affable Julien, MarieLou, or Estefania, guests dine beneath a vaulted stone ceiling.

From land to sea, wide pastures to lunar landscapes, and back again, Meyer's meals transport guests. Without naming (nearly) every component used, it might be challenging to communicate the subtle complexity of the chef's cuisine. Even the hors d'oeuvres are delectable, such as the tempura-style shiso leaf with a beef consommé coating or the bite-sized anchovy and eggplant pie, which is served with fried escargot dipped in squid ink. Every appetizer's play on textures (crunchy and meaty) is a true flavor explosion. Starters included mushroom crumble with subtly spiced brioche and mussels with delicious yellow kiwi on a bed of burrata perfumed with verbena. Two main courses were served after the starters, one of which featured tender Baie de Seine scallops that had been grilled and served with kohlrabi cabbage, apple juice made from pressing the fruit's peel, and konbanwa zest. Served with puréed broccoli and coriander curry, the second main course was a game dish of roasted Racan pigeon with millet and fermented cabosse fruit. A second dessert of lightasair rice pudding with yellow wine and a jellied milk veil over souffléed dry milk tiles and a poached pear, chartreuse, and carob sorbet served as our last course. Meyer and his team put on a genuine show here, one that leaves a lasting impression of tastes and sensations that transport you to other parts of the world with each bite. And topped off with the service, you'll be supporting the entire clan when the Michelin honors are announced.

Mimosa Restaurant Paris: *2 Rue Royale, 75008 Paris*

No introduction is necessary for the city's several restaurants' two-star chef Jean François Piège. His business endeavors have always been a success, and his most recent endeavor, MIMOSA, is no different. His restaurant is a laid-back tribute to vibrant Mediterranean gastronomy and is tucked inside the freshly rebuilt and reopened French cultural monument and museum, the Hotel de la Marine, situated on the Place de la Concorde in the city center.

Signature dishes like Mimosa eggs with sour preserved fish roe starters and grilled octopus baked in a wood fired oven or homestyle original spicy tomato meatballs for the main course are highlights. Another reason to visit is the French designer Dorothée Delaye's light and open interior. Piège's MIMOSA, a lofty restaurant with enormous floor-to-ceiling windows, velvet-upholstered banquettes decorated in the style of the 1970s, and a living tree in the middle, exudes a cheery Riviera elegance that lets us know summer is coming even on the gloomiest of winter days.

ADMO Restaurant Paris:
at Les Ombres au Musée du quai Branly Jacques Chirac, 27 quai Branly, 75007 Paris

Getting a table at ADMO should be on your list of things to do if you have plans to be in Paris before March 5. Alain Ducasse, the chef with the most Michelin stars to his name, and Romain Meder, who oversees the kitchen, co-created a 100day popup restaurant on the roof of the Quai Branly Museum. Meder formerly worked with Ducasse at the three-star Plaza Athénée and is also the brains behind the health-conscious café Sapid (see number 7 below). The culinary genius developed the idea of "naturalité," a cooking method that preserves the raw flavors of each ingredient, which serves as the foundation for the dishes here and at his former Plaza residences. He is approachable, genuine, and calm (he likes to get his creative juices flowing with Japanese zen music and bird song, or so we're told).

Albert Adrià, a co-creator of the renowned elBulli restaurant from Spain, is also involved in the initiative and completes the founding trio of the popup (Adrià, Ducasse, and Meder at les Ombres). Additionally, they are joined by Vincent Chaperon, a cellar master, and Jessica Préalpato, a pastry chef. It goes without saying that ADMO is a winning blend of culinary prowess, shockingly laid-back ambiance, and stunning views of the Eiffel Tower.

Beginning with the first amuse bouche of pressed caviar and almond celeriac milk, served like a yin and yang in a metal recipient with a spout you pour into your mouth, each of the six courses (as well as the seven amuse bouches and hors d'oeuvres) has intriguing experimental twists evoking pure nature with every mouthful. Other dishes include Brittany turbot fish lacquered with olive oil tank sediment cooked on embers with parsnip cooked two ways (under the ash and a pulp galette) and parsnip extraction vinaigrette served with a condiment of pomelo zest emulsi, crispy waffle with pollen toum and dried seaweed topped with sea anemone terrine and raw cream, and warm puffed lobster spaetzel pasta with creamy burrata and lobster cream made like Chef sommelier Alexis Bondel pairs the dishes with Dom Perignon champagne presented at various temperatures and other delicacies, further enhancing the experience with his vineyard anecdotes and deadpan humor. One to put in the calendar before March 5th.

Datsha Underground Restaurant:
57 Rue des Gravilliers, 75003 Paris

The sexy-cool atmosphere at Datsha Underground makes you eager to eat out once more. Step off the Marais backstreet and down a rabbit hole to a lair of hearty food packed with flavor created by Joao DaSilva and Vincent Bessy, served to patrons by a cast of dashing personnel wearing flowing black attire and providing impeccable service. The warmth of an ethereal atmosphere is supported by the sharp sound of delicate electronic music created particularly for the restaurant and emanating from hidden speakers as diners sit upon thick deconstructed marble tables. Svetislav Ekmesic's design for the room features centuries-old brick from the Austro-Hungarian empire and wood paneled walls brought from Serbia, the architect's native country, that are both softly lighted by slit lighting. Downstairs, under the space-themed sculpture in orbit, locals in the know congregate at the Spootnik bar, which is bathed in a seductive crimson glow and hosts a host of DJs on its tiny dance floor.

A limited, expertly prepared cuisine is served on plates that have been arranged with care. Consider the pressed beef tail with crunchy preserved cucumbers, or the half-cooked, half-raw vegetarian salad dish. These dishes, along with the lobster croquettes with yoghurt dressing, flame-grilled mackerel with its smoked mushroom broth, and the pork with grilled leek and sticky plum, were all full of flavor. The roasted cauliflower with vanilla and almond cream is a staple you shouldn't miss. His days as a rugby-playing optician are long gone, but Alexandre Rapoud, a less-than-thirty-year-old French entrepreneur with crescent moons and other mystical symbols tattooed on his neck and whose accent is laced with distant influences, created it. After spending time in Russia, he was inspired to create a location that might be anything.

Rapoud sought to build a place where Parisians might press pause and temporarily escape the daily grind. The word "Datsha" means "second home in the country" in Russian.

Bellefeuille Restaurant Paris:
5 Place du Chancelier Adenauer, 75116 Paris

Chef Julien Dumas' Bellefeuille restaurant is a must-visit location because it manages to be both upscale and unpretentious. It is located inside the recently renovated Saint James, Paris' only chateau hotel, and has all the belle epoque allure you could ask for. Views of the beautiful gardens are enhanced by the cheery handcrafted wallpaper, which has delicate plants swooping up to the high ceilings.

The six- or nine-course tasting menu is inspired by natural elements and takes the diner from the countryside to the coast before concluding with desserts made by head pastry chef Sophie Bonnefond. Try meals like slow-cooked exquisite river trout fillet with smoked ginger and trout eggs, as well as two-style green zebra tomato tartare wrapped in a nasturtium leaf, sorrel, purslane, and cardamom cocoon. Finish with a vine peach candied three ways with gavotte powder and some crunchy Brittany algae laced with chocolate.

When the building was constructed in the 1800s, a true library with antique books that roll all the way up to the ceiling was established, so make sure to arrive early so you may enjoy a cocktail there.

La Halle aux Grains Restaurant Paris

2 Rue de Viarmes, 75001 Paris

Even though the Halle aux Grains is located at the top of the Bourse de Commerce museum of art, executive chef Maxime Vergély's restaurant, run by father-and-son team Michel and Sébastien Bras from the Michelin-starred Le Suquet, is very much a stand-alone destination. The bright, airy space, which is crowned by a wave of glass, offers views of the St. Eustache Church, the undulating Canopée shopping mall, which is on the former site of the Halles food market, and the Beaubourg Contemporary Art Museum, which is a little farther away.

The restaurant is located in the former halle aux grains (grain hall), where grain would be evaluated and valued when the enormous circular building served as the city's chamber of commerce. As a result, the chefs have incorporated historical references into every aspect of the menu, from the floaty uniforms of the wait staff to the restaurant's logo to their specialized 30cuvées wines.

Order from the daily menu or order à la carte for the fresh celery spaghetti with pistachio and buddha hand or the seared scallops on a bed of parsnip cream to start at lunchtime, which is arguably the ideal time to enjoy the views. Then, either choose the hake that has been cooked in buckwheat or the meaty grilled chapon that is presented with barley pods. Finish with either the voile de kasha, a meringue made of chicory and chickpeas with sprouted herbs and coconut milk rice, or the biscuit coulant, often known as the fondant, which Michel Bras is credited with creating in the 1980s. After just one lunch, you'll be thinking about returning before you even get up from the table.

Sapid
54 Rue de Paradis, 75010 Paris

Last year, Romain Meder opened Sapid after leaving the famed kitchens of the Plaza Athénée. He brought his sous-chef Marvic Medina Matos and his inspiration with him. Sapid is a significant turning point for this sincere chef whose aim has always been to bring forth the natural flavors of the greatest ingredients he could find. Sapid is much more low key than the three-star Alain Ducasse stamped fine dining restaurant.

Meder, which is more of a canteen, offers mouthwateringly delicious, healthful meals with a concentration on vegetables. This is a place to keep in mind for eating properly without unnecessary additions because it is full of flavor, colorful, and is very reasonable. Try everything on the menu if you can. You can't go wrong with the roasted cauliflower covered in creamy scamorza, the stewed chickpea ragout, butternut and lentil bolognaise, or the sweets like homemade granola and olive oil biscuits topped with juicy kiwi fruit and farm-fresh yogurt dusted with seasonal fruit. At lunch or supper, diners have the option of eating at one of the long oak tables or taking out.

Auberge Nicolas Flamel Paris

51 Rue de Montmorency, 75003 Paris

An actual Paris landmark, this inn opened its doors back in 1407, when the city was still a maze of dingy, drab streets. The inn has survived, complete with its terracotta tiles and enormous oak beams, despite the fact that the city has changed much since then and undergone numerous renovations. That is, up until the establishment's owner, Michelin-starred chef Alan Geaam, hired Chef Gregory Garimbay to completely renovate it. Round tables with immaculate white tablecloths and sconce lighting are no longer present.

The open kitchen that is now located in the far wall of the dining room gives the impression that you are dining in Garimbay's living room. The only remaining indications of the restaurant's illustrious past are the original beams and the outside of a medieval auberge. Banquettes covered in thick wool fabric are arranged around teak wood tables to create a simple look.

A four- or five-course tasting menu that hints at the young chef's desire to earn one or more stars is available to diners in addition to an à la carte menu. The main dishes, like the meaty poularde Culoiselle from the Perche region and the flawlessly cooked lobster paired with acidic chard and golden chanterelle mushrooms, are highlights. Desserts like the chocolate cookie and the thickly sliced trompettes de la death mushrooms reveal the chef's rebellious side.

Limbar Restaurant Paris
8 Quai du Louvre, 75001 Paris

The talented young Norman pastry chef Maxime Frédéric (formerly at Paris' George V hotel) runs this cozy haven of tranquility at the back of the Cheval Blanc hotel lobby during the day, and cocktail whiz Florian Thireau does so at night.

You should put this place on your itinerary if you want to try Frédéric's Volauvent puff pastry, which was inspired by his grandmother's cooking, or his whole wheat croissant, which took at least two years to master and is lavishly stuffed with ham and cheese. Together with master baker Pierre Emmanuel Vargas, they scour artisan farmers for unique grains to experiment with and produce a variety of breads and pastries that you can eat there or take home.

Limbar is a calm area decorated in lovely open grain dark wood with bright red accents that is convenient for a quick lunch or pit stop while shopping at the Samaritaine department store just a few doors away or on the very busy Rue de Rivoli.

Le Relais Plaza Restaurant Paris
21 Avenue Montaigne, 75008 Paris

When three-star chef Alain Ducasse and the palace hotel Plaza Athénée parted ways last year, a new hire was made. Although Jean Imbert may be new to upscale establishments like the Plaza, his devoted social media following has carried him up the ranks and onto the Plaza's lap, where the clan hopes he'll direct a new generation of customers right to their door. And he's not performing poorly.

The thickly carpeted, wood paneled dining room, a piece of Art Deco history, is packed with patrons who are moms and daughters enjoying a break from shopping on Avenue Montaigne, Paris' most upscale shopping boulevard, for champagne and tomates farce. If large, round tomatoes roasted in the oven and filled with meaty garlic sauce aren't your thing, Imbert's grandma's flavorful, low-fat terrine will win you over. The robust Beaufort cheese quiche with spinach is a great option for vegetarians. If you prefer something a little more elegant, the fish dishes won't disappoint. As eager foodies wait for the next phase of Imbert's grand Plaza takeover the hotel's former three-star location the simplicity of Jean Imbert's satisfying dishes offer a lovely laid-backness to the neighborhood.

Liza Restaurant Paris

4 Rue de la Banque, 75002 Paris

While Liza's Paris headquarters is a fixture of the city, its new, simple furnishings, which feature summery palm tree print wallpaper reminiscent of Liza's Beirut restaurant located inside a historic castle, have been spiced up. The newly remodeled restaurant is a tribute to the proprietors' hometown of Beirut and serves as a constant reminder of the struggles faced by the city's residents.

Crunchy falafel and kafta, as well as the other mezzes, are still on the menu, delighting Liza regulars, a group of vegetarians from the worldwide fashion scene, local businesspeople, and people who know when something is good. In addition to an even heartier brunch and a mind-blowingly delicious sundae-style

Lebanese halva and carob ice cream finished with a slab of crunchy sesame biscuit, the chef has added a few new dishes like duck hummus, a more gastronomic take on the traditional chickpea dip, and tabboulé Teffe with apple. Regardless of dietary restrictions and mood, Liza's menu always has something for everyone, which is fantastic.

Maison Russe Restaurant Paris

59 Avenue Raymond Poincaré, 75116 Paris

The Maison Russe, which is nothing short of stunning, has brought attention to this frequently overlooked area of Paris. A hotel particulier of many storeys, decorated with hand-painted panels and tastefully renovated by Laleh Amir Assefi, who added plenty of natural light and color with plushly upholstered couches and an open fireplace, is hidden inside none other than Alfred Nobel's previous gothic-style home.

It was the home of chefs such Jol Robuchon in 1994, then Alain Ducasse, before turning into a beacon of Russian culinary pleasures including smoked salmon, caviar, and vodka. After afterwards, it was converted into a secretive upscale Chinese restaurant that served great Peking duck before being abandoned for many years. The latest acquisition of Accor, Paris Society, was snatched up by serial entrepreneur Laurent de Gourcuff, and the end result is excellent on all counts. A curious audience of locals with a variety of budgets as well as an international clientele with money to burn is drawn by the unique atmosphere and the appealing foods' different price points.

Drouant Restaurant Paris
1618 Rue Gaillon, 75002 Paris

The following address has been in operation for over a century, but recently hired Thibault Nizard, a former employee of Guy Savoy, has added some of his laid-back spirit to the kitchen, and Milan-born designer Fabrizio Casiraghi has updated the Art Deco interiors with his signature style, adding a little color and light. The Prix Goncourt and Prix Renaudot, two of the most distinguished literary awards in the nation, have always been presented at Drouant, a Paris institution that originally opened its doors in the 1880s. The private dining rooms, which are located above the main restaurant eating area and have tastefully decorated tables set up for entertaining city Alisters, are the main draw. As the first female president of the Goncourt Academy, Colette had lunch here every week with a guest, so be sure to ask to see it after your meal and don't miss the tiny boudoir-style dining room that bears her name.

The 28-year-old Nizard is carrying on Drouant's history with expertly created French brasserie dishes made with locally sourced food and cooked to maximize the flavor of each ingredient. Don't pass up the red mullet prepared by the chef, which is steamed, served with juicy grilled mushrooms, and topped with a meat jus and watercress flakes for a vegetal touch. Despite being young, this chef will go to the next level because to his devotion, simplicity, and grandmother's riz au lait with salted caramel butter.

Le Comptoir de la Traboule Restaurant Paris
1 bis Rue Augereau, 75007 Paris

The region around the Eiffel Tower can appear to be a no-land man's when it comes to fine dining if you don't know where to go. When you come across little pockets of cool with delicious food at the correct price, like Le Comptoir de la Traboule, you've got to take note. The 7th arrondissement is littered with pricey bistros serving up subpar renditions of French staples.

Jules Monnet, a chef and aspiring film director, opened this light-filled restaurant with outdoor seating on a peaceful street approximately 10 minutes' walk from the Eiffel Tower. Shareable dishes are listed on a chalkboard and include Japanese amberjack fish with caviar infused with bergamote and Basque pig belly roasted for 36 hours and served with parsnip and black garlic cream. Dishes are to be shared and are subject to daily modification. Desserts like the freshly baked fondant au chocolat are a must-have. A fantastic address to have on hand.

Le Petit Victor Hugo Restaurant Paris

143 Av. Victor Hugo, 75016 Paris

Le Petit Victor Hugo, or simply "PVH," is a revived brasserie with magnificent wooden paneled interiors that have been dusted off and brought back to life by designer of the moment Laura Gonzalez, who is also responsible for a number of other restaurant and hotel refurbishments. It gives diners a reason to travel over to this forgotten pocket of the 16th arrondissement of Paris.

Thanks to its stunning Art Deco design, which could have been taken straight out of the 1970s sitcom The Love Boat, this is the kind of venue that transcends space and time. You can have starters like caviar to tuna fingers with Thai sauce or Gillardeau oysters, and main courses like moules, scallops, and lobster risotto. Come hungry because there are ample amounts.

Montecito Restaurant Paris
2729 Bd des Capucines, 75002 Paris

However, Carrie Solomon and Nicolas Pastot, the couple behind the Montecito restaurant at the Kimpton Hotel, have made this road, which extends from the Paris Garnier opera theatre, a destination for supper. The expansive restaurant is buzzing with the light chatter of hotel guests and Parisians who have come to feast on the chefs' bright and cheery dishes that have traveled all the way from, as the restaurant's name lets on, sunny California. The restaurant was designed by French interiors outfit Humbert & Poyet and tapped for several eye-catching spots with floor-to-ceiling windows that slide open onto an outdoor courtyard.

You may anticipate hearty dishes like crispy fried chicken, grilled fish tacos with fresh chile and creamy avocado, and cheesecake to finish. On weekends, when the DJ starts playing and customers push back their chairs to dance on the temporary dance floor, you may burn off those tacos.

Villa Mikuna Restaurant Paris
2 Rue Frochot, 75009 Paris

In the past few years, the culinary scene in Paris has significantly expanded, going far beyond the traditional steak and frites. And one such location that serves delicacies all the way from

Peru is Villa Mikuna. Whatever you order, it will bring a little sunshine into your day. Consider tangy guacamole with roasted pineapple, anticucho de pollo (marinated chicken, aji panca, and huacatay sauce), or chicharron de chancho (crispy pork seasoned with Peruvian spices and served with fried cassava, grilled corn, and salsa criolla).

Aside from the food, Villa Mikuna's position inside the famed Villa Frochot, a former cabaret established in 1837 with stunning Hokusai stained glass windows, has to be its main selling feature. It's worth adding to the list for lunch or supper because the Pigalle district landmark was transformed into a pisco bar and restaurant last year with vibrantly upholstered banquettes and lots of plants hanging from the ceiling.

Magniv Restaurant Paris
37 bis Rue du Sentier, 75002 Paris

The next restaurant is located in the former space of speakeasy bar Le Fou in the bustling Sentier area, close to the theater-lined boulevards. It has been transformed into a slick establishment with a seductive Mediterranean-meets-Middle Eastern vibe that is always enjoyable to dip into, especially in the dead of winter, thanks to the acquisition of two former bartenders,

Benjamin Chiche and Cément Faure, and chef Kobi Villot, who oversees operations in the kitchen.

The flavorful food comes from all over the world, such as the Temani tacos with pulled lamb, carrot harissa, and tahina verde wrapped in a lachuch (Yemeni style crepe), the Tamnoun grilled octopus with soft, fluffy Jerusalem bagels and tangy tomato romesco sauce, or the vitello tonnato veal tartare in tuna sauce, a specialty of northeastern Italy. When you're finished, sneak downstairs to the bar for a drink where a DJ regularly spins upbeat music into the early hours beneath a battered bronze ceiling on a waxed concrete dance floor.

Café Jeanne Restaurant Paris
at the Park Hyatt Vendôme 5 Rue de la Paix, 75002 Paris

The Café Jeanne in the Park Hyatt Hotel is a handy place to have on hand when in the Place Vendôme region and is ideal for a quick pit stop. Formerly the hotel's depressing lobby, the area has been transformed into a full-fledged restaurant with a charming mirror-backed bar and a glass roof, all under the direction of Michelin-starred chef Jean François Rouquette.

Shoppers drop by for coffee, afternoon tea, or meals of oeuf parfait with butternut, fresh amberjack carpaccio, or tried-and-true fish and chips or steak and fries for lunch or dinner. The best thing about this place is that you can eat or drink whenever you like from seven in the morning until midnight every day without interruption, which is unusual in Paris where restaurants typically close after their scheduled closing times.

Yakuza Restaurant Paris
7 Rue du Helder, 75009 Paris

The Paris outpost of Portuguese chef Olivier da Costa's Yakuza restaurants is located in the Maison Albar hotel, which is tucked away near the Opéra Garnier and Boulevard Haussmann's shopping district. The chef's robust Japanese cuisine with a major Brazilian influence is served in this intimate enclave, the first outside of Portugal, which features seagreen velvet arm chairs you'll want to crawl into for the day.

Order the Taco Sakana with fish and guacamole, followed by black cod marinated in sweet miso or wagyu rump steak with black truffle pasta, from the comprehensive sushi menu. You must enjoy the iconic KitKat "Guaranteed Success" ice cream and chocolate snack shards for dessert. This Yakuza branch is a relaxed choice that is cozy and personal and feels exotic due to the personnel, who are a mixture of Portuguese and Japanese imports.

Thanks for Reading Paris Guide.

CPSIA information can be obtained
at www.ICGtesting.com
Printed in the USA
LVHW041035220223
739993LV00005B/14